ELL

MW01282138

Manchester University Press

British Pop Archive

Series editors
Doug Field, Tom Attah, Kirsty Fairclough

Drawing on a rich variety of sources including interviews, memoirs, recordings, images, press cuttings and other archival materials, the series reflects and expands the Manchester-based British Pop Archive, which recently launched to much acclaim.

Telling untold stories from music, popular (and unpopular) culture and counterculture, the series entertains and informs, while uncovering long-hidden secrets and delving into dusty corners for an audience of retro culture vultures, music buffs and curious souls.

The British Pop Archive series publishes collectible, desirable volumes that every music-loving and pop-cultural enthusiast reader will want to add to their own personal archive.

To buy or to find out more about the books currently available in this series, please go to: https://manchesteruniversitypress.co.uk/british-pop-archive-books/

STUDIO ELECTROPHONIQUE

The Sheffield space age, from The Human League to Pulp

JAMIE TAYLOR

Manchester University Press

The right of Jamie Taylor to be identified as the author of this work has been asserted in accordance with the Copyright, Designs and Patents Act 1988.

Published by Manchester University Press
Oxford Road, Manchester, M13 9PL

www.manchesteruniversitypress.co.uk

British Library Cataloguing-in-Publication Data
A catalogue record for this book is available from the British Library

ISBN 978 1 5261 8323 1 paperback

First published 2025

The publisher has no responsibility for the persistence or accuracy of URLs for any external or third-party internet websites referred to in this book, and does not guarantee that any content on such websites is, or will remain, accurate or appropriate.

EU authorised representative for GPSR:
Easy Access System Europe, Mustamäe tee 50, 10621 Tallinn, Estonia, gpsr.requests@easproject.com

Typeset
by Cheshire Typesetting Ltd, Cuddington, Cheshire

We cannot take in all the figures of the painting in one glance. Not only do the life-size proportions of the painting preclude such an appreciation but also the fact that the heads of the figures are turned in different directions means that our gaze is deflected. The painting communicates through images which, in order to be understood, must thus be considered in sequence, one after the other, in the context of a history that is still unfolding. It is a history that is still unframed, even in this painting composed of frames within frames.

Harriet Stone on *Las Meninas* by Diego Velázquez

Space is cold
Home is colder

All Seeing I, 'The First Man in Space' (lyrics Jarvis Cocker/vocals Philip Oakey)

To Laura

CONTENTS

PREFACE: YOUNG METEORS

Writing a short book that ties together the story of Ken Patten and the young musicians from Sheffield who, in some cases, looked to Ken for guidance and, in others, operated independently of his help, reminded me of the challenge faced by Hollywood executive Steven Bach and screen-writer William Goldman when they bought the rights to *The Right Stuff* by Tom Wolfe for half a million dollars in 1979 and then realised they had no idea how to turn it into a film.

The Right Stuff tells the story of Chuck Yeager, the American test pilot who became the first person to break the sound barrier in the rarefied air above the Mojave Desert in 1947. It also details the development of the Mercury Project, focusing on the courage and invention exhibited by the brash young astronauts who flew NASA's first manned space flights in the early 1960s.

Wolfe's writing talent enabled him to roll out these stories so they read like a romantic adventure or an elegy for a lost age of gallantry, camaraderie and ingenuity, but when the moviemakers tried to lift these stories and transfer them to the pages of a script, they turned to ashes under their hands.

On numerous occasions, they considered cutting Chuck out of the picture altogether, but he was such a strange and charismatic figure, a knight of the right stuff, that they couldn't imagine the story being told without him. Finally, Goldman located the golden thread that had would unite Yeager's legend with the impulsive, competitive jet jocks who followed his vapour trail through the atmosphere.

'The star of this movie,' he said, 'is America.'[1]

Ken Patten and Chuck Yeager were born in the same year. In 1941, when they were eighteen, they both joined the air force. They were both working-class lads: one from industrial Sheffield, one from the coal fields of Appalachia. They were both modest, self-taught enthusiasts, 'stick and rudder men' who devoted their lives to practical passions without fuss or the need for acclaim.[2]

Chuck Yeager eased the world into the transonic zone, breaking the sound barrier in his X-1 rocket plane; Ken Patten illuminated the way for Sheffield artists who wanted to explore sonic zones, as yet uncharted, in the field of electronic music and sound. I am well aware of the galaxies of significance that separate a human being travelling at Mach 1 for the first time and a human being sitting in his downstairs extension making a vocoder out of bog rolls, but I urge you to see these men, as I do, as twin engines, born in 1923, igniting the space age for all to wonder at.

The star of this story is Sheffield.

Chapter 1

DEATH OF A FUTURIST

All art constantly aspires towards the condition of music.

Walter Pater

The golden hour of Sheffield pop bloomed, perversely, in the hollow, death-marked era of *Threads*, Thatcher and mass redundancy. The hard work had been done in the seventies by cells of state-raised creatives with the drive and discipline to commit to a life governed by a tap room musical manifesto and a self-assemble synthesiser arriving in instalments through the post. Pop music pilgrims arriving in Sheffield, however, may struggle to locate its landmark sites. They are unheralded and unmarked yet still emit a faint, looped analogue pulse for those devoted enough to seek them out: the attic room in Lemont Road where Cabaret Voltaire first assembled, the house on Stanhope Road where 'Babies' came from, the condemned dead end in Barber Crescent where ABC conjured glamour out of margarine sandwiches and pure imagination. The most secret and sacred of all these signless places, however, is the Ballifield council semi that housed the studio owned by Ken Patten: panel beater, fly fisherman, waterskier, filmmaker and midwife at the birth of electronic music in the north.

A few years ago, when my friend James and I set out to tell Ken's story, it appeared to be a story on the verge of being lost. Vacant when we made our first visit, 32 Handsworth Grange Crescent has not been taken into the care of the National Trust; there is no custodian, no heritage trail, no blue plaque. The studio in the downstairs extension where the first recordings were made of the bands that became The Human League, ABC, Pulp, Heaven 17 and Clock DVA is now a compact family kitchen.

We both had personal connections to the Ballifield estate in Handsworth but no officially recognised investigative skills or nailed-on contacts who might help to shake the story from its slumber. My dad grew up on Old Retford Road and I had spent school holidays there being looked after by my Grandma Iris and Grandad Watson. In the late 1970s and early 1980s, I must have scuffed my way to Ballifield shops in the slipstream of grandma's shopping trolley countless times, unaware, as I passed Ken's house, of the alchemy that may have been at work behind the yellow front door.

When we started our quest, James was a solo musician in need of an enigmatic name to badge his new songs with. I knew that James had gone to school around the corner from Ken's house so I suggested that he should steal the unnecessarily exotic name that Ken had given to his own musical kingdom, Studio Electrophonique. By the time the name had been adopted, the mystery of Ken's life and work had us both in thrall and we decided to marshal our meagre resources to mount an investigation.

Death of a futurist

Our only leads at the outset were a photocopied picture of Ken's old business card (landline only) and the fortuitous coincidence that James's grandparents' best mates, Jeff and Ruth, lived in the semi that adjoined Ken's old house. The ache of the story never being told at all was all the impetus we needed and, one fine day, we set out to Ken's old address in an underpowered Nissan Micra with a notebook, a couple of cold fried egg sandwiches in foil and a wisp of hope.

The Ballifield estate was built in 1952 as part of Harold Macmillan's great postwar housing crusade. The houses are warm red brick and they are arranged in smart crescents and closes, describing a neat pattern of habitation around a central parade of shops and a pub, The Everest, christened to commemorate Edmund Hilary's Himalayan conquest. The pub is directly across the road from Ken's and we parked up with a view of both. I told James my dad's story about being taken to The Everest on the day it opened for a hot Vimto. James trumped this by recalling a family fun day hosted at The Everest in the late 1990s when he scored in a car park penalty shootout against Mel 'Zico' Sterland, the Sheffield Wednesday and England full-back.

Nothing faintly commemorative or fun appeared to be happening on the morning of our visit. The landlady of the pub lit a fag outside the tap room door and, as we got out of the car, the two pub dogs knocked past her legs and smashed violently into the fence. We tried not to flinch but were quick to put the Micra between us and the dogs. The landlady growled a rebuke that we hoped was aimed at the dogs and, when it was ignored, she threw her fag in the direction of the children's play area and strode towards the fence.

'They'll not hurt you, they're soft as owt.'

We smiled and edged towards the safety of Jeff and Ruth's garden gate. One of the dogs bolted up a slide and skittered to a halt in the concealment of a yellow plastic tunnel.

'And that one's thick as fuck.'

It was a relief that there was no one else about; James was wearing a corduroy jacket that a car park full of lunchtime drinkers would have made short work of. The estate world was a world we both knew well; a world of bandits, accumulators and days in lieu; a world of brown sauce, Adidas Hamburgs and the Meadowhall Sunday League. We knew it well but at a painful remove. We were perfect examples of Richard Hoggart's 'uprooted and anxious breed'.[1] We fancied ourselves as belonging, at last, to the world of sash windows, attic libraries and homemade salad dressings but we were ill at ease there as well. As the elder statesman, I had warned James that this would happen, yet there we were, caught in the tough filaments connecting past and future lives, pulled backwards and forwards yet still upright and knocking, for obscure reasons, at the house next door to Ken's.

Jeff opened the door, greeted James warmly, shook my hand then led us round to the side door.

'Go steady on that astroturf bit, it's slippy. Ruth's cousin went over on it not long since and cracked both wrists, he couldn't wipe his backside after.'

Jeff and Ruth are in their seventies. Jeff is one of those men who has worn a moustache for so long that his face has settled into place around it in awe. Even though the moustache is now grey and sparse, the illusion of luxurious

4

growth remains. Ruth muted *A Place in the Sun* and stood up to say hello with the remote still in her hand. She wore a loose summer dress and glasses. Jeff insisted that I sit in the best chair then nipped out to make a brew. The house was immaculate. James did his best to outline our vague motives to Ruth, observed from behind by a radiator shelf full of porcelain Buddhas and a stuffed dog.

'We were worried it was going to get to the point where no one knew anything about the studio anymore', he said.

Ruth settled herself into the settee beside him and sighed.

'Well. Yes. There's a lot of young 'uns moved on here a-lately and they wouldn't know.'

Jeff returned with the tea and perched on the arm of the settee next to his wife.

'Ken had died before we moved in,' he said, 'and that were, what, '93. And the thing what's happened now, well it's sad really because, when Lorna died, she never left the house to her daughter, she left it to this bloke who had the shop across the road. So no, we didn't know much about Ken but we did know Lorna.'

'We knew she were a funny bugger', said Ruth. 'I do remember she mentioned a boat, though, didn't she, what set afire. And I seem to think that Ken died in that accident and that his daughter got badly burned. I can't remember the daughter's name for the life of me. I tell you who will know,' she thumped Jeff on the leg, 'I'll give Linda Young a ring.'

As the closest family connection, James was thrust into the role of cold caller. Linda wasn't familiar with the firmament of stars that had coalesced in the skies over Ballifield back then but she was good value on the scandal and gore.

'Michele was the daughter. She used to live on Retford Road but she moved. God knows where she is now but she'd be the one to find. She were odd. She had that boating accident then, a few months later, the car she were travelling in hit a lorry that were carrying steel girders or something and one got her in the eye.'

Linda was on the speakerphone. Ruth interjected.

'Didn't it burst into flames?'

'That were the boat,' Linda said, 'I'm on about that car accident. If you can find Michele, she'll tell you more. She's not loopy, just a bit odd. Shafiq who Lorna left the house to, he could perhaps tell you more but he's another loop fruit and he's not back here that often.'

James kept her on the hook.

'Well, you must think we're loopy asking you about this.'

'She had a funny married name', said Linda. 'What were it now? Something like Humperdink. Humpel ... something like ...'

'Well don't worry', James reassured her. 'At least we know her first name.'

'Umpleby!' The dam burst. 'It's Umpleby. Michele Umpleby.'

'Well,' James smiled, 'we should be able to track her down with a name like that.'

'He were a quiet bloke were Ken,' said Linda, 'a quiet bloke. But, as I say, I think he were the only sane one out of the lot.'

We thanked Linda and finished our tea as Jeff and Ruth asked after James's Grandad Mel, who hadn't been feeling himself lately. As we moved to leave the front room, Ruth remembered something and stood up from the settee to rummage around in a tin that sat on top of the fire.

Death of a futurist

'Here y'are, look. We've still got this little love-heart pebble what Lorna gave us on our wedding day.' Ruth held out her palm, showing a small, smooth pebble. 'She said she found it when she were walking on the beach with Ken. She kept it all that time and then gave it to me and Jeff when we got married. Just a little pebble.'

Reassured by Jeff and Ruth that Ken's old house next door was vacant, we decided to have a snoop around. The front garden had been paved to make a drive but a walk into the back garden allowed us to imagine the house as it would have looked in the atomic age when Ken's visions began. The heavy iron washing poles, planted aslant in the long grass, bore the thick lacquered overpainting of the years, and the extension that Ken had built to house Studio Electrophonique still looked newer than the rest of the house even though it must have been there now for fifty years. James leant a loose flagstone against the wall of the extension and stood on top of it, muscling up to the window-sill on his forearms.

'See anything?' I asked.

'Fridge freezer', he replied.

'What if all his gear's still up in that loft?'

'Well it's got to be somewhere.'

The only picture we had seen of Ken's studio was a photograph of Stephen Singleton, Mark White and David Sydenham arranged artfully in a nest of cabling, reel-to-reel tape machines and closed-circuit TVs. The picture of the three teenage musicians was taken in 1979 when Vice Versa travelled to Ken's to record their *Music 4* EP. A year later, two of these men would play their part in one of the most audacious manoeuvres in British pop, spinning the threadbare electronic experimentation of Vice Versa into the gleaming, white-scratch-funk of ABC.

We knew that Ken had recorded bands in this tiny room for at least twenty years and we were convinced that there must be many stories to tell. I was tortured by the image of lofts all over South Yorkshire concealing the artefacts we were after and by the fact that I had no radar to detect them. Through the 1970s and 1980s, hundreds of bands trooped out to Ken's to capture their art on tape and, although only a handful were launched into the pop orbit, they all knocked on that front door with the same creative commitment, preparing with a gulp to expose their unformed artistic frailties to a middle-aged stranger in a C&A cardigan.

Looking through a roll call of these bands, one can only imagine the range of micro-genres Ken had managed to coax onto tape: The Electric Armpits, My Pierrot Dolls, Blue Ice, Bangkok Shock, Grasping the Pineappleness, The Naughtiest Girl Was a Monitor and Systematic Annexe, whose track 'Death Trades' was recorded by Ken in 1984 yet failed to arouse the interest of those compiling *Now That's What I Call Music 4*. Ken received all these bands with an encouraging practicality and never balked at their mad ideas or musical ineptitude. The tape made at Ken's by The Future in 1977, for example, contained a track called 'Looking for the Black Haired Girls' featuring Adi Newton growling lyrics about the Son of Sam murders in New York City over a backing track of bleeps and distortion manipulated by Martyn Ware and Ian Craig Marsh. These formative forays into the world of sound production and creative expression from the artists who later formed Clock DVA, The Human League and Heaven 17 were patiently patched together by Ken with little care for convention or, indeed, for Lorna, doing her knitting on the other side of the louvre doors.

Ken was an honest worker, well accustomed to putting a shift in at his garage and, to him, the work he did in the studio was no different; if you were going to take hard-earned money from young musicians, you were going to do your best to give them the tape they dreamed of.

These were the tapes we dreamed of finding as we left Jeff and Ruth's house with a faint lead but still no real idea about what had happened to Ken or the recordings his studio had magicked into existence. Our next step was to find the artists who had put their trust in Ken at the outset; the ones whom Ken had boosted into stardom and the ones who, perhaps, had been left behind on the launchpad. Céline wrote that 'kids are like years, you never see them again', but we were groundlessly hopeful that we would track them down and see what had become of the kids of the space age.[2] Perhaps we would even be allowed to gaze upon some relics: mouldering tape boxes and handwritten manifestos that mapped out what the route into the future had looked like back then.

We knew, of course, that Ken had been dead for many years and that a search for the hardware that had comprised Studio Electrophonique was probably as foolish and futile as a search for the final resting place of the Ark. Ken never sought attention or praise and his work had never been catalogued or explored. While his gauche apprentices were rubbing gold lamé shoulders with Andy Warhol, guesting on the Band Aid single or shifting units with *Penthouse and Pavement* or *The Lexicon of Love*, Ken had already shifted back to his own unit under Norfolk Bridge, knocking out dents in his garage.

Some of the artists we met are older now than Ken was when he was presented with their futuristic masterplans in the 1970s and 1980s, yet we noted a distinct correlation in Sheffield's artistic attitudes across the generations. Creative people in Sheffield have always cracked on with their work, away from the cultural gaze and, often, without the training, education or equipment that would normally be a prerequisite before the impulse became an action. People in Sheffield are, famously, makers and, if they can't afford to buy the latest means of artistic production, they will make something or make do with something else.

'Part of that Sheffield thing', said Martyn Ware, 'is being producers of product rather than being delicate artists who are maybe too delicate for the world and need approbation all the time. That's not a Sheffield thing at all.'

Ken started his odyssey into sound by cannibalising two old tape recorders so they would do something they weren't designed to do. These traditions were handed down and honoured by artists such as Cabaret Voltaire, The Future, Vice Versa and others who, like Ken, found themselves existing in a grey, cheerless city but found within themselves the capacity to dream up singular visions where Sheffield could, for a time, be left behind.

This is the story of Sheffield in the space age; Sheffield characters and the character of Sheffield. Ken Patten returned from the Second World War and settled down to family life in Ballifield; to the wider world, his life rolled out evenly, an adventureless tale. His inner life, however, was a perpetual engine of ideas and invention, ignited by the rocket ship glamour of the atomic age and fuelled by the ungraspable allure of the sounds of tomorrow. In the 1970s and 1980s, a new generation of creators, charged by the cathode voltage of TV, science fiction, pop music, art and the Apollo moonshots, made Sheffield the unlikely epicentre of a movement defined by Ken's principles of tape manipulation, DIY sonics and a general determination to make machines bend to the will of the artist.

Sheffield in the space age was, for many, a desperate place but, as Kierkegaard said, 'given a possibility, the desperate man breathes once more'.[3] The advent of relatively affordable electronic musical devices after the Second World War made the creation of music possible for many imaginative but untrained artists, persuading even those in a city as modest as Sheffield that they could add their visions to the time capsule.

Referring to Sheffield as a modest city is not to suggest that it is a small or insignificant place, but rather that its people don't like to go on about the wonderful things they are capable of. In 1982, for example, acts from Sheffield made up 5 per cent of sales in the UK singles chart but, of course, they didn't like to mention it. Glenn Gregory of Heaven 17 captured the grounding effect of being a successful working-class Sheffield artist perfectly when he recalled the greeting he habitually received from his dad's steelworker mates when he used to visit the local pub at the height of his fame.

'Whenever I used to go to The Bridge Inn, which was my dad's local, they used to shout, "Here y'are, look. Fuckin' Beatles are here."'[4]

Although the impulse to downplay or diminish any creative pursuit is hardwired into most people from Sheffield, there are some stories that cry out to be told. Ken wouldn't have countenanced the idea of making a big deal out of one of his 'hobbies' but, when the cultural map of Sheffield is spread out before you, the blast circles his work generated can still be traced today. For this reason, I decided to tell his story for him.

Chapter 2
BALLIFIELD YEAR ZERO

A child's eyes register fast. Later, he develops the film.

Jean Cocteau

A vintage Austrian Eumig cinefilm projector whirs into life in the loft of a Sheffield terraced house. The blinds are drawn so that a projected square of flickering light can play over the bare wall. The leader runs through the machine then a homemade test card flashes up, a colourful classroom tableau with Blue Meanie posters surrounding a blackboard upon which the words 'KenPat Productions' are printed in Elizabethan font. The card fades into a dark blue title screen with glossy red plastic letters arranged across it to spell out *Apollo Eleven Moon Landing* then cuts to a domestic front room, wallpapered in vertical stripes from the beige spectrum, where a middle-aged woman in horn rimmed glasses is standing awkwardly. Beside her is a black and white TV set and, in her hands, she holds a single sheet of paper and a large globular microphone. Before she can speak, a toy poodle enters the shot and begins to paw at her leg.

A couple of months after Ken filmed the moon landing on his telly, David Bowie would appear on Top of the Pops for the first time, cashing in on the same event by rush-releasing his single 'Space Oddity'. It would be his only hit for three years and the film of this performance has been destroyed.

It would be fair to say that David Bowie, Stanley Kubrick and Ken Patten had a considerable hand in shaping the artists of the Sheffield space age. Whether Kubrick had a hand in the cinematic framing of the 1969 moon shot is less certain, but what we can safely assume is that he wouldn't have composed an opening shot featuring his own earthbound wife and dog as the voice of ground control. As we watch, Lorna picks up the dog with her script hand and starts to speak. No sounds emerge.

By this time, James and I had been working our way methodically through a Heron Foods carrier bag full of cine film reels for two hot weeks in a cramped attic. We had collected them from Ken's daughter, Michele, and her ex-husband, John, after tracking them down to a suburban house in Parson Cross. The carrier bag was full of Super 8 film reels, loose or in orange Kodak envelopes self-addressed to Ken at the fabled Ballifield address. Some were labelled in biro in the neat caps-lock script of the working man and some had intriguing and oblique titles printed on the back such as: *Banger Racing, US?*, *No 2 Peep* and *Body Beautiful*. The bag also contained unlabelled sound reels which, in our optimistic moments, we dared to believe may contain unheard melodies from another age.

Without a suitable projector, we had to content ourselves with the occasionally unspooling to squint at a few frames in the pale light of the Velux window but Ken's reels demanded a greater level of commitment. Specifically, six days with a 'collection only' projector on an eBay watchlist, a last-minute snide bid and a day return to Wigan on the train to go and fetch it. James did most of the leg work and had now burned through three projector bulbs in the heat of the August attic, blinking through hours of Ken's holiday vistas, terrified of missing the moment when the oxide ghosts of Studio Electrophonique would be cast onto the wall to live again.

One of the promises we made to Michele and John to convince them to loan us the reels was that we would try our best to digitise the footage so they could have a look at Ken's films for the first time in fifty years. We didn't want to let them down as they had shown unwarranted faith in us and, also, because we were slightly terrified of them.

Our first meeting was surreal. We were told to arrive at an appointed time but, when we did, no one answered the door. A mouldering, moss-green Toyota Camry sat on the drive and the front bay window had a bed sheet pinned up as a curtain. We knocked again and the stained-glass image of a riverside cottage shivered in the door frame. Two dead spider plants hanging from either side of the door turned ominously as a car drew up at the end of the drive. It was a taxi carrying Michele and John. They emerged with some difficulty but no explanation; Michele, grey-haired in a fern-print dress, John with thick-lensed glasses, a zip-up black leather jerkin and sandals. We introduced ourselves with the customary awkwardness as they unlocked the door and led us in.

Just inside the front door, like the monolith from *2001*, stood an unplugged upright fridge freezer and a scrum of man-sized teddy bears guarding a grandfather clock. As we edged around into the front room, John had already settled himself in the only upholstered chair. Three tubular camping chairs had been set out for the interview, so we sat, Michele upright and expectant in front of the gas fire and beneath a shadeless standard lamp, James and I hunched among large cardboard boxes labelled 'Lighting – Do Not Crush'.

Michele hitched up her sleeves and fixed us with a blank look. Behind her on the fire were a pair of galleons in full sail, a family of porcelain foxes and a brass elephant. The pre-interview negotiations had been with John and we weren't sure how Michele would take to a couple of weirdly enthusiastic strangers scrounging about in her memory banks. She had already cancelled twice at the last minute so we were grateful that she had decided to give us the benefit of the doubt this time. As we tried our best to explain our project, she nodded and turned a white envelope over in her lap.

'Most people knew that my dad was the music man,' she said, 'that he was capable of playing a tune and having friends round for a tinkle on the guitars. His mum had composed music for church sermons and dad also had this gift. He could pick up a banjo or a guitar and play most things. He made his own amplifiers and they asked him to be in the RAF band. There's a picture of him here in the RAF with his banjo.'

Michele slid a slim deck of photos out of the envelope and passed across a worn shot of a teenage Ken in an RAF trio. She smiled for the first time as we looked at the picture and our factories of admiration began to hum.

'In fact,' she continued, 'he was busy cleaning his banjo strings when I was born.'

We handed the picture back and she folded it back into the pack.

'I wish I had a more to show you. Sadly, my mother left all her possessions to the man who had the shop across the road. I wasn't left a ha'penny.'

Michele had sad stories to tell but she also told us some joyful ones. She had an impressive theatrical delivery when she got going, impulsively bursting into regional accents or unsettling us with sudden swoops into sorrow or climbing outrage when our faces weren't ready for it. The main things I remember from that first afternoon at the Umplebys', as the room grew dark around us and no one thought to put the light on, was the pantomime laugh that crowned most of Michele's tales. Often accompanied by an artful unfurling of the fingers or the head thrown back, it was the deep, resonant joy of a genie released after years in the dark.

We came away from the first visit with a tentative bond of trust, a carrier bag full of film reels and the stories that frame this account of Ken's life. A few weeks later, in the attic with the newly acquired cinefilm projector, we watched Michele's mum, Lorna, introduce the dawning of the space age on 20 July 1969 from her front room with a dog in her arms and a black and white television on beside her. We can't retrieve the sound so we are left to imagine how Ken and Lorna scripted this momentous event. Sheffield, like the rest of the Western world, was enchanted by the first moon landing. Martyn Ware was thirteen in 1969 and remembers the glamour and possibility of the time:

It's hard now to impress on people how all-pervasive the space race was for our generation. It was the embodiment of optimism and we don't have anything like that now. Back then, the future seemed quite rosy and there was a general belief in the world that we should keep pushing forward because we would all benefit from progress.

Adi Newton, Ware's collaborator in The Future, was also marked by the gravity of the first moon landing:

I didn't see it but I heard it on the radio. I was on holiday with my mum and dad in Wales and everyone on the site was out in the open, listening to it being broadcast. Everyone was silent. It was seen as a monumental feat. The idea of the future was fascinating.

The year of the first moon landing was also the year that other Sheffield artists received their first booster shots of great expectation in the form of a visit to the cinema to watch a rescreening of Stanley Kubrick's *2001: A Space Odyssey*. Jarvis Cocker persuaded his mum to take him to the Cinecenta on his sixth birthday to watch it with his pal John White, while Glenn Gregory was taken on a school trip from Hinde House to watch it at the Gaumont in Barker's Pool. The experience appears to have been enlightening and misleading in equal measures. Jarvis came away from the film convinced that the future would naturally unfurl in the manner suggested by Kubrick's vision.

Shortly after this glimpse of the interstellar future, Jarvis contracted meningitis and was seriously ill in hospital for some time. He was placed in isolation and, although he could receive gifts and cards, he was allowed no human contact. When he recovered, the toys he had been sent were destroyed as infectious waste. The only one he was allowed to take home was a cheap moulded plastic astronaut that could be boiled and returned to him free from contagion. Jarvis still has this figure, a token of invincibility and imagination.

Sheffield's natural tendency to withdraw from the pull of the future was only brought home to Jarvis years later when he was reduced to traipsing around the city's rain-soaked streets trying to sell his possessions:

The people at NASA were saying that, by 1984, we'd all be living on different planets or whirring around on space stations and there didn't seem to be any reason why we wouldn't. But in 1984, when I was twenty-two, I distinctly remember tromping around Sheffield with a yellow portable washing machine trying to sell it to get the money for some food. It was pissing it down and I thought to myself, Jarvis, you were supposed to be living in space by now. I never even got a bike when I was young because I was convinced I'd be whizzing down the shops with my personal jetpack. I didn't think you'd need a bike if you were living on the moon.[1]

Adi Newton credits Kubrick and *2001* in particular as being a defining influence on his formative years as an artist.

'It was a radical, incredible piece of work. So immense, mythical, magical. Everything's in there: it's dystopian, it's funny, it's absurd, it's serious, it's savage.'

Film, and the films of Kubrick in particular, had a profound effect on Sheffield's early electronic artists. Kubrick himself termed *2001* a 'machine ballet' and the often wordless beauty and precision of the musical passages, along with the stainless, synchronous, geometric set design, must have inspired young devotees such as Glenn Gregory to believe that they would soon be swapping their Hinde House School blazer for a brave new world of warp-speed chic. Film critic Alexander Walker noted the boundless nature of Kubrick's vision and the almost lysergic liberation of the sequence where Mission Commander Bowman embarks on a cosmic ride through his own evolution. The film, he stated, and this scene in particular, seemed to take the viewer 'beyond the boundaries of the imprisoning present'.[2]

Although Adi, Glenn, Jarvis and Ken could shut out the imprisoning present of Sheffield in the darkness of a cinema auditorium or in the cloistered sanctum of a home studio, the crumbs of homegrown cultural nourishment were hard to find in 1969. But it's always the quiet places you have to watch out for. Like Zurich, the calm, blank eye of Europe's storm, where Dada was allowed to flourish in the petri dish of the Cabaret Voltaire in the middle of the First World War, Sheffield was also capable of breeding some original artistic life in prosaic surroundings.

A photograph in the *Sheffield Telegraph* from the late 1960s shows the exterior of the Sheffield Playhouse on Townhead Street, a theatre converted from the old Temperance Hall. The photograph is in black and white and the people in frame look stooped and preoccupied. They do not marvel at the large billboard advertising the play *It Happened in Irkutsk* by Alexei Arbuzov. If the play's director were outside plugging the show to passers-by, it is difficult to imagine how a twenty-second pitch or even a free ticket would help to swell the audience with local shoppers. The play tells the story of a Russian crew foreman who drowns while excavating a dam in Siberia, a hard sell when Jane Fonda is starring in *Barbarella* across the road at the pictures. This attempt to introduce working-class Sheffield to a coarse diet of austere and challenging European drama was a politically noble one and the creatives responsible for this movement were the same people who would help to launch the native space age of Sheffield art in the decade to come.

Chris Wilkinson wasn't raised in the same circumstances as the young Sheffield artists he later encouraged. There weren't many kids on Sheffield estates with the middle name Umfreville but Wilkinson certainly had a keenly felt vocation to elevate those kids' lives through theatre and experimental art. He was born in 1941, the great grandson of Walter Wilkinson, the founder of Orwell Park Prep and Boarding School in Suffolk and, after attending his great grandad's school and subsequent studies at Lancing, he accepted a place at Bristol University to work towards a degree in drama. He came to Sheffield in 1962 to work as a repertory actor at the Playhouse, featuring in plays throughout the 1960s that tested the palate of Sheffield theatregoers with the city's first taste of works by Pinter, Brecht, Pirandello and Sophocles.

The radical nature of the Playhouse was not stark or even readily apparent but its artistic director, Colin George, and his wife, Dorothy Vernon, did introduce several ideas in the 1960s that nudged the Sheffield art world out of its torpor. They started a Saturday morning theatre club for local children that acted as a testing ground for the Meatwhistle project that would follow in the 1970s, steered by Chris Wilkinson and his wife, Veronica. They also formed connections with eastern European artists and organised regular trips and exchanges so that the staid and stolid chromatic templates of provincial theatre could be remade and remodelled with tools and techniques that had the alien glamour of the Eastern bloc.

A Playhouse production of Shakespeare's *Macbeth* in 1970 starred Nigel Hawthorne in the title role as a shaven-headed killer wearing an eye-catching costume designed by Polish artist Józef Szajna. The costume emerged from the prop cupboard to play its own part in Sheffield pop history when Phil Oakey bought it some years later from a theatre sale and took to wearing it in his everyday life.

Martyn Ware remembers this spectacle. 'It looked like it was a carapace of insect scales in various textures of black fabrics, combined with ludicrously built-up shoulders. It took some balls to wear it in public, but he pulled it off.'

The first stirrings of radical art at the Playhouse came from these cultural exchanges and from the pen of Chris Wilkinson, who was writing plays of his own. The titles alone prompted outrage and consternation when they were added to the coming soon listings: *Strip Jack Naked*, *I Was Hitler's Maid* and *Plays for Rubber Go Go Girls* were a considerable psychic leap from the typical three-act fodder of Rattigan and Priestley.

The final show at the Sheffield Playhouse, on 26 June 1971, was, in fact, a production of *I Was Hitler's Maid* starring Alun Armstrong in the lead role. Promotion of the show had been edgy and salacious, with the *Sheffield Star* promising/ threatening 'Sheffield's First Full-Frontal Nude Male' and, on the night itself, a determined old woman brushed aside the front-of-house manager with a brusque, 'Don't tell me what I can and can't do!', when he tried to dissuade her from taking her seat. Those in attendance reported that Armstrong had, in reality, been sheathed in white long-johns throughout, but the spirit of mischief and misrule had been kindled.[3]

A teenage attendee on closing night remembers an uneasy blend of art-school hippies and middle-aged professionals in evening dress manoeuvring around each other in a foyer where promotional merchandise such as 'Hitler's rubber duck' and 'Hitler's favourite bedtime story' were on display. The same audience member also recalls the lasting trauma of one scene where a female character wearing a flesh-toned body cast beneath her clothes was attacked by two male characters, stripped, then disembowelled, resulting in coils and clots of animal innards being ripped from the prosthetic pouch and flung around the stage.

At the show's end, before switching off the Playhouse's neon sign for the final time, Colin George mounted the stage and read some of Prospero's verse from Shakespeare's *The Tempest*:

Our revels now are ended. These our actors,
As I foretold you, were all spirits and
Are melted into air, into thin air …
We are such stuff
As dreams are made on, and our little life
Is rounded with a sleep.

In the interregnum between the Playhouse closing its doors and the Crucible Theatre opening up down the road, those in search of artistic excitement would be hard pushed to find any. Richard H. Kirk, who would soon resurrect the spirit of Dada in Sheffield with a new incarnation of Cabaret

Voltaire, looked for glimmers of danger and invention and could only find it in the proto-art-rock of local band McCloskey's Apocalypse. Formed in 1968, this trio of Ray Higgins (vocals/guitar), Mick Wilson (bass/violin) and Dave Seville (drums) were almost famous for staging the world's first rock opera; their performance of *The Redemption of Gaylord McCloskey* at the Sheffield City Hall was only a few weeks behind The Who's premiere of *Tommy*.

Kirk had seen them at the Sheffield Festival in 1969 and was impressed by the improvised, impromptu, absurdist antics of their singer. Higgins would eat live goldfish on stage and chew through chunky dimpled pint pots mid-song. At one gig, during their Friday night residency at the Minerva Tavern in town, an audience member recalls Higgins attempting some ill-advised fire-breathing during a cover of 'The Seeker' by The Who which set fire to someone's afro in the front row.

McCloskey's Apocalypse had even blurred the lines between radical performance art and conventional theatre when they starred in a Playhouse reworking of Shakespeare's *A Midsummer Night's Dream* – 'Words by WS, Music by McCloskey's Apocalypse'.[4] The counterculture was moving north and it was no longer the harmonious, rainbow-striped music hall psychedelia of The Beatles and The Monkees. The acid had gone brown in the basement and the culture that took root in Sheffield's art squats and common rooms was more attuned to the sexspacemagick of Hawkwind, Presuming Ed and the portentous day-after-tomorrow science fiction of Michael Moorcock and J. G. Ballard. Underground ideologies and inspirations hatched in the communes of Ladbroke Grove were soon to find a breeding

ground in an area of Sheffield's city centre traditionally characterised by the industry of 'little mesters', master craftsmen
who toiled in the dark, cramped brick workshops around
West Street and Devonshire Lane. For years, these workshops had produced the finest blades, scissors, tools and
cutlery on the face of the earth but, as mass production
made steel products cheaper, global economic forces drove
the little mesters from their dens and in rushed the young
artists, chancers and layabouts to take their own place at the
workbench.

Although the repurposing of industrial workshops for
electronic and artistic creativity was some years away, one
vital cultural resource embedded itself in this declining quar-
ter of the city centre before the 1970s began when John
Wade opened Rare and Racy at 166 Devonshire Street in
1969. An independent book and record shop that would
nourish the outermost branch line of any art lover's literary
or musical road map, Rare and Racy took possession of an
old bookie's office and, over time, filled three Victorian storeys with enough print and vinyl ammunition to fire a dying
industrial city into creative orbit.

The shop is now closed and empty, although the sign
remains. I remember the shop as if it were a lung; full of entic-
ing paperbacks on looming shelves, in free-standing piles on
the twist of a staircase and in darker, further rooms on the
upper floors where customers could squint and peer but not
venture. Each step between the canyons of books felt like it
might bring a listing stack of Kerouacs down on your shoulders as the floorboards warped and gave with the concen-
trated weight of the ideas bearing down on them. The owners
had decided to keep the old bookies' hatch as a counter,

facing customers on a raised platform as they walked in. The music that emerged from this hatch during the forty-odd years of its function as a portal into new dimensions was a playlist of the most esoteric, abstract and challenging compositions known to mankind. The records in my collection whose inner sleeves are stamped with the Rare and Racy logo, a beatnik cartoon character in shades holding a cane and wearing a sandwich board reading: 'To the Learned – Books and Records Bought, Sold and Exchanged', are from the tame end of the selection they offered: *So Tough* by Carl and the Passions, Love's *Electra Masters* and *The Open Mind of John D Loudermilk*. The records that were played behind the hatch, however, were more likely to be by John Cage, Xenakis or the Mahavishnu Orchestra.

'Unlike most bookstores,' said local NME journalist Andy Gill, 'where there'd be this hush like in church, there'd be this cacophonous racket of free jazz or it'd be John Cage playing. Sun Ra was a shared love. They only liked avant-garde jazz, contemporary classical European avant-garde and old blues, so you'd hear Skip James or Charlie Patton wheezing away at you while you shopped.'[5]

'I first visited on a shopping trip to town with my mum', said Jarvis Cocker. 'I've travelled all over the world and I've never encountered a place like it. Nowhere have I heard music like they played in Rare and Racy.'[6]

This shop would become a well of inspiration and sustenance for the generation who would soon be mooching around the city, educating themselves with whatever they could pick up from John Peel, late night BBC2, the central library and the music press. Martyn Ware, who lived just across the road from Rare and Racy in the brutalist

26

playground of Broomhall flats throughout the 1970s, remembers the shop as a cultural life raft:

Rare and Racy was a key element in my education because you could buy stuff speculatively and cheaply and not worry about it because, if you didn't like it, you could take it back and get half your money back. I'd say 90 per cent of the stuff I bought there, I'd never heard of before. I bet no one ever went up to the counter and said, 'What's that you're playing now? I like that' because it was usually deeply experimental jazz but, to me and my friends, it was our de facto education in terms of learning stuff for ourselves rather than being taught.

This experience was a common one. Like Ken, whose passions diverged from theirs but were equally innovative, the young musicians of 1970s Sheffield were all autodidacts foraging for knowledge in a cold climate or seeking out communities of sympathetic companions where interests could be developed or explored without ridicule or intimidation.

Approaching the Rare and Racy serving hatch with a carefully selected Panther edition of William Burroughs' *Nova Express* or a vinyl copy of Tomita's *Snowflakes Are Dancing*, it was only a small leap to imagine the shop assistants crowded into the small, elevated booth as astronauts busy at the controls of a lunar module. Through the airlock, money could be exchanged for a new weapon in your cultural armoury and, although the sounds that clashed around you were redolent of a dying satellite being lashed by electric cables, you could smile, thank them and return home, one day closer to a life where art was normal and the city outside just something to be endured.

Chapter 3
THE ANALOGUE TRACE

True modern works of art are made, not by artists, but quite simply by men.

Francis Picabia, *Jesus Christ Rastaquouere*

The crisp sound of footsteps upon a concrete floor echo eerily in a vast underground chamber. 'I must get to the capsule, I must!' cries a voice. Reaching a tall, steel stairway, our adventurer begins to climb to the open hatchway in a rocket's side. The hatch clangs into place and, in short time, there is a spine-chilling whoosh and the giant rocket is on its way. No! This is not a science fiction novelist's nightmare, it's a brief account of my impressions on hearing a tape recording made with some imagination and a great deal of trickery by Sheffield guitarist Ken Patten. The tape made by this thirty-seven-year-old Yorkshireman, who started his fretted activities on the banjo before becoming addicted to the plectrum guitar, also contains strange noises popularly associated with a BBC brand of space serial and multi-recorded guitar plus echo. So let's meet Ken Patten and see for ourselves what lies behind the tape just described.[1]

The analogue trace

BMG is, according to the masthead, the oldest and most widely read fretted instrument magazine in the world. It stands for banjo, mandolin and guitar and, in December 1960, its tape-recording columnist, Jeffrey Pocock, gave Ken's innovations in sound their first public airing.

Ken, returning from RAF service after the Second World War with a love of music and radio technology, had moved on from the banjo after buying Lorna a guitar then learning how to play it himself when she showed little interest. He joined a local guitar club but soon became more interested in recording technology, building himself a collection of tape machines with various ingenious fitments that enabled him to attempt multitrack recording of conventional music and, increasingly, futuristic sketches featuring homemade sound effects. Pocock was very taken with Ken's methods:

The weird effects of his interplanetary mission are obtained by feeding back the recording to be added to itself in a decreasing signal while the astronaut's footsteps are made by the disillusioning expedient of lightly tapping the microphone with a pencil. With equipment as versatile as Ken's, the effects obtainable are many and varied: shrieks, whistles and frightful crashes give no clue to their simple origin, being magnified out of all proportion by that pulsating extra dimension.[2]

Added dimensions praised in other audio periodicals of this era included pouring lead shot into a drum to simulate rain, slapping the side of a large cardboard box with a wooden lath to approximate a gunshot or, most laborious of all, an eerie squeak conjured by simply 'tying a six foot length of fairly stout string to the handle of a door, procuring some powdered resin, sprinkling the resin on a folded cloth of around six inches square and pulling the cloth along the taut string'.

Ivor Hillman, lead singer of 1980s Rotherham futurists My Pierrot Dolls, remembers one of Ken's magical homemade solutions to a pre-digital dilemma:

Ken always had these ingenious ideas for creating sounds. One of our songs was called 'Mirrors Don't Lie' and, halfway through the song, there was meant to be the sound of breaking glass. Now Ken obviously didn't want to break anything in the house but he did find a glass vase that was full of pebbles so he shook that over some mics on a coffee table over and over again until it sounded spot on.

Ian Helliwell's research for his book *Tape Leaders* uncovered a previously unheralded generation of tape recorder enthusiasts, active in clubs and correspondence networks across Britain in the 1950s and 1960s. Ken was one of these 'hobbyist' innovators, subscribing to magazines such as *Tape Recording Monthly* and sharing ideas through the post and at the occasional regional meeting of the tape clubs that had sprung up to satisfy interest in new sonic possibilities for the home or shed.

Until Helliwell's book appeared, the common response to an enquiry about innovation in postwar British tape technology would be to trot out the names of Daphne Oram, Delia Derbyshire and other well-known pioneers associated with the BBC Radiophonic Workshop. Helliwell went deeper, discovering a whole new strata of amateur enthusiasts such as F. C. Judd, Malcolm Pointon and Cyril Clouts who had

1 Ken playing his guitar in the room that would become Studio Electrophonique, 1961

amassed wonderful personal collections of taped sounds but never released or distributed them. Helliwell contends that 'the ownership of over two million tape recorders in Britain by the mid-60s represents a futuristic post-war folk music, a garden shed musique concrète movement, responding in a DIY, make-do-and-mend manner to the climate of modernity and science fiction that had gathered pace since the end of the Second World War'.[3]

Helliwell also noted the elitist attitude that pervaded in all areas of music during the postwar years; an establishment-led, class-driven determination to diminish the efforts of independent, self-taught, non-music readers who were seen to be encroaching on professional airspace. At the British Electronic Music Concert at the Queen Elizabeth Hall in London in February 1969, Francis Regnier of the Paris-based Group de Recherches Musicales was asked to comment on 'people who think of electronic music as an amateur's hobby carried on in one's attic'. Regnier replied loftily, stating that 'it would be very difficult indeed for us to conceive that any attempt at composing electronic music in amateur conditions could be taken seriously'.[4] Although it was true that the stamp of professionalism and academia was almost always required in order for a piece of avant-garde music to reach the airwaves or to receive public distribution, thousands of enthusiasts like Ken persevered in 'amateur conditions', pursuing their own visions without the need for financial reward or critical acclaim.

Despite the depth of research undertaken by Helliwell, Ken's experiments on tape after the war, and later with Studio Electrophonique, seemed to reside in an even deeper seam of obscurity. The mission to excavate the details of his life's work was left to us.

Margaret Thatcher once said that 'any man who finds himself, beyond the age of twenty-six, on a bus can consider himself a failure'.

I composed many passages of this book, in my head, on the ninety-seven bus into Sheffield. If you can achieve the necessary detachment from the huffing and puffing of fellow passengers and avoid a grand mal seizure as the low morning sun strobes in your peripheries through the passing terraced streets, it is possible to train the mind on ideas and beautiful prose. But when it's dark and January cold on the top deck and the low branches hit the windows and drag like chains across the groaning hull of a ghost ship in the rain-clogged bus lanes of Abbeydale Road, it's hard to hold anything in your head except perhaps the nagging suspicion that Margaret might have had a fair point. After all, art is one thing, life is another.

I tried my best to find out about Ken's life while working full time in an office job in Sheffield city centre. The office was just behind West Street, equidistant between Western Bank Library and the Central Library. Every lunchtime, after a morning of posting emails directly into the void, I would walk briskly to one or the other, eating limp sandwiches straight from the foil on the way. If you're prepared to put the hours in on the microfiche machine and your idea of the creative life is a few years spent reading all the back issues of *BMG* for a chance sighting of your quarry in print, there's not much that can top this routine.

I picked up some interesting stories during these months in the archives. *Tape Recording Monthly* was marvellous; half the pages were devoted to advertising space for the latest gear: hulking Elizabethan tape recorders, slim Panatella microphones and classified tape-to-disc services from around the country. The other half was reserved for adventures in tape land, readers' letters and doom-laden editorials outlining the inevitable dystopian hijacking of tape technology for nefarious purposes in the near future.

The editor's column in the June 1957 issue is entitled 'Some Proportion' and predicts a future where advances in tape science render the world illiterate:

Stories on tape for children? How long before books are put on tape for adults who are too lazy to read for themselves? How long before people start handling their correspondence on tape instead of with a pen? How long before they decide it is no longer necessary to learn to read and write? This vision of 1984 may seem like a far-fetched nightmare of the intellectuals but, in our enthusiasm for tape, we must keep a sense of proportion and use it intelligently.[5]

Or this 'Glimpse of the Future' from January 1958, where taped bodily rhythms reduce mankind to the level of the performing ape:

Doctors will certainly build up an album of your respiratory and heart sounds and who knows where it will end. In an American laboratory, electrodes were embedded in the brain of an ape. The animal was made to wave his arms and the nerve impulses were captured on tape. Later, when the tape was played back, the ape repeated his original arm-waving motion. A very solemn thought with which to leave you this month.[6]

Even the national competitions organised by the magazine each year seemed to favour entries with an apocalyptic bent. The British amateur tape-recording contest, which Ken was to enter with some success in the 1970s, began in 1958 and was often crowded with quite dreary bucolic offerings such as 'Starlings at Dusk' or 'Sounds of the Morris Men'. The winning entry from 1965, however, meshed perfectly with the editor's fatalistic technological death spiral when 'Mushrooms', composed by student enthusiast Richard

Partridge, swept both the Amphlett Shield and the Emitape Challenge Cup.

This taped rendering of global nuclear annihilation featured a laconic voiceover from a crazed US president, excerpts from Louis MacNeice's poem 'Prayer before Birth' and a final cataclysmic atomic blast created, in Richard's own words, by 'dropping a metal wastepaper basket onto the concrete landing at the bottom of my echoey staircase then replaying it at a speed eight times slower. Lovely!'[7]

Sheffield was especially susceptible to apocalyptic visions. Cabaret Voltaire founder member Richard Kirk believed a city full of hulking industrial furnaces and steel silos was the ideal training ground for junior dystopians:

I remember watching loads of science fiction in the 60s, like *Doctor Who* and *Quatermass*, and all these strange things always seemed to happen in old gas works or industrial environments. Sheffield had an otherworldliness about it. You might see an alien or a giant blob creeping across the floor glowing bright green from radioactivity.[8]

The library that most suited the mood of an imminent nuclear strike or alien invasion was my basement booth in Western Bank library beside Sheffield University's Arts Tower. A common trope that I had heard many times was that a city's soul can, in part, be weighed by the function of its tallest building. For many years, since its official opening in 1966, Sheffield's tallest building was the Arts Tower, a twenty-storey monolith to the advancement of creative pursuits. Sheffield is surrounded by hills and, wherever you stand on the city's rim, the Arts Tower draws your eye as the natural magnetic centre of the landscape. It was opened by the Queen Mother on the same day that she opened Hyde Park Block B, the infamous and now demolished citadel that stood sentinel behind Park Hill flats. She obviously didn't want to endure two separate trips to Sheffield if something more streamlined could be arranged.

Without wishing to labour the *2001* analogy, the stark slab of the Arts Tower came to function as a beacon of inquiry and possibility, drawing, as we shall discover, artists such as Phil Oakey, Cabaret Voltaire and the writer Barry Hines to worship at its foot. The race to build the brutalist colonies of Hyde Park, Kelvin, Broomhall and Park Hill, however, resulted in a brand of futuristic socialism that 'was imposed rather than agreed' and created hives of space age hibernacula that would satisfy Kubrick's eye for design but would not stand the test of time.[9]

Martyn Ware grew up in the rising shadow of the Arts Tower as it was being constructed. The month before the Queen Mother cut the ribbon, he watched his beloved Sheffield Wednesday on the coin-driven TV for the first time, losing 3–2 to Everton in the FA Cup Final. Ware grew up on Hope Street in Netherthorpe, a working-class network of cobbles and terraces just down the hill from the university. His dad was fifty when his youngest son was born and worked as a toolmaker at Joseph Thompson's on Townhead Street, just down the road from the Playhouse. When he was twelve years old, Ware visited his dad's workshop for the first and only time:

He didn't really want me to see where he worked and, when I went there, I understood why because it was the grimmest

2 Hyde Park and Park Hill flats in the late 1970s

thing I've ever witnessed. It was an appalling place to work. He was very proud of his job because it was very skilled but that was definitely the moment when I thought to myself, I am never ever, in my life, going to work in a place like this.[10]

Shortly after this visit, Ware's dad was forced to take early retirement through ill health and missed out on his full pension entitlement as a result. He'd been smoking eighty Capstan full-strength a day and breathing in ground steel dust for most of his working life. 'When he got to eighty years old,' Ware recalls, 'he did move to filter tips but, after a few weeks, he started breaking the tips off.'

The looming Arts Tower aside, Ware's early cultural exposure took place largely beneath the bedclothes, listening to the shifting waves of static that carried the sounds of Radio Luxembourg into his Hope Street bedroom. Although he had inherited a stack of Motown records from his much older sisters (the eldest, Maureen, was twenty years older), the sounds that enchanted young Martyn were the sounds of the future: *Junior Choice* on Radio 2 featuring Sparky and his Magic Piano, a talking instrument with a robotic vocoder voice, and The Beach Boys' 'Good Vibrations', featuring a theremin that sounded like a death ray signal from an interstellar fleet. Ware's Supermarionated TV diet of *Stingray*, *Fireball XL5* and *Space Patrol* also primed him for the imminent leap into the galactic beyond.

On the southern edge of the city, in the bedroom of his parents' house in Totley, Chris Watson was absorbing a similar dose of enchantment over the airwaves. A founder member of Cabaret Voltaire, Watson felt captivated by the lull and surge of the longwave radio.

'It seemed to be coming from another galaxy', remembers Watson. 'It had that analogue warmth to it and the harmonic shift and pulse of the stations fading in and out was very seductive.'

In 1965, when Watson was twelve years old, his dad's mate, an electrician perfectly named Ernest Sockett, got hold of a Japanese-made National reel-to-reel tape recorder from Wigfalls Electricals as a birthday gift for Chris. Soon, Watson was busy recording birdsong in the back garden and seeking out more sophisticated examples of musique concrète on Radio Three. From this unlikely outpost on the edge of the Peak District, Watson was soon marvelling over the compositions of Stockhausen and, in particular, Pierre Schaeffer's 1948 *Etude aux Chemins de Fer*, which Watson believed contained 'the pulse of life' and led directly to Kraftwerk's *Trans Europe Express*. One of many synchronous temporal coincidences that led to the development of the Sheffield space age happened when Ware was invited to the twenty-first birthday party of Chris Watson's girlfriend, Maggie, in July 1977. Cabaret Voltaire had obviously installed or hijacked a sound system with some power and little regard for the neighbours in Coppice View, Crosspool, as Ware remembers arriving at the party and being immediately awestruck by the sound of *Trans Europe Express* rattling the French windows and seething through the privet hedge. Ware was struck bodily and imbued with fresh sonic purpose. 'It changed my perception of how physical electronic music could be.'

Chapter 4
UNTRAINED/UNDAUNTED

There are two worlds, or rather two distinct ways of looking at the same world and these can be called The Inspired and The Uninspired. It is the task of the artist to connect them.

Colin Wilson, *The Outsider*

Sheffield at the dawn of the seventies was not an inspirational place. The pall of a past world sagged and glowered above corrugated factories, industrial fallout cloaked the city with ash and grim-faced men at bus stops wore overalls that were infused with machine oil and potted meat. The papers were full of bomb scares, house fires and Thalidomide babies. Buses crawled through wet streets under grey skies past black trees over brown rivers alive with brewers' yeast and tetanus. Swamped carrier bags moved like spectres under the city's bridges and the water was choked with scrap. In the town centre, spavined pensioners bent to consider dog ends in the metal tread of escalators, carrying them down to underpasses where clerks sat on benches in brown nylon suits eating cheese and onion sandwiches under dim, deoxygenated corporation fishtanks. In strip-lit office blocks, workers stared into the street from tiled stairwells listening for the first creaks of concrete cancer. The mood was moustaches and verrucas, buckled filing cabinets and erupted flagstones, lunchtime strippers at the Hofbräuhaus, sweat stains, bad breath, four sugars in your tea and tinned boiled potatoes and stewing steak in your pantry at home.

It was easy to feel like you had a hard life, coming face to face with The Uninspired each morning when you splashed your face with cold water, when you caught yourself in the mirror in the bogs at work or in the window reflection of the bus taking you home. One of the ways to avoid misery, then as now, was to create your own world as an escape from the drudge. In 1970, Ken Patten was at his peak as the definitive British hobbyist of the age. In addition to his full-time job at the garage, providing for a wife, a daughter and a toy poodle, he was also providing a mobile recording service for local schools and church choirs, creating comedy film sketches for the cine club, playing in a guitar group, making his own fly-fishing tackle and building a powerful speedboat on his front drive.

With all his hobbies, Ken was determined to research, study and construct the most professional equipment for optimum performance. His cine camera rig was semi-professional. Most amateurs had a machine that held a 25ft spool of film; Ken's held 100ft and had an anamorphic lens that enabled him to shoot in CinemaScope. In the reels of film we sat through in the attic, among the holiday footage and the local parades, were carefully staged comedy skits in the style of Eric Sykes's *The Plank* and slow-motion surrealist sequences of his daughter, Michele, dancing in his back garden in shades and snakeskin boots:

Studio Electrophonique

When I was about five, dad got a movie camera and that was a big deal in them days. He joined the Sheffield Cine Club in the 1960s and it was quite a homely affair up there in Pitsmoor. Dad used to drive there in his slippers, or his 'house shoes' as he would call them. When it snowed, he'd come out with his camera and the kids would go past on their sledges and wave. He was always busy with something. He worked full time in the car trade then, at night, he'd go into the lounge and, bit by bit, he built up his recording equipment until, in the early seventies, he bought the corporation house and built an extension on the back so he'd have more room for his gear.

The first recordings credited to Ken are from around this time; snapshots of creative expression in the South Yorkshire hinterlands captured, Alan Lomax style, on his improvised mobile unit. These field recordings were a school musical version of Charlotte Brontë's *Jane Eyre* in the mining village of Thrybergh, Rotherham, and a performance by the Doncaster Wheatsheaf Girls' Choir which Ken also arranged to be pressed to vinyl on the Deroy label as *Singing for Pleasure Vol. 2*. He also did some recording for Radio Sheffield when it launched in 1969, capturing the 200-strong Sheffield Cathedral Choir on two channels in return for free use of their studios on a Sunday.

There are many film reels from this time that celebrate Ken's growing fascination for powerboating and waterskiing. In these films, Ken looks every inch the dashing English rake, blending Graham Hill's square-jawed swank with the jaunty athleticism of a trim, middle-aged secret serviceman on amphibious manoeuvres.

Untrained/undaunted

Ken and his family had been going on holiday in the caravan to Laneham in Nottinghamshire for years. There was a field beside a broad section of the River Trent where bank holiday campers could enjoy the waters in the looming shadow of the Cottam power station and, after a few brave pioneers had launched basic river craft, a crew of the holidaymakers decided to ask the county council if they could buy another field, build a proper slipway and start a boat club.

In time, when the proposal was granted, this group, which included Ken and his family, became organised and proficient. Club wetsuits in black with waspish yellow piping were ordered, a diving pontoon was floated in the middle of the river and waterskiing with ever more sleek and powerful boats became the pursuit of choice. Footage of waterskiers young and old, often on each other's shoulders, standing on kitchen chairs, iron bedsteads or, alarmingly, navigating the choppy backwash of monstrous black coal barges, suggests that this was a time when a risk assessment meant checking that you hadn't forgotten your fags, lighter and a paper-stoppled milk bottle full of red diesel.

When Ken had finished building his speedboat on the drive, it was named *Mischievous* after his daughter and transported by trailer to the slipway at Laneham. Michele's story of the Easter bank holiday weekend of 1970 is, on its own, enough to usher in a raft of health and safety reforms:

We'd been members of the boat club at Laneham for a few years and people used to love to have a ski behind the boats we had but all that had to stop when I was seventeen because the boat that my dad had built exploded with me

3 Ken, wife Lorna and daughter Michele outside 32 Handsworth Grange Crescent, 1957

and dad sat right on top of the inboard engine. We were blown up into the air, aflame both of us, and then down into the River Trent which, luckily, put out the fire. I went unconscious and went to the bottom but the guy who had been waterskiing behind us, George Cliff, who had a timber shop down in Darnall, kicked his skis off and dived down to save me. Thank God he could do that. My dad wasn't as badly hurt and he could stand up and get out. They got me to the riverbank, the ambulance came and we were both rushed to Retford Hospital to see to our burns. After that, he sold the boat, sold the skis and said 'never again'. From then on, it was mainly music.

When we heard this story and tentatively suggested that it could've been worse, Michele quickly put us right:

Well it did get tragically worse, because two and a half months after, when I'd just gone back to work, the car I was being driven in by my boyfriend went under an articulated lorry and I went straight through the windscreen, straight into the back of the lorry, straight into a coma, fractured skull, brain damage, lacerations, the lot. And this was when I was still getting better from the skin grafts. I was in Hull Hospital for I don't know how long and, when they let me out, they said: 'If she hasn't fully improved in two years, that's how she's going to stay for the rest of her time.'

The French poet Arthur Rimbaud said, 'one makes oneself a visionary by a long, immense, ordered derangement of the senses'.[1] After this calamitous sequence of events, Ken retreated into a world he could fully control, the world of sound within the safe confines of his downstairs extension. The emotional and psychological impact the accidents had on Ken can only be guessed at, but what is clear is that he spent the early years of the seventies engaged in more solitary pursuits, experimenting with tape technology, hunting for new sounds, stockpiling audio gear and constructing machinery of his own design.

During the same period, one of the young pioneers of the electronic age was opening his eyes to the cultural world and beginning his own long, immense, ordered derangement of the senses through art, music, fashion and politics. A founder member of Cabaret Voltaire, Stephen Mallinder was born in Sheffield on New Year's Day 1955. His dad died when Stephen was only four years old, so he was raised by his mum and sisters on Delf Street in Heeley, a working-class terrace of red brick Victorian houses near the city's main bus depot at Olive Grove.

Although he had no formal training in music, his father's legacy became a subconscious driving force. 'I never got to know my dad but, in a weird way, I think he might've been the reason I ended up doing music. He used to play the violin and, as a child, I had this fascination with the violin that was still under my mum's bed.'

After attending St Wifrid's Primary School in Millhouses, Mallinder won a scholarship to De La Salle Catholic College which meant a bus journey to Pitsmoor each day, unaware that his collaborator-in-chief, Richard Kirk, was living close by at the top of Burngreave Road. While Mallinder's education was conducted under the rigid supervision of monks, an early interest in popular music was encouraged by older relatives:

Untrained/undaunted

The first record I bought was 'Sweet Talking Guy' by The Chiffons when I was about fourteen. When we were teenagers, we didn't have any money so records were really just the family record collection. My brother-in-law was into Bo Diddley and had Johnny Cash *Live at Folsom Prison*, and my aunty had some Joe Meek records like 'Johnny Remember Me'. The difference came when I met Richard.

Mallinder and Kirk met at The Ark at Crookesmoor, a soul night organised by the Metcalfe twins, Peter and Paul, and hosted at St Nathanael's church hall on the corner of Roebuck Road. The three DJs, Paul, Andrew and Nev, played a mixture of Motown, ska and what would eventually become Northern Soul, attracting teenage aficionados from all over the city. The pair would also go to Sheffield Wednesday matches together, hang around in pinball halls such as The Crystal Rooms and mooch round town looking for something to steal:

We'd go and nick records at Violet May's on Matilda Street, shoving them up the back of our Harrington jackets because she'd prosecute you if she caught you. We'd swap records at school and we were into stuff like The Drifters and Sonny Charles and The Checkmates.

As with every youth movement, the look was crucial. Mallinder and Kirk adopted the soul boy suedehead look immortalised on the covers of tatty New English Library paperbacks by Richard Allen. Sexy Rexy's in the Haymarket in town was reliable for many key purchases but others were hard to find or impossible to afford.

'We wore Levi's Sta-Prest,' said Mallinder, 'Ben Sherman or Brutus button down shirts, Bata monkey boots. I wanted a pair of Royals but I couldn't afford them. We went around in Crombies or blue Marks & Spencers raincoats. We used to have to shoplift to get some of it.'

Although Kirk went to Ashleigh School near Manor Top, the two met up regularly to explore new cultural haunts such as The Heartbeat Club above the Silver Blades ice rink on Queens Road. The Heartbeat Club specialised in Motown and soul and DJ Barry Campbell had amassed an enviable collection of US imports such as The Contours' 'Just a Little Misunderstanding' and The Elgins' 'Heaven Must Have Sent You'. An additional attraction was the fact that Double Diamond pale ale only cost one and eleven (10p) for a half pint.

The desire to soak up as much passionate, vital music as possible soon developed into a need to witness live performances first-hand. Mallinder's lack of money couldn't be allowed to stand in the way of this mission to receive a mainline transmission of soul whenever the big hitters were in town:

When I was fourteen, I went to see Martha and the Vandellas and The Four Tops at the City Hall. I went up and shook hands with Martha Reeves when she was on stage and ended up getting pulled away by the bouncers. They didn't throw me out, they just said, 'Go and fuckin' sit down and don't get up again.' Next time, I had to break in with my friend to see Booker T and the M.G.'s. It was the matinee performance and we kept sneaking in then getting slung out. We eventually sneaked back in through a toilet window and made it up to the balcony to see them. We saw a bit of Jimmy Ruffin and Blue Mink too.

This fervour to connect with something soulful and emotive was raised to a fever pitch by further tantalising glimpses of a world beyond Heeley Bottom. An older lad called Mick Grudge who lived on the next street won a scholarship to play basketball in the USA and, later, Mallinder discovered that Mick was playing saxophone in a United Artists funk band called Brass Construction. His daily bus route from Heeley to Pitsmoor also took him past Peter Stringfellow's King Mojo Club where soul legends such as Wilson Pickett, Tina Turner and Stevie Wonder had appeared live as recently as 1967.

Mallinder's urge to create and expand his horizons also included self-navigated routes through art and literature. He started painting Mondrian copies in his Delf Street basement and haunting Highfields Library, working his way through the lurid hobo jazz odysseys of Kerouac and Kesey then decelerating into the blank-eyed dreadscapes of Sartre and Camus.

Walk north-west from the beatnik aisle at Highfield Library, through Sharrow, Ecclesall and Broomhall, and you will come upon the grand façade of King Edward VII School where Martyn Ware met Phil Oakey in 1970.

Ware had passed his eleven plus and was well aware of his privileged position at a school where masters wore gowns and escape through academia was possible if you gave yourself up to the current. Oakey arrived in the fourth year, an incomer from the midlands with what seemed, to Ware, to be a spectacularly liberated approach to life.

'The great awakening was meeting Phil', said Ware. 'The intellectual rigour of where he was coming from was fascinating. He taught me a lot and I looked up to him. He was more worldly than me. It felt like a blossoming of taste. Things I'd never come across like Frank Zappa and experimental jazz.'

Oakey's early life had been very different to Ware's; his dad, Ralph, had brought the family to Sheffield so that he could take up the role of Head Postmaster. They settled in a large, comfortable house on Crimicar Avenue in Fulwood and Phil, as the youngest sibling, was allowed to please himself. Until their meeting, the pair had very different cultural palates: Ware was into the Gothic doom of Deep Purple's *In Rock* and Black Widow's 'Come to the Sabbat' whereas Oakey was committed to the progressive art-rock of The Nice, Curved Air and Van Der Graaf Generator. Oakey was also obsessed with modern science fiction and passed on to Ware his infectious enthusiasm for the skewed visions of Michael Moorcock, J. G. Ballard and the New Worlds group.

'That was the blue touchpaper', said Ware. 'The idea of taking literary, music and film influences and not being frightened of chucking them all into the same pot was a big part of making The Human League what it became. The friction between playfulness and the profound is what always turned us on.'

Like Ware, Oakey had much older siblings and his parents were often away. The relative opulence and the air of bohemian transgression in Oakey's house when the pair had the place to themselves opened up Ware's worldview and widened his hitherto blinkered range of experience.

The house became a crucible where embryonic ideas were formed and where raw material for future projects could be absorbed. It was even on the route of the school cross-country run, enabling a few of the lads to dip out of the PE lesson and tune out on Phil's beanbags, smoking weed, reading *Oz* magazine and listening to King Crimson until it was time for a steady jog back to King Teds.

As Ken was building his studio and the young artists of the electronic age were busy stockpiling influences, the music map of Sheffield was still a virtual blank. Local music journalist Andy Gill, who worked at the Virgin record shop on The Moor in the 1970s, tried to explain the reason for this void:

Unlike any other city of comparable size, Sheffield lacks the basic machinery for indigenous musical growth. Manchester, Liverpool and all these other provincial outposts possess local studios and small clubs prepared to act as a platform for local talent, as well as the myths, legends and general mystique of earlier musical enterprise which helps guarantee hope in current activities.[2]

At the start of the decade, ex-Gas Board operative Joe Cocker was the only musical artist from Sheffield who had attained worldwide acclaim. This was largely due to his high-profile appearance at the Woodstock Festival in 1969 and the big budget bacchanal of the *Mad Dogs and Englishmen* Tour, which plugged him into the big time but ultimately left him drunk and strung out on heroin back at his mum's house on Tasker Road, Crookes. Gill noted this as his lament continued:

Sheffield has only the rotting memory of a bloated gas fitter made good, and what clubs there are can't afford to put on local bands because of a strange psychological barrier which prevents local gig-goers from admitting that homegrown talent can be as good as that from out of town.[3]

Without the infrastructure necessary to nurture new bands in their infancy, it would be up to the artists of the space age to create their own environments for self-expression. As electronic equipment became more portable, intuitive and affordable, bedrooms, lofts and suburban extensions would be increasingly requisitioned by the untrained yet undaunted musicians and engineers of tomorrow in the hope that the open architecture of machinery and the common spirit of exploration would lead them, liberated, out of the past.

Almost 200 years before, another English visionary, William Blake, articulated this innate urge to break with cultural convention in *Jerusalem: the emanation of a giant Albion*:

I must create my own system or be enslaved by another man's. My business is not to reason and compare, my business is to create.[4]

Chapter 5

THE DÉCOR OF TOMORROW'S HELL

Where I lived was with my dada and mum in Municipal Flat Block 18A, Linear North.

Alex DeLarge, *A Clockwork Orange*

On the 13 January 1971, Stanley Kubrick's film version of Anthony Burgess's novel *A Clockwork Orange* was released in UK cinemas. For cinemagoers familiar with his sci-fi masterpiece *2001: A Space Odyssey*, Alex, the antihero of this new film, played by Malcolm McDowell, must have struck them as being a closer cousin to the risen apes of *2001* than to the serene fallen angel that was the Star Child.[1] For the young artists of Sheffield, this story of teenage power and the personal sanctities of art and friendship among the concrete colonies of the near future had a seismic impact.

'It was an exposition of true youth power', said Martyn Ware. 'Every adult was cast as a fool in that film. That's why it appealed so much.'

The film featured themes that were of obvious appeal to young northerners: a charismatic Yorkshire actor in the lead role, extreme violence, sexual freedom, drugs, friendship,

53

mad fashion and loud electronic music. Slightly less obvious but uniquely applicable to the self-taught artists of Sheffield was the film's treatment of art and its purpose. *Time* magazine's film critic, Robert Hughes, considered this upon the film's release:

At issue is the popular 19th century idea, still held today, that Art Is Good For You, that the purpose of fine art is to provide moral uplift. Kubrick's message, amplified from Burgess's novel, is the opposite. Art has no ethical purpose. There is no religion of beauty. Art serves, instead, to promote ecstatic consciousness. The kind of ecstasy depends on the person who is having it.[2]

This idea, relating to Alex's passion for the high art of Beethoven curiously coupled with the low cunning of an alley cat, chimed with the Sheffield artists who were keen to throw out the old notion of the revered artist and who felt they too had been left to seek out their own artistic heroes in a world as bleak as Alex's. Sheffield bands such as Heaven 17, Clock DVA, Molodoy, Durango 95 and Moloko even signalled their affinity with Kubrick's vision by naming themselves after elements from the film.

Martyn Ware must have watched *A Clockwork Orange* and felt a presentiment of his own domestic future. The shots of Alex returning to his family home in Municipal Flat Block 18A were filmed at the newly built Tavy Bridge Centre at Thamesmead South, London, a vast brutalist estate designed by Robert Rigg. Martyn and his family had recently been rehoused from Burngreave to lodgings in the newly constructed Broomhall flats in the centre of Sheffield, a system-built colony to rival the one depicted in the film.

The décor of tomorrow's hell

During the lifespan of the British housing boom of the 1950s and 1960s, planners and architects moved from the warm, red brick tradition of estates like Ken's at Ballifield to the cold modernist hives of Broomhall without much concern for the long-term happiness of the residents or the longevity of the constructions themselves. Lynsey Hanley, who grew up on a 1960s estate on the outskirts of Birmingham and writes on the subject of social housing, believes that city architects of the era were 'hypnotised by modernism and Le Corbusier' and had turned housebuilding 'from the crowning glory of the welfare state to mass-produced barracks'.[3]

Early publicity for these new estates was not ideal. The architects themselves, who generally lived in leafier zones behind the front lines, appeared to be in competition with each other to see who could raise the most awe-inspiring battlements. James Dunnett, the designer of the Balfron Tower in London, stated that his intention was for the block to inspire 'a delicate sense of terror'.[4] Construction techniques in these new blocks were often untested and corners were sometimes cut with the quality or quantity of crucial materials. When a gas explosion at the Ronan Point tower block in Newham, east London in May 1968 caused concrete walls and floors to collapse, domino-style, down through twenty-two storeys, killing four people, many started to question the safety and sanity of such 'muscular, masculine, abstract structures with no concession to an architecture of domesticity'.[5] Ronan Point had only been completed two months before the explosion.

Broomhall flats were designed to be built using the same concrete panel construction system used at Ronan Point. As a result of the London collapse, eleventh-hour changes dictated that gas heating was to be outlawed in the Sheffield development. The electric underfloor heating and hot-air blowers that were installed as a substitute, coupled with the cold metal window frames, made it very expensive to keep the houses and flats warm enough in winter. The flats were physically suspect and psychologically disorientating. As with many similar designs of the age, raw poured concrete was used, which was often porous and locked in the damp, corroding bolts and reinforced steel bars until rust bled brown through the skin of the building. Identical balconies, walkways and stairwells connected identical blocks, 'like concrete magic carpets or fractals, each leading from one to another in a self-generating whirl, first numbing then dulling the mind with their similarity'.[6]

The French situationist Guy Debord devised a method of classifying the feelings that were inspired by walking

4 Broomhall flats, late 1970s

through certain places. His psychogeographic conclusion found that places with the widest view of the sky induced feelings of happiness and freedom, whereas cluttered, confined areas with dark corners of 'perpetual night' made people anxious and afraid.[7] George Orwell, who visited Sheffield and hated it, believed that the city's council-built estates had 'an uncomfortable, almost prison-like atmosphere and the people who live there are perfectly aware of it'.[8]

It is too easy, however, to wheel out the writers and philosophers and lament what became of these ill-conceived estates. One must remember that Orwell and Debord never lived there either. Admittedly, when my dad used to drive us past The Domino pub on Broomhall flats in the mid-1980s, looking for a spot he could park in to avoid city centre charges, the estate did look like a grim, grey, listless interzone, all leaking membranes and squat, cancerous bulwarks. The playgrounds between the blocks looked like they had been configured from concrete tubes and steel piping left over from the flats' construction.

To Martyn Ware and his family, however, who moved in to 17 High Victoria shortly after the complex was built, the flats were perfect. They were built in the very centre of the city, close to West Street and the university, and although the flats looked like a vast gritty mausoleum, each block did face onto a square of landscaped greenery where the kids could impale themselves on railings or rake open their knees on the edges of roughcast slabs. The futuristic blocks were six stories high and were named, incongruously, after various ancient luminaries: Victoria, Wellington, Monmouth, Cavendish, etc. Addresses on the bottom deck were 'Gardens', those sandwiched in the middle were 'Rows' and those at the top, like the Wares', were classified as 'High'.

Everyone looked at Broomhall flats from the outside and thought, this is a potential shithole, but for us it was luxury. I loved living there and my parents did too. We were on the upper deck and you walked straight in and the bedrooms were on that floor with the living rooms and the kitchen downstairs. This was quite handy from a teenage point of view because it meant you could bring girls back without disturbing your mum and dad.

To imaginative teenagers such as Ware, the dramatic scale and symmetry of the modern flats didn't deaden or demoralise. Growing up in the midst of modernisation and rapid change, pop culture daydreams helped to nourish a rich inner life which could be projected onto these brutalist backdrops through an exotic lens.

'I lived on Broomhall flats for a while when we had the rehearsal space on Devonshire Lane', said Adi Newton. 'I used to look out of this semicircular window on the top floor and there was like a zone of wasteland and then Broomhall flats beyond. It reminded me of Berlin or something, a no-man's land and then these brutalist, eastern European constructions.'

The soundtrack to *A Clockwork Orange*, by Wendy Carlos, was an accompaniment to life in the inner city and an introduction to the synthesiser sound that would be central to The Human League's creative template.

'Wendy Carlos was an absolute inspiration,' remembers Phil Oakey, 'it was the first time we'd ever heard that absorbent, synth-based sound.'[9]

The dystopian rhapsodies of Carlos aside, Ware was also attracted to the theatrical retro glam of artists such as Sha Na Na and Alice Cooper (his first vinyl purchase was *Pretties for You* in 1969). Although the atom-bomb detonation of Roxy Music was still a year or so away, Ware and Oakey, like Ferry and Eno, were unafraid of raiding the pantomime wardrobe for outlandish outfits in fur, foil and leopard print. If Alex from *A Clockwork Orange* could be into Beethoven and Gene Kelly, and Bryan Ferry could wander around Newcastle pretending to be Humphrey Bogart or Charlie Parker, why couldn't Martyn Ware and Phil Oakey strut out of Broomhall flats in green fun-fur jackets and silver boots as if they were central to a J. G. Ballard narrative about time storms and orgasmic implants?

Chapter 6
WAR CHANTS

When I was a child. I thought,
Casually, that solitude
Never needed to be sought.
Something everybody had,
Like nakedness, it lay at hand,
Not specially right or specially wrong,
A plentiful and obvious thing
Not at all hard to understand.

Philip Larkin, 'Best Society'[1]

Equally exotic but less futuristic is the cultural journey of John Marsden of Bannerdale, Sheffield. John's story is a good example of the singular nature of each musical obsessive and serves to illuminate the connective threads that bind Sheffield artists and their legacies together.

One of the most intriguing spools of film that we discovered in the Heron Foods carrier bag was a silent version of a song called 'Little Brown Girl' performed on Hawaiian guitar by a man in a dicky bow with a handlebar moustache as a woman in Pacific island regalia played the ukulele and danced beside him. Ken's hand-made credits named these performers as John Marsden and Kalena, The Maile Hawaiians. After some elementary Googling, we were delighted to discover that John still lived locally and was commonly regarded as one of the world's foremost authorities on Hawaiian music.

We swooped to make contact and quickly discovered several Marsden characteristics that made him, in an instant, one of our favourite people. First, he answered the landline with a formal 'Sheffield 4937', which threw me momentarily as I believed I had mistakenly dialled the year 1953. Second, John doesn't have a mobile phone or a computer. This may not seem obviously endearing or admirable but, when you consider that he has one of the most wide-ranging and revered collections of Pacific island vinyl in the world and is in constant postal correspondence with global enthusiasts in the pursuit of rare and rumoured recordings, his resolve to do it the hard way is astounding. On one of our visits to see John, we asked him what he did after recording the first album made at Ken's studio in 1972. John said he had started to research a book about Felix Mendelssohn's Hawaiian Serenaders, a popular band from the 1940s. When we asked if he a copy lying around that we could have a look at, he told us that he was still writing it but was nearly there, 900 pages in and fifty years later: 'I just need to double-check some of the details of the radio broadcasts they did, and then write the introduction.'

When we asked if he had a publisher lined up, he said he didn't. This is a commitment to art that swallows up decades and has no earthly reward.

In Ken's promo film from 1972, John is around thirty years old, a tall, rangy crooner with a medieval fringe and a smart blue blazer. When he opened the door to us fifty years later, he still had the height and reach of a lap steel cruiserweight but the moustache had paled and the hair was in wild white professorial tufts around his ears. He led James and I into the lounge where he'd pre-heated the room with two out of three panels of the Misermatic gas fire, asked us to take a seat then left to make us all a cup of tea.

On top of the gas fire were piles of correspondence and a big box of Cook's matches. The bookshelves at either side of the fire were crowded with books on two ill-matched topics: extinct birds and James Bond films. Surrounding the TV were listing piles of E240 VHS tapes and various bulky remote-control units. A sparse, silver tinsel tree stood between the TV and the front window. It was Christmas in Bannerdale.

John returned and placed a wickerwork tray of tea down on the table. He'd even got some mince pies in. He hitched up his loose jeans and sat down on his regular chair beneath an oil painting of a beautiful dark-haired woman. There were holes in his socks. James pointed out the painting.

'Is that the same woman as the one in the film?'

John craned his neck towards the wall.

'Yes, that's my wife, Karen', said John. 'We're separated now. She lives in Shrewsbury. She only called herself Kalena for the shows.'

'Was she from Sheffield too?' asked James.

'Yes', said John. 'Well, originally, she was from India but we met in Sheffield and we played in the clubs for years. We started out with the pops-and-Polynesian set-up, you know, regular pops then hit 'em hard with a Polynesian segment. She used to dance with the Māori Poi Balls and do the Samoan Knife Dance. She still cringes when she watches this. She'd only been dancing for about a year at this point.'

With a remote in each hand, John was trying to cue up the version of 'Little Brown Girl' that had full sound and vision. A blast of 'King Creole' came from the TV along with a shot of some young Teds dancing in a pub lounge. James has a pathological obsession with vintage guitars and, as soon as the pub band were in frame, he couldn't stop himself.

'He's got a Burns Nu-Sonic.'

'Yes, that's me,' said John, 'I've still got that upstairs.'

'Nice. Who's that singing?' asked James.

'Steve Denton', said John. 'He was a Presley-type singer. Very good. I played in The Steve Denton Band for about ten years after Karen got tired of what we were doing. We used to get Teds and rockers following us from all around South Yorkshire', said John. 'Then Steve dropped it on us by suddenly announcing he was leaving on New Years Eve 1989 at The Gatefield Club just down the road. Ten years of practice and a diary full of work for the following year and he goes and announces that.' John paused the video on a freeze frame of Denton on one knee. 'So that was it really for the live music. The heart went out of it, really, and then Karen announced she was leaving too. As I say, we're still married, funnily enough.'

John finally navigated to the opening sequence of 'Little Brown Girl', filmed at the Sheffield Cine Club on Barnsley Road, Pitsmoor on 21 January 1972. The film opens with some up-tempo porn funk and an ogrish modulated voice announcing the song's title over a chalk line drawing of a female Hawaiian dancer. Ken is heard next, the only record we have of his voice, a brusque Sheffield roll call of the performers:

John Marsden on Hawaiian steel guitar, bass guitar and vocals, Ken Patten on backing guitars, Kalena on hula dancing and ukulele. The track 'Little Brown Girl' was taken from an LP produced and recorded at Ken Patten's studio, Sheffield.

The lilting strings of the Pacific are then heard as Ken nudges his cine camera through a fern plant and the viewer emerges into an island glade conjured from a wintry back room in Pitsmoor. The pair mime their way through the track in front of a backdrop that I foolishly attempt to identify as Egyptian.

'No,' said John, 'I actually brought that along. It's an authentic Māori batik.'

Karen, or Kalena, looks full of joy but, wearing just a pink bra top, a green-tinsel hula skirt, a red lei garland and a flower in her hair, perhaps she was just hoping for a one-take deal in the January chill. The performance ends with pleasing symmetry as Ken performs a reverse dolly with his camera, moonwalking back through the fronds of the fern before fading to black with the dramatic crescendo of a multitracked choral war chant as a full stop. John pointed one remote and stopped the tape.

'Now that chant at the end there, the war chant,' John said, 'that's the one Ken won the shield for in that competition.'

As part of Ken's involvement with his local tape club and his correspondence with magazines such as *Tape Recording Monthly*, he had gained the expertise and confidence to start entering his own compositions in the annual British amateur tape-recording contest. Ken travelled to London to be awarded the Kodak Shield for his submission of the Hawaiian War Chant and qualified for the 22nd Rangliste Palmares International organised by CIMES which took place in Paris in 1973. Due to work commitments under the arches at Norfolk Bridge, Ken couldn't attend the international leg but he was placed eighth in this category and won a smart Swiss Nivada wrist watch.

John ejected the tape and stood up to retrieve it.

'In fact, I'm sure I've got some pictures upstairs, certainly of the shield', said John. 'You're welcome to have a look.'

Following John up the gloomy twists of his staircase, we were unprepared for two things: the scale of his record collection when he switched on the landing light and the fact that he had a large Girls Aloud poster Blu-Tacked to the facing wall.

Every wall of the long room he led us into was filled, floor to ceiling, with shelves that bowed under the weight of rare Pacific island vinyl in neat manila sleeves. Thousands and thousands of apparently identical records whose provenance was known only to John and, presumably, the neat row of red ring binders in the centre of the display.

'This is just the vinyl,' said John, 'the CDs, DVDs and videos are in the other room, but that's in a mess. And there's more unsorted stuff up in the loft with all the magazine back issues and what have you.'

'I wasn't expecting this when we arrived', said James.

'These ordinary houses,' said John, 'you never know what's inside. It's strange isn't it, to think of the secrets that some of these places hold?'

John didn't like to talk about himself. When we realised that we had stumbled upon another suburban Sheffield semi with almost as much mystique as Ken's, we were full of wonder and questions. John said he was happy to dig out the photos for us but, if we really wanted to know about his life, he would type us a few notes up. He was true to his word on this and, a few weeks later, we received, through the post, two closely type-written sheets of paper with any errors Tippexed out and corrected.

John had lived in Bannerdale and Banner Cross all his life. He'd grown up on Gisborne Road and one of his closest childhood pals was Michael Wilson, later Mick Wilson of McCloskey's Apocalypse. Michael and John grew up in comfortable houses and their childhood pastimes served as foundation courses for their future pursuits. John's dad, who ran an electrical business, helped them rig up curtains and lights in Michael's large basement to put on variety shows for the neighbours. At this point, John was learning the piano and the mouth organ. Michael, who was keen even then to inject the showman spirit into his endeavours, asked his own dad to rig up a trapeze in the basement and this became a more edgy element of the show, with Michael careening through the gloom with nothing beneath him but the poured concrete floor.

John comes after Ken in the chronological lineage of Sheffield sound-hunters but before Chris Watson and Martyn Ware. They were all enchanted in their youth by exotic compositions beamed into the monochrome north on long-distance radio waves. John acquired a tape recorder in his teens and quickly became obsessed with taping anything that struck him as strange or otherworldly; recording the sound of a theremin from the TV was one of his earliest triumphs. This passion soon morphed into a love of atmospheric string sounds and, in the fifties, he drove his parents mad playing and replaying the zither theme from *The Third Man* on the family piano.

Before leaving Sheffield for Manchester University, John's interest had developed into a more general fascination with the Pacific islands. The solitary nature of this obsession found a like-minded community when John spotted the June 1958 issue of *BMG* magazine in the window of Barratt's Music Shop in Manchester. The Hawaiian guitarist Jules Ah See was on the cover and the world that opened up inside the magazine's pages led John to buy a Selmer Novelectric Single Six Hawaiian guitar from Barratt's and commit himself to a life of cultural discovery.

John met Ken through the tape club section of *BMG* magazine in the 1960s. By this time, John was working in the architectural drawing library at Sheffield Town Hall while practising his musicianship and writing a Hawaiian guitar column for *BMG*.

Back in the present day, in one of his red ring binders, he had located the photographs of his visits to Ken's studio: 'As I said, we'd met through the tape club and things just drifted on for a bit then Ken got this idea that he wanted to record some Hawaiian songs and make a film.'

In one picture, there are two young, dark-haired women wearing bulky headphones in a backing vocal pose in front of the studio window blind while Ken, in an orange polo shirt, is in the foreground hitting 'record' on one of his machines. In another, Ken stands with a young Polynesian man, both in blazers, holding the kind of wooden shield you might be awarded for winning Players' Player of the Year for the under-12s.

'So that was the prize he won for the "Hawaiian War Chant"', John pointed out. 'It was actually broadcast on Radio Sheffield too. Standing with Karen there is Margaret Bower, or Moana as she was known. With the shield there, that's Danny Tigilau, who was from Samoa but lived in Chesterfield.'

'So, did you make the album before the film?' asked James.

'No, we recorded "Little Brown Girl" then made the film and then, during the first half of 1972, we recorded the other tracks with Ken. He was a terrific plectrum guitarist and he played on all the tracks. The way he could just play unfamiliar material straight through just by following the charts I'd brought along was amazing. Quite what Lorna felt about the dregs of Sheffield traipsing in all the time, I don't know. She was houseproud but friendly. I think we ended up pressing 100 copies of our album, which we called *Trade Winds*, and I did go back to record at Ken's after that, but only a few times. The last time I saw him must have been a year or so before he died. This picture here', John shuffled out a picture of a grey, reduced-looking Ken in a V-neck Le Shark jumper standing next to John and a younger man wearing glasses and a thick black beard, who is clutching a shellac 78 record. 'Through my correspondence, I'd been in touch with Bob Brozman, who was an American guitar player and ethnomusicologist. He made a famous study of National resonator instruments, quite famous anyway. He played in Robert Crumb's band, the Cheap Suit Serenaders. Anyway, Bob was making a documentary about the Tau Moe Family, a very famous Polynesian band, and he wanted to use a certain song to open the film. He knew that I had one of the surviving vinyl copies of the record, which was called "A Journey to a Star" so he came over and I took him to Ken's studio so he could get a decent copy from one of Ken's machines.'

'He came all the way from America to tape one of your records?' asked James.

'Not exactly,' said John, 'I think he was on a tour and playing somewhere nearby.'

'Did you go and sit in?' I asked.

'Oh no, I'd stopped performing by then. By that time I'd moved into research, and that's the priority nowadays.'

'Well, thanks for helping us with our research,' said James, 'we were worried that the people who worked with Ken at the start might not be around.'

'Well, the threads disappear,' said John, 'that's what I've found.'

We said goodbye and left John to his Christmas of research, records and Tippexed correspondence. He banged the front door twice to make sure it was shut.

While Ken and The Maile Hawaiians were occupied transforming a cold room in Pitsmoor into an island glade, exotica from another source was being introduced to Sheffield's youth a stone's throw from John Marsden's home.

Max Omare was the owner of Shades nightclub which stood halfway up the hill between Hunter's Bar and Banner Cross. The club was directly below the Greystones Bingo Club so the loud music wasn't allowed to start until the last game had been called. Various themed nights and live gigs in the early 1970s exposed young Sheffield artists to new music and new cuisine, as Max's goat curry was available as a punchy antidote to the Fray Bentos fare on offer at home.

Shades was the venue that brought the members of Cabaret Voltaire together. While studying for O-levels and A-levels, Richard Kirk and Stephen Mallinder had drifted apart. Mallinder was still toiling under the stern gaze of the De La Salle monks while Kirk was attending Ashleigh Technical School.[2]

Wednesday night was student night at Shades.

'It was a leftfield night', said Mallinder. 'We used to call the DJ there "The Hassle Man" because he didn't like being hassled to play records. On other nights it was more like a Jamaican club, we went to see Desmond Dekker there once. But on Wednesdays, The Hassle Man would play stuff like Can and the Velvets and Roxy.'

It was during one of these Wednesday nights that Kirk and Mallinder met Chris Watson through mutual friends. Watson was studying at technical college by then and, according to Mallinder, this proved to be a factor that cemented the friendship:

Chris and a few of the other lads were at technical college so they could get us all fake student IDs. This meant we could get into the student union to see bands. We used to go to gigs most Friday nights, get pissed on cheap beer then have a mustard-eating competition in the lower refectory. We wouldn't buy any food, we'd just dare each other to have a big spoonful of mustard. We had very broad musical tastes but things that were edgy or working class or a bit fucking mad were the thing.

War chants

By this time, Mallinder had been given a guitar by one older brother-in-law and a reel-to-reel tape player by another. His reading had expanded into the astral (Huxley's *Doors of Perception*) and the uncanny (Grass's *The Tin Drum*) and his heart was set on an education in the arts:

I'd been for an open day at the art college at Psalter Lane and I thought it was great but, when I got back to school the next day, I had to go and see my careers teacher, Brother Serenus. When I told him I wanted to go to art college, he just said, 'No, you're not doing that. Only drug addicts and homosexuals go to art college.' I wanted to say, 'Exactly!' but I didn't. To get my own back on the Brothers, I was offered a place at Manchester University then turned it down at the last minute to become a labourer in the steel works.

Chapter 7
THIS IS TOMORROW

From now on, we want to shit in different colours.

    Tristan Tzara, 1st Dada Night, Waag Hall, 14 July 1916

As the Apollo moon landings became more of a bore, flickering across TV news bulletins worldwide yet failing to deliver on the promise of the first, Sheffield began to wonder if the leap into the future would ever happen. In the three years between July 1969 and the final lunar mission, in December 1972, the world had expected more than grainy footage of tentative jaunts in the Lunar Roving Vehicle or a couple of six irons floated onto the apron of a crater. I was born two months before the most depressing achievement of the space race, when Apollo 17 took five mice to the moon then brought four of them home to be euthanised and examined for cosmic lesions. The fifth died of boredom before the 75th orbit was completed. As this act of haruspication was taking place in Cape Canaveral, the portents for Sheffield moving into an era of interplanetary exploration and colonisation seemed distant.

'The sixth man on the moon,' Jarvis Cocker recalled, 'who obviously doesn't get remembered very much, was a bloke called Ed Mitchell. He claimed that, when he was standing on the moon, he sent out all these telepathic thoughts that people on earth were supposed to be able to pick up on. I didn't get anything coming through myself, though.'[1]

My dad was on strike with the workers at Presto Tools when I was born in October 1972. My family lived in a maisonette on the Lowedges council estate on the southern rim of the city. My dad and his workmates called Presto Tools 'the dripping factory' because that was all you could afford to eat if you worked there. The McGee family, who ran the firm, wouldn't allow workers to join a union until a principled firebrand called Sylvia Greenwood tried to unionise the shop floor and provoked general unrest among the management. When the bosses still wouldn't recognise the union, Sylvia led the workers out on strike. My dad had to go home and tell my mum that he wouldn't be bringing any wages in for the foreseeable future. They had a new baby and a toddler and a newly rented TV from DER in town. The idea was that solidarity would see Sylvia's army through, but there were a handful of strike-breakers who tainted this notion. One Friday, as my dad stood around a burning oil drum at the factory gates on Penistone Road, a bloke they called 'Wendy' Whitby, who'd not been working there long but had chosen not to join the strike, came out of the factory door and waved his wage packet at the striking workers. The bosses gave in after about three weeks and the union was recognised. 'Wendy' Whitby didn't last long after the workers went back in. Nobody would speak to him and two or three times a week he'd find his overall pockets filled with the grease that they used to lubricate the machines.

Bus travel was standard in the 1970s as we had no car. I remember bus-seat upholstery, the bristly kind that resembled tarantula hair and the faux-leather stitched design, easily gouged to expose its foam innards. I remember colour-coded paper bus tickets that my dad would roll expertly to an impossible tightness and beyond until their molecules failed and they lay in two pieces on the chair arm alongside his perfectly spherical meditative balls of Blu-Tack. I remember the charnel smell of the bin chutes at the bottom of each concrete maisonette stairwell and the angles of housing blocks channelling wind into sudden supernatural vortexes of litter and leaves. I remember the looming tower of the Atlantic flats and the railings beneath, bent into a violent V by the falling body of a teenage suicide. I remember footballs with all their panels peeled off. I remember nosebleeds, grass stains, dog shit and scabs.

Trips to town were a chance to wander the newly constructed municipal concourses of the space age. The town hall extension was built in 1977 and featured an exterior casing that would have suited a lunar base: each window erupting from the exterior wall like a sarcophagal pod. It soon became known locally as the Egg Box and was attached to the blackened Victorian edifice of the old town hall by an umbilical airlock walkway. The interior was even more futuristic. The vast Rates Hall on the ground floor was studded with tiled information hubs and galactic-scale hexagonal hive lighting straight from the Kubrick mood board. A visit to the Vulcan restaurant upstairs was a chance to survey the smoking urban wastes from the comfort of a sleek modernist observation post. It had canted floor-to-ceiling windows, lozenge pad lighting and raw concrete struts between diners. The only thing that spoiled the illusion of striding through an off-world colony were the people who filled up these places. Spaces that looked so sleek and futuristic on the architect's drawing board didn't account for the fact that the same spaces would soon be full of Sheffield pensioners shuffling about in headscarves and flobbing on the floor. If Stanley Kubrick was scouting for locations for a late 1970s near-future epic, he would seize on the angles offered by the Egg Box, especially the uniformed, peak-capped custodians of the information booths, but he would insist on the removal of the careworn mums and the kids in greasy snorkel parkas hanging from pram handles.

Outside the Egg Box, the verdant tranquillity of the Peace Gardens envisaged by the town planners was also compromised by the congregational patterns of two particular Sheffield subcultures.[2] The benches arranged around the ornamental lawns and the central fountain were either loaded with the seeping, gibbering forms of alcoholic tramps or thick with bolts of loppy, denim-clad rockers straight from the lyric book of future Sheffield proto-punks Musical Vomit:

> From my denim undies to my denim whip,
> I've even got a bird with denim tits,
> I've got a denim mind![3]

To misquote H. G. Wells, no one would have believed that sonic revolutions were likely to have their beginnings in a city like mine. Yet across town, intellects vast and cool were hatching their plans.

In the November 1972 issue of *Practical Electronics*, there was a Project X advertisement encouraging intrepid enthusiasts to send off for a build-it-yourself Dewtron synthesiser. Chris Watson and his dad, Alec, signed up and were somewhat underwhelmed by initial deliveries.

'It started with two blocks of brown resin with six coloured wires sticking out of it', said Watson. 'Sometimes the packages arrived and the components weren't identified in the packaging so you didn't know what they were supposed to do.'[4]

Undeterred, the father and son team persisted with a new module each month until the contraption started making interesting noises. Around this time, Watson acquired an Akai 4000 tape recorder and a reference book that would provide years of invaluable guidance: Terence Dwyer's *Composing with Tape Recorders*. His dad also boarded out the loft at Lemont Road so that Chris could mess about with his new gear without getting in everyone else's way.

By 1972, Chris had moved on from technical college to an apprenticeship at the GPO in Sheffield as a telephone engineer. It was here that he met David Bower, whose younger brother, Paul, became a Zelig-like, Forrest Gump figure in 1970s Sheffield, knitting together the threads of various highly influential artistic projects. The Bowers grew up on Langdon Street, Sharrow and had a tough childhood. Their dad, a toolmaker, had a chronic lung condition exacerbated by working conditions and died when the kids were still at school, leaving their mum to manage on her own with the boys and their sister. Paul passed his eleven plus and went to High Storrs School whereas David attended Newfield Secondary Modern and worked hard to secure his role as an apprentice engineer. David married at twenty-two and was lucky enough to take possession of one of the new flats in the same Broomhall complex as Martyn Ware and his family.

Chris Watson and David Bower would often spend time at the newly-weds' flat recording music and tape compositions, including an a cappella version of David Bowie's 'Five Years'. Along with the friends they met at Shades, there was a common urge to transgress the staid and hidebound rituals of Sheffield life.

'There were probably about half a dozen of us at that point', said Mallinder. 'Mick Ford, who had the "Meatwagon" van with the blacked out windows, and Dave Walmsley, who had a Chevrolet Impala with the fins on the back.'

Newly taped compositions made at Bower's flat were literally road tested on the Sheffield public by attaching large speakers to the back of the 'Meatwagon' and blasting them out on suburban streets.

'We were interested in the sounds themselves,' said Watson, 'but also in seeing what kind of reaction we'd get. It attracted attention.'[5]

During this formative period, Kirk and Mallinder were rekindling their bond and seeking out new interests. Mallinder recalls the layabout life:

A big part of it was just having the time to fuck about. From our late teens, we probably saw and spoke to each other every day for twenty years. Back then, we'd go to town every day and wander round the second-hand shops and the army stores, just killing time. We were proper working-class flâneurs. We'd make a cup of tea and a toasted teacake last an hour in a café or the Wimpy then we'd go home for our tea then meet up again at night outside the Classic Cinema in Fitzalan Square. We'd do that most nights and, if someone had a car, you'd take off and go to a pub for half then drive around Derbyshire for a bit. Sometimes we'd go to the film club at the university on a Sunday night and watch something like *La Jetée* or a Buñuel film or Fellini's *Satyricon*, films like that. Or go and watch a Warhol film at the Library Theatre. I remember we used to get kicked out of Rare and Racy just for loitering about. It wasn't really an idle life because we were picking things up and learning. What people do now digitally to find information, we were doing physically by walking about and looking into the edges of these artistic worlds.

The loft at Lemont Road soon became the locus of these artistic explorations. David Bower opted out due to the responsibilities of married life and partly due to the fact that the others didn't like the way he tuned his guitar properly. What had started out as half a dozen mischievous experimental pranksters was soon reduced to a core trio of Watson, Kirk and Mallinder who now assembled twice weekly at the loft to distil their disparate ideas into taped compositions. This cramped 10ft by 6ft pyramid of space became, in essence, their shared teenage bedroom or a magpie's nest where scraps of cultural treasure could be gathered and repurposed. The fact that this fraternal group went on to create music was really only down to Watson's existing equipment and expertise.

'It could have ended up being anything really', said Kirk. 'It could have been film, it could have been literature. We chose music because of its immediacy.'[6]

Watson had become adept at making tape loops fifteen or twenty feet long using his Akai machine and domestic items such as toilet roll inners to wind the tape around.

This is tomorrow

'They were just experiments', said Mallinder. 'It wasn't like we set out to be brave and radical. We were just doing it for ourselves for a laugh. It was the process we were interested in, not the end result. It was like being in a laboratory of sound, capturing mad experiments on tape that gradually built up. There wasn't any idea that we were a band. We were just fucking about.'

I have lived around the corner from Lemont Road for over twenty years and used to walk the kids to the library and the park past number eighteen. I would often stop and gaze at the house in wonder, knowing it was the birthplace of something original and magnificent while people passed me on their way to the Co-op, thinking I must have had a stroke, and my children strayed onto the road, unreined. The legend that enthralled me was, however, some distance from Mallinder's memories of the domestic realities of the loft era:

Me and Kirky would get the forty-five bus and knock on Chris's door. His dad would answer the door and shout, 'Chris! Melvin's here!' He called me that for years. We'd say hello to his mum and the dog then scuttle up into the loft. It was a drop-down ladder and you'd have to squeeze yourself up there. It's a wonder the ceiling didn't collapse with the three of us and Chris's equipment. By then he'd built a two-oscillator synth with its own patching system, we'd got a TEAC four-channel recorder, Richard had bought a clarinet, I bought a bass and we just used to pick things up in junk shops to use. We'd do an hour or so in the loft then nip over to Totley shops for a beer if we had any money then back into the loft for a bit, then back home on the bus. We did that twice a week for two years, religiously.

Setting aside environmental influences and the impact of film, literature and art, it was the musical trinity of David Bowie, Marc Bolan and Roxy Music that provided the fuel to launch the Sheffield space age. Nineteen seventy-two, in particular, was the year that Brian Eno's squalling sci-fi gadgetry, Bryan Ferry's glint-eyed, greased vibrato and the freeform glam theatrics of Andy Mackay left indelible marks on all the artists who made music in the city during the coming decade.

Although they probably weren't aware of it when they tuned in to watch Roxy Music perform 'Ladytron' on *The Old Grey Whistle Test* in June 1972, Sheffield's young artists were bearing witness to a perfect distillation of the pop culture ingredients that they would later raid for their own projects. Unlike the young Sheffield bands of the era, Ferry and Eno were products of the radical art schools of the 1960s. Ferry had studied under Richard Hamilton at Newcastle and was unafraid of linking music, art, film and commerce in the way that Hamilton and Peter Blake had with The Beatles and Andy Warhol had with The Velvet Underground.[7]

Roxy's shiny sonic sleaze was a brash, clever, intoxicating blend of pop art, science fiction, Hollywood glamour and atomic age machinery. The concepts and lyrical content drew heavily on the collage art of The Independent Group, which included Ferry's mentor, Hamilton, and the Scottish surrealist Eduardo Paolozzi. Hamilton's 1956 work *Just what is it that makes today's homes so different, so appealing?* and Paolozzi's *Bunk* collages both used 'found' materials that juxtaposed American advertising, Hollywood gossip magazines, *Popular Mechanics* periodicals and imagery from the macho world of war and weaponry to hint at a world to come where drone warfare would scroll down a screen just ahead of a miracle hair-loss cure.

Paolozzi in particular was a modest, unheralded visionary whose life and work links directly with all the key influences later brought to bear on the Sheffield space age. Born in Scotland to parents who were Italian immigrants, Paolozzi and members of his family were interned as enemies of the state during the Second World War. When he was released at the age of sixteen, Paolozzi discovered that his father, uncle and grandfather had been killed by a German U-boat attack as their ship was heading to a prison camp in Canada. Not only did Paolozzi later become friends with Dada artist Tristan Tzara in Paris in the late 1940s, he also worked with Michael Moorcock and J. G. Ballard on the *New Worlds* sci-fi anthologies and with Peter and Alison Smithson in The Independent Group. The Smithsons were northerners (Alison, like Ken, was born in Sheffield in the 1920s) and, as a team of architects, they were at the forefront of the modernist or new brutalist school that dominated urban regeneration projects like the ones at Broomhall in Sheffield. Together, they designed the Robin Hood Gardens estate in Poplar, east London and featured, along with Hamilton and Paolozzi, in *This Is Tomorrow*, a landmark art exhibition at the Whitechapel Gallery in 1956 which included early pop art posters along with dystopian sculptural installations.

Echoes of the work of The Independent Group can clearly be seen in projects by Sheffield artists who discovered their work in the 1970s. Concepts for work such as Heaven 17's *Penthouse and Pavement* and *The Luxury Gap* and Phil Oakey's collaboration with Giorgio Moroder on 'Together in Electric Dreams' play with satirical ideas about capitalist, consumerist desires and expectations, and the tightening embrace of technology, and could have served as collage titles for Hamilton or Paolozzi in the late 1950s.

It would be a push to claim that all of these cultural links were sifting through the receptive sensors of key viewers in Sheffield front rooms on that night in June 1972. They were more likely to be wondering why a guy with a rock'n'roll haircut and a green Bacofoil shirt with a stiff Ming the Merciless collar was playing the accompaniment to a lunar time storm on an oboe, why a spectral hand in golden gloves was troubling some dials on an industrial console and why a singer who looked like a narcotised hybrid of Arthur Seaton and Anna Karina was singing in a Jacques Brel voice about the pursuit of sex robots.

Eno, in full leopard print, alien-cranium majesty at the controls of his EMS VCS3 was, apparently, deemed too startling to reveal to the viewer until four minutes into the song when he is first glimpsed oscillating wildly as Phil Manzanera, in compound insectoid goggles, assists him in feeding the melody of the song through a sonic wormhole.

To the impressionable hearts and minds of Sheffield, the arrival of Roxy Music was everything, all at once.

'I measure all pop stars against that performance', said ABC's Mark White.

In the same month as the Whistle Test and the debut album, Roxy headlined a free six-band gig at Sheffield University, accompanied by bands whose names alone suggested that they now belonged to the patchouli-drenched past: Superslug, Trees, Home, Capability Brown and Warhorse may have been heavy on the substance, but the young Sheffield artists were here for the glamour and style that would facilitate their dreams of escape.

With the release of Roxy Music's debut album and Bowie's Ziggy transformation, it suddenly became acceptable for northern blokes to wear make-up and women's clothes. Some, including Bowie's own band, were initially reticent but soon relaxed into it when they realised their new look gave them an androgynous cachet beyond the scope of the typical hetero rocker from Hull. Martyn Ware remembers the dawn of glam:

I started off going to the Castle Market to buy Harrington jackets and Oxford bags but, when things moved onto glam, we just wanted to dress like our heroes. I started customising my clothes. I'd buy a white T-shirt and stick a silver bangle to the front with glue, thinking I looked like something out of *Doctor Who*. Then I got the green fun-fur jacket and some high-waisted loons. Me and Phil used to go to the sales in women's clothes shops and buy platform shoes. I had several pairs, as the heels used to break off and you'd have to hobble home through town with one leg two inches shorter than the other. We looked so far off the charts that we never got any grief, not even from the beer monsters. They didn't know what to make of us. It was a Sheffield working-class thing. You go to work all week in your normal clothes then play out your fantasy life at the weekend.

By the time Roxy Music played Sheffield again, at the student accommodation block Ranmoor Hall in November 1972 (admission price 50p), the younger artists in Sheffield were starting to assert their independence and individuality.

Phil Oakey had decided to drop out of school instead of staying on for his A-levels. His parents told him he needed to get a job so he went to work in the university bookshop at the base of the Arts Tower. This job allowed him to express his new sartorial urges and indulge his established love of science fiction.

'I would go to work in purple velvet trousers and high-heeled shoes', said Oakey. 'They let me do the sci-fi section as long as I kept the maths section in order.'[8]

Shortly after this move into the world of work, Oakey's parents retired and moved away from Sheffield, leaving Phil to fend for himself in his self-created world of fantastical fiction, flamboyant fashion and fast motorbikes. He moved into a small flat in Middlewood and quickly turned it into a repair shop. One day, a Triumph Thunderbird engine he was fixing on the kitchen table tipped over and fell out of the flat window, burying itself in the scabby grass verge like a meteor. His look veered from transvestite chic to galactic chic to biker chic but, somehow, he went about his daily business in Sheffield without molestation.

'Nobody messed with Phil,' said Ware, 'he always looked kind of tough and greasy and covered in shit because he'd bought his first motorbike when he was sixteen.'[9]

Oakey would take Ware out on the back of his BSA Beezer or his Norton Commando into the wide open spaces of the Peak District, an experience that awakened a sensual rush of feeling in Ware and cemented their bond as a pair of unshackled romantics.

Don't be fooled into thinking that the materialisation of Roxy Music and Ziggy Stardust ushered in an age of universal tolerance and acceptance, however, even in Sheffield's artier regions. At a Faust gig attended by Martyn Ware at the City Hall in October 1972, a local in the crowd, who struggled to understand the art in Werner 'Zappi' Diermaier drilling into concrete slabs while the keyboard player played on a pinball machine, shouted, 'It's fucking shit this, get off!' Zappi, feeling that his freedom to create had been unfairly judged, jumped off the stage to discuss this and was promptly chinned. The gig was cancelled and everyone had to go home. Sheffield had not yet committed to the great leap forward.

Chapter 8
KNOCK THREE TIMES AND
ASK FOR BIG JAKE

They are the we of me.

Frankie in *The Member of the Wedding*
by Carson McCullers

Ken's beginnings were far removed from the dreams of space and sonic invention that he would later explore. His parents, John and Trixie, first encountered each other in a story straight from the rejection pile beneath D. H. Lawrence's desk. Michele related this tale:

John was a farm labourer and Trixie was from a rich family of jewellers. She had servants, maids, horseman, the lot. And she'd been to a Swiss finishing school. Trixie's family wanted to arrange a marriage for her with a rich banker from London but she didn't want to, so one day she absconded with the horse and carriage and ended up out near some church in Hillsborough. She was black-haired, dressed like a queen and, when the service ended, she stayed behind while the congregation were serving teas and coffees. That's when she noticed this man, shabbily dressed but very handsome.

Knock three times and ask for Big Jake

He was short because he'd been in a very bad farming accident and it had shortened his legs and made him a shorter
person than he should have been. Anyway, this man made her
a cup of tea and two weeks later they decided they wanted
to get married. Her parents were furious, of course, but they
still went ahead, lived on the farm where John worked for a
bit and then, when my dad was born, my grandad decided he
was going to try his hand at being a painter and decorator
and moved a bit closer to Sheffield.

Ken's early years were spent at 126 Alnwick Road in
Hollinsend and, as a teenager, he lived next door to his
grandparents at 35 Gleadless Avenue. He joined the RAF
just after his eighteenth birthday in 1941 and completed
his training near St Andrews in Scotland. He soon found
that two of his burgeoning interests were well catered for
in the armed forces. His mother and his Auntie Elsie, who
was a successful opera singer, had passed on their affinity
for music and composition and soon Ken was playing the
banjo in the RAF band. He was also very quick to pick up
new skills relating to radio and communications technology.
    When I say 'pick up', I mean 'develop' but I also mean
'petty theft'. Evidence of Ken's use of items requisitioned
from the government can be found in one of Jarvis Cocker's
stories from Studio Electrophonique:

During a break in recording, we were just chatting and someone mentioned the ELO song 'Mr Blue Sky' and Ken said,
'You know what makes that robotic voice in "Mr Blue Sky"?'
and we said we didn't. So he goes, 'Vocoder. Do you know
how much they cost?' and we said we didn't so he said, 'Set

you back about two grand, one of them. Do you know how much mine cost me? 50p. Do you want to know how I did it?' So we said: 'Yes Ken.' So he told us this story about when he was in the RAF.

He said they used to use special microphones for communication in planes because all the background noise made it impossible to use normal ones. They had these things called throat mics that were strapped onto your throat to pick up the vibrations when you spoke. He said, 'I kept some of them mics from the war and what people don't know is that microphones and speakers use the same principle, just in reverse. So what I did was, I got a keyboard, plugged these throat mics into it then fastened them to my throat and then, when I played a chord and opened my mouth to form the words, it sounded like a robot, just like a vocoder. Now all that were free because I had them from the war. Do you want to know why it cost 50p?' and we said, 'Yes Ken, we do' and he said, 'Well, it's very quiet, the robot voice, so what I had to do was get two toilet roll tubes, Sellotape them together and put it to my mouth to make it louder.' So that was where the budget had gone, two toilet rolls.

As well as giving him a technical schooling that would later enhance his musical pursuits, the RAF also gave Ken a glimpse of an exotic world beyond Sheffield. He met Lorna during his training and they married shortly before he was shipped to India in 1944. It is important to stress at this point how devastatingly handsome Ken was in his early twenties. His official RAF portrait inscribed with a loving message to Lorna could be an RKO studio portrait introducing Hollywood's latest Brilliantined Beau. Shots taken on the subcontinent depict a lean, bronzed, Errol Flynn figure in pristine white shorts, Captain Blood with a clipped moustache and an immaculate side parting. The tales he related to his daughter from these adventurous days illustrate how Ken's time in the East exposed him to an intensity of experience that he couldn't have imagined as a working-class youth in Sheffield:

When he got off the boat in Calcutta, he said it was like a hot oven had hit him. The stench and the heat and the people begging in the gutter, in Calcutta, and straight away my dad felt sorry for them. Later on, he said he met some Anglo-Indian millionaires who would open up their homes in the foothills of the Himalayas to dad and these handsome RAF pilots. They'd have racing horses and beautiful daughters and my dad would go there on his leave.

Ken sailed back from India in 1946 and was discharged honourably from the RAF. He began work as a panel beater, repairing damaged vehicles, and eventually opened his own garage in one of the arches beneath Norfolk Bridge in Sheffield city centre. When the council built the new estate at Ballifield, Ken and Lorna moved in at number 32 Handsworth Grange Crescent and domestic life began.

Stanley Cook, a relatively unknown Sheffield poet and schoolteacher who was born the year before Ken and died the year after, wrote a poem called 'Pigeon Cotes on Penistone Road'. When my mum passed her test in the seventies, we got our first family car, a Mini with holes rusted through the floor so you could see the road rushing along

5 Ken's RAF portrait, 1943

beneath you. Sometimes, we'd go in the car to pick my dad up from his work at Presto Tools on Penistone Road. The pigeon cotes referenced in the poem's title were ranged across the embankment opposite his factory like a ramshackle estate knocked up out of offcuts, pallets, nails and wire mesh. My dad used to have me on that poor people lived up there and that, if I didn't watch myself and get on at school, I might end up joining them.

Cook's poem celebrates people like Ken; hobbyists who take great pride in their pastimes even if glory never comes their way:

Sometimes, to someone, pigeon fanciers,
Backyard mechanics, rabbit breeders,

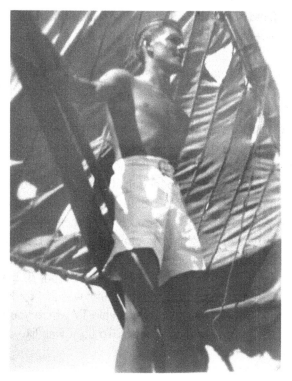

6 Ken in India, 1944

Hermit chrysanthemum growers on allotments
And trumpet players in silver prize bands
Are/were/will be great.[1]

The formation of Ken's creative kingdom spanned many disciplines and hobbies and was an eccentric blend of cutting-edge innovation and kitchen-sink domestication. Mike Day, known to all as Daisy in his time as singer of Sheffield post-punk band Tsi Tsa, recalls the generational gulf between Ken and the young artists of the time.

If I was to describe Ken, I'd say he was kind of like Harold Wilson, that kind of generation. I remember him sitting there in a three-piece suit, or certainly two pieces of it, or wearing a cardigan. He was your typical northern older man. I'm not sure he was even that old when we met him but, to us, he seemed a million years old. He had some cool stuff though. The bulk of the work happened upstairs in a trippy room covered entirely in curtains to create a very dead sound. You'd record your guitar, bass and vocals separately in there then, at three o'clock, everything stopped for tea. Mrs Patten, who like many northern housewives of that time had been invisible in the background, would appear with a pot of tea and some biscuits. We got a bit excited but it was just for Ken. In the studio downstairs, there was a little TV where you could watch the guys recording upstairs. To us, it was like a sci-fi movie.

Approaching the house on Handsworth Grange Crescent was an exciting yet disconcerting experience. Outwardly, it felt like you were dropping in on an elderly relative but, from previous experience or local hearsay, you knew you were about to cross the threshold into a world of ideas and possibility.

John Mayfield, founder member of The Naughtiest Girl Was a Monitor, remembers this routine:

The process was always the same when you arrived at Ken's: you rang the bell, the poodle would yap, Ken would let you in, his wife would say hello and you'd go through into the studio. Sessions were evenings and weekends usually. Ken's wife would occasionally pop her head around the door to hand Ken his tablets and say, 'Make sure you take them before your tea.' Ken would always have his pipe with him, lit or unlit, and he'd always have his carpet slippers on. It was like working with your favourite uncle. Despite his appearance, Ken was quite futuristic. He was proud of the fact that he'd built his own synth and vocoder. He had a Roland CR-68 drum machine too, which was quite expensive in those days.

Ivor Hillman recalls the clash of cultures as his band, My Pierrot Dolls, tried to fuse Rotherham and Rimbaud in a house where Louis L'Amour paperbacks and John Wayne gunslinger movies were more in vogue:

We formed in Rawmarsh and started out as The Frozen Ones but I thought we needed a French name to compete with your Visages and your Depeche Modes. Ken was a legend to all the local bands. I remember when you parked your car or your van up outside Ken's, you'd go up to the front door and he had a sign on it that said, 'Knock three times and ask for Big Jake'. A few of the tracks we recorded with Ken got played on Radio Hallam and put on a compilation album called *Subtle Hints*. He also helped us get some songs ready for a TDK Battle of the Bands competition at Sheffield University. I was working at Dale Farms yoghurt factory at the time and we took a coachload across to cheer us on. When we ended up not getting placed, it all kicked off. It was in the paper the next day and I think the headline was something like, 'Battle of the Bands Ends on a Sour Note as Yoghurt Workers Fight it Out'.

Studio Electrophonique

Rob Coupe, guitarist in Woodhouse's The Electric Armpits, recalls the details of his visit to Studio Electrophonique with the lucidity of a dreamer being asked to recall their time in some lost domain:

We were a bunch of weirdo misfits: the tallest kid, the fattest kid, the short kid with the big nose. Even though we were only eighteen-year-old schoolkids, Ken seemed to take us totally seriously. You'd have to take your shoes off first but it was so exciting to walk into his studio and see that big reel-to-reel machine and the VU meters swinging up and down. He had all sorts of equipment tucked in here and there: a Powertran monophonic synthesiser that he'd built himself, a spring reverb in a bit of drainpipe. It was pretty tight with all the band and Ken in there together. Maybe ten foot by ten foot. You had to kneel to operate the mixing desk.

I remember Ken's wife sitting in the dark in the other half of the lounge watching TV. I also remember that we took along a few bottles of fizzy water to keep us refreshed. We took Evian, sparkling, with a hint of lemon. We felt ever so sophisticated sipping it straight from the bottle. After the session, I think we listened to the cassette in the car in the pub carpark and argued about who was going to take it home. I think the general idea was that Ken ran you a tape off with the idea that you'd return at a later date to mix it properly. I don't think we went back to mix it, we just thought that were it.

Pulp were two years above us at our school and Jarvis's sister, Saskia, was in my class. We thought if they could get on the radio from a tape they'd done at Ken's, that it was open to anyone with a bit of enthusiasm and talent. As it happens, we just got rejection letters from all the major labels and a pleasant note from Frank Sidebottom.

We went to Ken's one last time to record a Christmas single. We were quite naïve though because I think we recorded it on something like December 23rd and came away with a tape that no one had heard and we had no way of promoting with one day left until Christmas Day. We were just sat there in the pub looking at this cassette. So I think only our parents heard it and, by the time we played it to people in the New Year, it was pointless and obsolete.

Adding to this curious mixture of art and domesticity, and further enhancing Ken's claim to be the lodestone of all Sheffield's cultural developments in the 1970s and 1980s, is the fact that a teenage Sean Bean often popped round to Studio Electrophonique to pay his dad's garage bill. The actor, whose mum still lives around the corner from Ken's, grew up in Ballifield and, according to Michele, was proud to be seen being driven around by his dad in a classic car:

His dad was a director at a foundry he'd set up. He'd bought himself a Rolls Royce so, naturally, Sean wanted to be dropped off at school in it. If his dad scratched the car or had a bump, my dad would fix it up and Sean would be sent round to pay the bill. He'd come round as a surly teenager, knock on the door and say, 'I've brought t' money for me fatha's car'.

In 1973, while Sean was still at school weighing up the prospects of a City and Guilds welding course at Rotherham

College, a council arts initiative was being promoted in Sheffield's secondary schools that captured the attention of some of the other young artists in the city.

Glenn Gregory was born in 1958 and grew up as an only child on the Flower Estate in Shiregreen. His dad was a steelworker and his mum worked as a secretary at the Northern General Hospital. He attended Hinde House School but didn't enjoy the drudgery of the lessons or the prospect of following his dad into factory life. He wanted to be an actor. One morning in assembly, the head teacher read an announcement:

Without much enthusiasm, from him or the audience, he read that there was going to be a theatre arts workshop in town and was anyone interested? I stood up but he didn't see me so he just carried on reading the other notices as about 500 sneering fifteen-year-olds stared at me. One of the other teachers must have drawn his attention to me and he stopped and said, 'Yes Gregory, what is it?' and I said, 'I'm interested', and he said, 'Interested in what, boy?' So I had to go and see him after assembly and I'm sure he thought I was trying to pull some kind of scam because he was saying, 'This is at the weekend you know. You don't get any time off school.'

You couldn't shift for Arts Laboratories back then. Bowie had emerged from this scene in the late 1960s and, in 1970, J. G. Ballard had staged his *Crashed Cars* exhibition at the New Arts Lab in London. The new Sheffield arts workshop was organised by former Playhouse actor and playwright Chris Wilkinson, his wife, Veronica, and their colleague, Justin Downing. They were somehow able to badge it with the suggestively carnivorous name Meatwhistle, which was a polari term for an appetising penis, and launched the project at the polytechnic on Pond Street in Easter 1973.

The ambitious plan was to gather young people from some of the toughest comprehensive schools in the city,

7 Glenn Gregory of Heaven 17 in his nan's garden on the Flower Estate, Shiregreen, 1973

find a space for them to meet and swap ideas, then stage a week-long festival of art and free expression at the Crucible Theatre. The nightly headline production at this festival would be Peter Weiss's controversial *Marat/Sade*, a play that featured the Marquis de Sade directing lunatics in a play within a play about the assassination of Jean-Paul Marat during the French Revolution. The Wilkinsons had secured funding for the project as a development of the existing Earthworks scheme devised by John King. The purpose was to encourage the wider representation of disadvantaged kids in every aspect of the arts world.

On the first Saturday at Sheffield Polytechnic, Glenn met Ian Reddington, who would later join the Royal Shakespeare Company and star as Tricky Dicky in *Eastenders*, and Mark Civico, who would go on to form the less illustrious but highly influential proto-punk band Musical Vomit. As soon as the core of committed Meatwhistlers was established, the Wilkinsons moved the operation into the Holly Building, an old Victorian school behind the City Hall. This became known as 'the workhouse'.

One of the first activities in preparation for the performance of *Marat/Sade*, a drama set within the confines of the Charenton Asylum in 1808, was a fact-finding trip to Grenoside Mental Hospital to soak up the mannerisms of the disturbed.

The Meatwhistle festival itself took place between 16 and 21 July 1973 and, in addition to the headline performance, it included all sorts of irreverent fooling about, instigated by the kids and organised by a young theatre manager with infinite tolerance and the untoppable name Roger De Wolf. Warm-up skits from De Wolf's itinerary include *Twinkie*

8 Veronica Wilkinson, artist and founder of the Meatwhistle arts project, 1976

Hour, *Bleen Thrape*, *Spray-on Theatre* and *Workhouse Beanfeast*.

'*Bleen Thrape* was very violent', recalled Mark Civico. 'It was just an excuse for us to make loads of weapons. We spent hours in the craft room at Holly Street making maces.'[2]

For Glenn Gregory, who was cast as one of the four singers in the headline play, his involvement in Meatwhistle was life-changing. As the build up to the week at the Crucible intensified, Gregory stopped going to school without telling his parents and committed himself to a life in the arts.

'It turned out to be absolutely the best thing that ever happened to me', said Gregory. 'It was a place of freedom and fun. It was eye-opening, life-affirming and just brilliant.'

The summer that Meatwhistle took over the Crucible, Martyn Ware dropped out of his A-levels at King Edward's

9 Chris Wilkinson, actor, playwright and founder of the Meatwhistle arts project, 1976

and got a place on a trainee managers' course at the Sheffield and Ecclesall Co-op. On his first day at the training centre, he met Paul Bower, younger brother of David, and they became friends, bonding over David Bowie. Soon, Ware was dispatched to his trainee role at the Gleadless Townend branch but, after a few months of boning bacon and handing out free cheese to needy pensioners, he packed it in for a more future-facing role as a computer operator at Lucas Industries just off West Street. In an improbable coincidence, the role vacated by Ware was filled by Glenn Gregory, who went on to complete his training with new pal Paul Bower and later encouraged both of them to join him at the Meatwhistle workhouse.

10 The hand drawn timetable for the first Meatwhistle arts event 1973

Studio Electrophonique

One of Gregory's last memories of Hinde House School was an appointment with a visionary career adviser:

She said to me, 'What do you want to do?' and I said, 'I want to work in the theatre', and she went, 'Oh dear. Let me have a look.' So she went through this card index and picked one out and said, 'How about this?' and she handed me a card and it was for a vacancy to be a trainee manager at the Co-op. I'd love to question her now about the line of thinking that led her to that. That careers adviser probably saved my life because I met Paul Bower at the Co-op and that's how him and Martyn Ware found out about Meatwhistle.

Following that path of logic, the Hinde House careers adviser who suggested the role at the Co-op was probably responsible for the entire Sheffield space age as, without her advice, the members of The Future, Heaven 17, Clock DVA and The Human League would never have met.

A futuristic band that emerged from Sheffield without the bohemian boost of a council arts lab or the help of a soothsayer in the school careers office was Vice Versa. As 1973 became 1974, founder members Mark White and Stephen Singleton were developing similar cultural identities in different postcodes. Mark, like Pulp and The Electric Armpits, went to City School. His parents were from the Manor and Arbourthorne estates and his dad, perhaps as a herald of an age of music about the joys and perils of automation, had a job 'designing machines that made other machines'.

Stephen was growing up on Bowood Road in Sharrow Vale with relatively restricted access to pop culture:

It may seem a little odd to say this, but my parents couldn't afford a television, so the only source of entertainment in my house was a radio. I listened to a lot of music. I loved songs and stories within songs, things like 'Distant Drums' by Jim Reeves, 'Green, Green Grass Of Home' by Tom Jones and 'Strangers In The Night' by Frank Sinatra. Eventually my parents got a television and the first time I heard electronic music was the *Doctor Who* theme music. I just thought: 'Oh my God, what's that?' it was mysterious and scary.[3]

The musical awakening for Singleton was the axle-greased glam transformation of Tyrannosaurus Rex into T. Rex in the early 70s:

I went to school down at Hunters Bar with Joe Elliott from Def Leppard and we were both really into football but then we got really into music. We went from playing football every lunchtime to asking if we could borrow the school record player and taking in singles to play on it. T. Rex were like our Beatles or Stones and that was the first gig I went to at Sheffield City Hall when I was eleven. It looked incredible. It sounded like nothing I'd ever heard before. I was like: 'What the fuck? Imagine if I could be in a band.'

Mark was equally taken by Bolan's power and presentation. He asked his parents for a guitar and received a cheap, steel-stringed acoustic from a shop on Chapel Walk:

The action was so high I'd go as far to say that it was impossible to play. It was like cheese wire on my little fingers and the sounds I got out of it sounded nothing like Marc's guitar.

I just didn't understand the difference between electric and acoustic guitars.

The impact made by T. Rex on young Sheffield artists during their regular visits to the City Hall in the early 1970s was felt viscerally as a three-pronged attack of raw guitars, iridescent glamour and the poise and beauty of Bolan himself. Those, like Martyn Ware, who attended the 1974 Truck Off tour gig in Sheffield, however, were treated to an unexpected fourth prong:

It was the most exciting opening to a show ever. The chords from 'Twentieth Century Boy' rang out across the darkened auditorium, then a big fifteen-foot star began to lift from the stage with Bolan strapped to it playing his guitar. I was only about five yards from the stage and Bolan was wearing a sparkly bolero top and these black Spandex tights. Suddenly, I noticed something hanging out of his shiny trousers. It looked like a pair of joke-shop bollocks, completely hairless. I thought it must be a practical joke, but he did leave the stage after that song and came back on wearing different trousers, so it must have been his actual bollocks.

The look soon became as important as the sound and, although fashion risks in Sheffield were not subject to the same levels of exposure as those experienced by Marc Bolan, glam music and film changed how people presented themselves to the world.

'Wearing star jumpers from the Castle Market was our version of going to Savile Row', said Mark White. 'There was one boy I knew who had a burgundy Levi's corduroy jacket with matching trousers, and I was very jealous about that.'

'I didn't wear school uniform like everyone else,' said Stephen Singleton, a student at High Storrs School. 'I ended up wearing a white suit like David Essex in *Stardust* and I wore Adidas training shoes. There was no turning back.'[4]

Although glimmers of stardust could be made out in the soot and steam of Sheffield in 1974, it was still a world where new art and ideas had a battle for survival against the hardwired traditions of northern life.

Even in the Arts Tower, a bastion of cultural advancement and exploration, some artists were unwilling to decommission the old structures of Sheffield life before others plugged in and began again at year zero. It is remarkable to think that, on certain days in 1974, four or five great Sheffield artists were milling about on the wide concrete esplanade beneath the tower, stung by the blasts of spray that the wind whipped off the top of the ill-conceived fountain feature. I bet no one even held the door open for them.

Phil Oakey, of course, was high priestess of the science fiction section of the university bookshop, admiring the hermaphrodite swagger of Michael Moorcock's most infamous creation but not yet convinced of the wisdom of going full Cornelius when he still had the maths section to minister to.

Chris Watson, still a telephone engineer, had read in the local paper that the university music department owned an EMS VCS3 synthesiser identical to the one used by Brian Eno on *The Old Grey Whistle Test*. Although Watson had no academic claim to set foot on the clanking paternoster lift that would take him to the sanctum where the machine was housed, with dogged enthusiasm and resilience, he eventually dug out a contact when he met Bob Dickinson at a Sheffield Musicians Co-operative performance of piano pieces written by Philip Glass and Steve Reich. Dickinson, who was studying music at the university and later went on to play in Magazine, finally managed to grant Watson an audience with the fabled synth. His first contact with the machine was tentative; it had no keyboard, just a joystick to control timbre and pitch, many dials and a solitaire grid of red and white pegs that could be added, moved or removed with electronically thrilling results. Having secured Dickinson's trust, Watson started visiting the synth twice a week, often in the evenings with Richard Kirk, to make taped recordings of their exploratory efforts. The other academics they bumped into were snooty about the common, unlettered folk clambering all over their tower.

'We'd be there at night,' said Watson, '[m]aking these weird and wonderful noises. The academics were totally po-faced and serious. Not the sort of department that would encourage you to make pop music.'[5]

Meanwhile, on the ninth floor of the tower, writer Barry Hines was trying and failing to write a book to order. His early successes, *The Blinder* and *A Kestrel for a Knave*, had been written while he was still a PE teacher, driven to literary endeavour in snatched moments of inspiration. Now he was a proper writer, wallowing in the idle luxury of an academic fellowship, two years in an ivory tower, grafting to chip something credible out of something so comfortable. The view from the ninth-floor window looked north over the Netherthorpe terraces where Martyn Ware grew up, taking in the new tower blocks, the concrete barricade of Kelvin flats and the factories beyond. During blocked hours, Hines would examine the old and the new from on high:

Knock three times and ask for Big Jake

This is what I can see directly below me: a cluster of terraced houses, some of these houses empty and boarded up, but there's still life down there. People stand and talk in the street, dogs and cats walk about, somebody keeps pigeons in one of the outhouses and there are tubs of plants growing in the backyards. Next to these houses are four tower blocks of flats. Very neat, they are. Nobody keeps pigeons in there, or dogs or cats. Somebody might keep a budgie in a cage. There's a paved area between the flats and a circular ornamental pond. It must have looked good on paper, a pond on the new village green. I bet they thought people were going to flock round there and natter together like they did when they lived in the terraces. They thought wrong.[6]

The book that Hines was trying to write was *The Game-keeper*, a novel about modern serfdom on a ducal estate in South Yorkshire that he eventually finished and published in 1975. The book examines the incongruity of working-class people struggling to make a living on a modern council estate that borders aristocratic acres of private land. The gamekeeper, George Purse, is an ex-steel worker who summons all his pride, energy and skill to breed and rear game birds so that the duke and his privileged cronies can kill them for their sport. Class issues aside, the book examines a particular strain of modern northern life: young people in an industrial landscape seeking satisfaction and escape by reconnecting with the rural rituals of the past.

Sheffield in the 1970s was certainly a place where futuristic notions existed alongside fugitive country pursuits. My dad, for example, went to watch the first performance by The Human League at Psalter Lane art college in 1978 but he also worked in a tool factory and kept two ferrets in a hutch in our garden in Lowedges. He bought the ferrets via mail order from an advert in *Exchange and Mart* magazine. They arrived on a train in a wooden crate and my dad had to pick them up at the station and bring them home on the bus. They were bandit polecats, blonde with a black stripe across the eyes. He called them Snitch and Snatch after a couple of Lord Snooty's pals from *The Beano*.

At the weekend, he'd put the ferrets in cloth money bags that my mum had brought him from her work at the Co-op Bank, stick the beasts in his poacher's pocket and sneak around the De La Salle estate at Beauchief with his pal and a pocketful of purse nets. The ferrets were sent down rabbit holes and the rabbits were caught in the nets, killed with a blow to the back of the neck and taken home for the family pot. He had a shotgun and permission to shoot wood pigeons on a local farmer's land, he had an outhouse full of fishing tackle and the house always smelled of homemade tutti-frutti carp bait. Ken's cine films used the most advanced and professional equipment he could afford but often depicted carefully staged tutorials in ancient techniques such as crafting and tying flies for catching trout. The old ways ran beneath the new, but at the heart of all these pastimes was pride in the mastery of an art or skill.

Hines looked down from his high window and considered the tug of the past and the lure of the future, unaware that the artists of the space age were busy below him in the tower. He knew, however, that if you were a working-class artist from a city like Sheffield, you had to teach yourself, believe in yourself and make sure things got done regardless of the vantage point.

'Writing is nothing to do with pretty views', he wrote. 'It is to do with commitment. If you know what you're writing about and what you're writing it for, you could write it in a cellar.'[7]

Chapter 9
MUSICAL VOMIT

Dada is not despair or protest but a rebellious feeling of joy inspired by new discoveries.

Werner Haftmann

On 28 May 1974, Ken and Lorna were featured in a half-page spread in the *Sheffield Star* beneath the headline 'Pay Goes Into Liquidation'. Their daughter, Michele, remembers the event that led to this canny piece of self-promotion.

My parents were going on holiday so, on the way home from work, my dad took some money out of the bank and, when he got home, he took his work trousers off and left them on the side without telling mum he'd left ninety nicker in the pocket. My mum thought she'd do a quick wash before they went away so she put the trousers in with the rest of the things without checking the pockets. Soon after, she started to notice all these soggy pound notes floating to the top of the washing part of the twin tub. She screamed and stopped the machine, drained the tub and tried to rescue this money.

Musical Vomit

Some was in shreds, some was just pulp but they collected it all and tried their best to dry it out.

The staged photograph that accompanies the newspaper story shows a rumpled, world-weary, fifty-year-old Ken scratching his head with one hand while the other aims a hairdryer at a pegged-out line of tatty pound notes. At the other end of this washing line of cash, Lorna, with a sculpted helmet of Marge Simpson hair, hams it up with an expression of extreme vexation and outrage.

The staff reporter, beneath a subheading that reads 'Ken's £90 holiday money takes a washday plunge', detailed how Ken had set about reassembling the shredded notes, embarking 'on the longest and most complicated jigsaw he had ever tackled. Now, for Ken,' the writer continued, 'the moment of truth will come when the experts at the Bank of England decide how much of the £90 can be salvaged.'[1]

According to Michele, it was Ken himself who alerted the local news desk to this washday calamity, sensing, perhaps, that the ensuing regional publicity and exposure could be leveraged to promote his studio work. If this was the case, then Ken was right. The staff reporter sent to cover the soggy cash story was given a quick tour of the downstairs extension that housed Ken's nest of electronics and subsequently told colleagues at the *Sheffield Star* and Radio Sheffield, who then made their own visits to Ballifield to find out more about Studio Electrophonique in the following months.

One article by Lindsey Cook, in the *All Sorts of People* local colour column, had the headline 'A Serenade of South

Sea Sounds' and reported on Ken's work with The Maile Hawaiians and his victorious entries in the British and European tape-recording contests. Ken was also pictured in this article, fiddling with the controls of the machines on his wall of sound in the extension, giant headphones on and a full ashtray and pipe in the foreground. The Radio Sheffield feature, fronted by Tony Capstick, even led to some freelance engineering work for Ken at the station, recording tracks and sessions for local bands.

A local band Ken never managed to capture on tape was Musical Vomit, formed in 1974 at the Meatwhistle work-house on Holly Street. The group was put together by Ian Craig Marsh and Mark Civico, two students from Myers Grove School whose aim was to act daft on stage and annoy as many people as possible. Apparently named after a quote from a live review of an early Suicide gig, Musical Vomit's earliest incarnation was disrupted when Ian was expelled from school for plotting to electrocute the head-teacher. At the time, he was living in Walkley and com-pleting A-levels in Physics, Biology and Chemistry with an ambition to study cybernetics and genetic engineering at university. His expulsion from school also meant a temporary hiatus from Meatwhistle and Musical Vomit, as his parents insisted that he should find a job.

'Ian was a very weird character', remembered Civico. 'He would do things like nail roadkill to the noticeboard or make garden gnomes and fill them with gunpowder and blow them up. He was quiet but very rebellious.'[2]

During this enforced sabbatical from Meatwhistle, Ian worked on a market while hatching more ambitious schemes:

I started up a business called Aurora Astrological Analysis. I'd figured that there were fifty-five million people in Britain and if they all gave me a quid I could retire. So how could I get everybody to give me a quid? I decided that people would pay a quid for a genuine personalised horoscope but not making them personalised at all, just wording the ad very carefully, getting a solicitor to check it all out and just having the dozen very basic standardised ones. I just booked ads in various magazines like *Prediction* … I think I made about thirty quid. I still get some very weird letters from Nigeria, like the ones I used to get from women asking for very detailed advice about their personal lives. I used to write back and give them advice … I was about 17 at the time.[3]

Civico moved quickly to recruit new Meatwhistlers as replacements and set about creating a band that paired the retro doo-wop glam of Sha Na Na with the transgressive stagecraft and lyrics of Alice Cooper and Divine.

Band members adopted alter egos and employed method-acting rituals, slipping into character as they slipped on their tinfoil underpants and blood-stained, banana-enhanced tights and slapped each other about to generate the mad blood necessary to deliver self-penned songs such as 'Laxative Lament' and 'I Was a Teenage Necrophiliac'.

Gigs in 1974 at the workhouse, Burngreave Methodist Church Hall and the university drama studio were performed by a rotating line-up of Mark Civico (Trigay Thug), Ian Reddington (Romany Bowls), Glenn Gregory (Borstal Communications), Paul Bower (Rocky Coastlines), Mal Veale (Captain Zap) and Nick Dawson (Cliff Face). Reddington, notably, played a washboard he had named 'Aural Punishment'.

Studio Electrophonique

Claims that Musical Vomit were the first British punk band have some validity when the stage show at the drama studio gig is considered more closely. Promoted as a rock opera entitled *Musical Vomit Lost in Space*, the curtains opened to reveal a spotlit toilet below a tall portable lighting rig. In a room behind the stage, the members of the band finished slapping each other, opened a few cans of vegetable soup and filled their mouths with the cold slimy chunks of broth. A pre-arranged bribe meant that, upon the band's entry, some of the girls from Meatwhistle would prostrate themselves across the front of the stage, screaming with hormonal abandon for their idols. As this chaos greeted their arrival, Trigay Thug climbed the swaying scaffold while the rest of the band watched in a tight circle around the toilet beneath. Reaching the top, Trigay paused then vomited his mouthful of soup down through the air into and around the toilet bowl. The band, splattered by collateral cubes of carrot, then delivered their own portions of vomit into the spotlit porcelain before kicking straight into two brand new songs, the self-explanatory 'Vomit Down the Toilet' and the more sensual and sensitive 'Self Abuse'.

Revulsion was the general reaction but, incredibly, the band were invited to play at the Bath Arts Festival in the summer of 1974. The previous year, a sci-fi musical called *Quondam* had represented Sheffield at the festival as the offering from Meatwhistle's predecessor, Earthworks. A foolhardy curator in Bath booked Musical Vomit as this year's northern selection and, soon, the band were finessing their set and making travel plans. Paul Bower, who knew four or five chords on the guitar and was considered by the others in the band to be something of a virtuoso, was relied upon to set Civico's taste-testing lyrics to music, often the night before a gig.

Three of the band crammed themselves into Justin Downing's red Reliant Robin three-wheeler while the others had to hitchhike from Sheffield to Bath. The car had to be rescued repeatedly by the AA after it broke down three times on the way. A photograph of one of the breakdowns shows Justin and Glenn both barefoot on the hard shoulder. Inevitably, the hitchhiking contingent managed to arrive first. At this point in 1974, Downing, who later changed his name by deed poll to simply 'Justin', looked exactly like Jesus and, between him and the band, the artistically suspect decision was made that he should open the Musical Vomit set with an improvised speech in role as a quasi-mystic cult leader who demanded money from the audience to fund his spiritual retreat. Although a young Poly Styrene from X-Ray Spex was in the audience and later expressed the view that Musical Vomit were the first British punk band, the set didn't go down well and proved to be the band's final gig. Glenn Gregory and auxiliary member Simon Hall had dyed their hair especially for the gig and planned to hitchhike straight from Bath to a Meatwhistle camping holiday in Abergele. It rained throughout the long journey and they eventually arrived in Wales with their entire heads stained indelibly in bright blue and green.

Shortly after the demise of Musical Vomit, Paul Bower invited Martyn Ware down to Meatwhistle and facilitated the meeting of the future members of Heaven 17.

'I walked in,' remembered Ware, 'and I was wearing white flares, a white T-shirt, silver platform boots and a diamanté cat collar. I made the New York Dolls look like butchers.'[4]

'I was wearing jeans with 24-inch bottoms and gold baseball boots,' said Gregory, 'I knew immediately we'd get along well.'[5]

Ware was still living with his parents on Broomhall flats. Keen to robe himself in Sheffield's vision of the space age, he had clad the inside of his bedroom with purple polystyrene fruit trays from the local greengrocer. This achieved the twin effect of reducing the sound of his stereo bleeding through the walls and making his room resemble a womb-like chamber on a long-distance galactic mission. Thanks to his new and relatively well-paid job as a computer operator, he had also managed to acquire the first LED wrist watch ever seen in Sheffield:

I remember seeing an advert at the cinema. It was for something like Milk Tray and this suave guy had an LED watch with a black face and red numerals and I thought, that is the coolest thing ever. I think Sinclair brought one out and I got it. It was a pain in the arse though because you had to press the button to see the time. I thought it was the future.

Both Ware and Ian Craig Marsh were now working as computer operators, Ware at Lucas Industries and Marsh at Spear and Jackson. In 1974, however, the computer age still involved devices built on an industrial scale. The computer monitored by Ware, for example, filled an entire room yet held only sixteen megabytes of memory. His duties including changing over tapes and heavy magnetic disk drives as big as washing machine drums.

'I used to work night shifts,' said Ware. 'It was boring. There was nothing to do at night apart from watch the machines printing off payroll sheets.'

Musical Vomit

Marsh, meanwhile, had served his parental punishment and was allowed to rejoin the Dada-esque experimentation at the Meatwhistle workhouse. Strangely, Kirk, Mallinder and Watson were also about to invoke the spirit of Dada when selecting a name for their own artistic project. It appears that many of the young artists in Sheffield became aware of Dada separately and through various entry points. Chris and Veronica Wilkinson were certainly key influencers at Meatwhistle but music and pop culture led others back to the raucous, convention-busting artists of the past.

'We started to become aware of Edgard Varèse and musique concrète,' said Mallinder, 'and then, through David Bowie, we'd heard of William Burroughs and Brion Gysin and the cut-ups. We were all aware of Dada. I'd been painting for years and Richard was into art and surrealism. There were also weird TV influences like *The Outer Limits*.'

At the time of the phone call between Richard Kirk and Chris Watson when the name Cabaret Voltaire was settled upon, Kirk was completing his foundation year at the art college at Psalter Lane. Undoubtedly, it was here that his passion for outsider art was revitalised and his affinity for artists such as Picabia, Duchamp and Dalí crystallised. One story claims that Kirk was nicknamed Salvador at college and, during certain practical workshops, burly sculptors would chuck plaster and clay at him to puncture his artistic reveries.

The parallels between the Dada movement and the art that developed in Sheffield in the 1970s are obvious. Both were fuelled by young people who were tired of what had gone before and who wanted to disabuse the world of the notion that artists were formed of a special nature relating to

117

pedigree and privilege. Both were also largely based on the principles of contradiction, provocation and general pissing about. Marcel Duchamp's call to 'use a Rembrandt as an ironing board' neatly encapsulated the liberating quest for anti-art that drove both movements.[6]

Dada sprang from the iconoclastic, absurdist work of writer Alfred Jarry and gained early notoriety through the nihilistic visions of Francis Picabia in Barcelona and the ironic and innovative creations of Duchamp and Man Ray in New York during the First World War. These artists were intent on destroying the idols of the art establishment but were on this path unaware of the official birth of Dada in Zurich.

Hugo Ball, a German writer deranged by the madness of the war, had convened a group of similarly disillusioned émigrés, objectors and agitators from across Europe and was looking for a venue from which they could vent their primal disgust and delight. Together with his partner, Emmy Hennings, they found a nightclub at 1 Spiegelgasse and the first Cabaret Voltaire evening took place on 1 February 1916.

The name Dada has multiple meanings and even the dada-ists themselves argued over its origins. Some said it was a child's term for a hobby horse, some said it was Russian or Romanian for 'Yes/Yes' and some said it was the term used for the tail of a sacred African cow. Whichever is true, the name came to embody a new, unencumbered movement that expressed 'primitiveness, the beginning at zero'.[7]

Artists such as Tristan Tzara, Hans Richter, Richard Huelsenbeck, Hans Arp and Marcel Janco were drawn to this liberated salon where all forms of art, literature and music were accepted. Together, they organised the movement into a credo that echoed Italian Futurism with its violent language, striking design ideas and radical manifestos.

Paul Bower, who later became the Hugo Ball of Devonshire Lane with his *Gun Rubber* fanzine, was drawn to the powerful art but suspicious of the politics.

'We liked the futurists,' he said, 'but we didn't like their fascism.'

The performances that took place at the Cabaret Voltaire prefigured the often bizarre dramatic and musical work undertaken at the Meatwhistle workhouse sixty years later. On the first Dada night on Spiegelgasse, Hugo Ball was carried on stage dressed in a stiff blue cardboard cylinder and a witch doctor's hat to recite an abstract phonetic poem; sixty years later in Sheffield, Mal Veale was carried on stage inside a wardrobe with two armholes and a mouthhole before being handed a saxophone and improvising in the guise of his alter ego, Captain Zap.

Almost as amazing as Sean Bean living around the corner from Ken Patten in Ballifield is the fact that, while the authorities and locals in Zurich were outraged and appalled by the goings on at 1 Spiegelgasse, Lenin and his pals were living at No 12 planning world revolution and no one seemed that bothered.

Picabia arrived in Zurich in 1918 and tried to breed a more rigid and serious attitude among the Dada pranksters, eventually leading the movement to Paris where it was 'devoured and digested' by surrealism under the hand of Picabia and André Breton. By then, the fun had gone out of it.[8]

'Meeting Picabia,' Hans Richter said, when asked about the impact of Picabia on the Dada movement, 'was like an experience of death.'[9]

119

Studio Electrophonique

Pure, spontaneous movements, whether in Zurich 1916 or Sheffield 1974, cannot last forever. In both cities, a band of artists and enthusiasts had brought their own individual skills and personalities to creative causes ungoverned by money, rules or critical praise. Both movements also served as a breeding ground that gave new artists the confidence and permission to break with convention and to treat what had gone before as raw material to be mocked or remoulded.

Paul Bower, who later formed Sheffield's first punk band, 2.3, remembers the reaction of Meatwhistle's founder when the country was outraged by the punk explosion of the 1970s: 'When punk first came along, Chris Wilkinson got it immediately because he understood the need in art for things to be shaken up.'

One of the first tapes distributed by Cabaret Voltaire featured a track called 'She Loved You', a terrifying nine-minute version of The Beatles' standard slowed down and denatured so that it sounded like a David Lynch nightmare enhanced by the proximity of a Black and Decker strimmer.

When Paul Bower promoted a 1977 Cabs gig at the Crucible Studio, this song was performed live and provoked an extreme audience reaction: 'I was stood in the doorway and a guy ran out shouting, "Pull the plug! Have you heard what they're doing in there?" He couldn't believe that someone would have the nerve to treat a song like that in such a sacrilegious way.'

In some respects, Dada was the perfect template for the artists of the Sheffield space age to follow. It meant freedom, it meant spontaneity and, more importantly for those who had nothing in the way of training, education or money, it meant nothing.

Dada alone does not smell: it is nothing, nothing,
  nothing
It is like your hopes: nothing
Like your paradise: nothing
Like your idols: nothing
Like your politicians: nothing
Like your heroes: nothing
Like your artists: nothing
Like your religions: nothing[10]

The idea that Ken was a student of Dada is an academic stretch but his determination to create his own artistic output without financial backing or any proximity to the entry points of the art world is evident in the rare photographs of his studio that exist. Shots of the band Tsi Tsa show members posing against Ken's wall of machinery and the only space not covered by a device is taken up by a scrap of paper displaying a quote from Mother Teresa.

'We, the unwilling, led by the unknowing, are doing the impossible for the ungrateful. We have done so much for so long with so little, we are now qualified to do anything with nothing.'[11]

Chapter 10
ADOLPHUS RISING

He shows the way to things never seen before: he is the rock
on which the foreseeable comes to grief.

André Breton on Man Ray

The Dada artist Hans Richter classified the movement's gal-
vanising trinity as Francis Picabia the 'passionate destroyer',
Man Ray the 'tireless inventor' and Marcel Duchamp the
'detached anti-creator'.[1] A parallel assessment of space
age Sheffield might substitute Cabaret Voltaire for Picabia,
Ken Patten for Man Ray and Adi Newton for Duchamp.

Adi joined the Meatwhistle workhouse after making
friends with Glenn Gregory on a commercial design course
at Granville College in 1975. Adi, who joined the college
as Gary Coates, was quickly christened Adolf, then Adi, by
Gregory because his side parting brought to mind a certain
German dictator.

Adi grew up on the Manor Park estate then moved to
Burncross just before entering Ecclesfield secondary
school. Adi's dad was a long-distance lorry driver and his
mum looked after the house. He had always been a keen

reader as a child, losing himself in books about myths, mysteries and lost civilisations. His interest in sound and music was stoked when his dad gave him an old tape recorder to experiment with. A life-changing trauma occurred, however, when Adi was fourteen years old, severing his links with the normal teenage world of school and pals and, at the same time, unlocking creative urges that had lain dormant:

I had an accident and fractured my skull which meant I was off school for a long time. We were messing about in some old buildings and I tried to jump from one building to another and I grabbed this window frame and it fell out. I fell onto this pile of bricks and one of them punctured my skull in two places. I ended up in hospital with blood clots on my brain. It was pretty serious. They shaved all my hair off and I had this big scar. I had to stay off school during my last year and I only went in to do art. I had a really good art teacher. She encouraged me a lot and never forced her opinions on me.

With the guidance of his art teacher, Adi won a place at college then transferred to Psalter Lane to satisfy a renewed obsession with painting. His accident, it seemed, had triggered an undeniable need to create and an insatiable appetite to learn about creators of the past:

It was a bit like Joseph Beuys when he crashed his Stuka in the Crimea in the Second World War and damaged his skull. These Tartar tribesman took him in and wrapped him in felt and smeared him with fat and he recovered and started doing all these art works with rolls of felt with fat smeared on them. They say skull impacts can have an effect on you but they don't know how or why. Like the guy who got struck by lightning and could suddenly play the piano. It's a strange and mysterious place the brain; they think the patterns might be like snowflakes, never the same twice as they scan from alpha to theta frequencies. It's a whole realm that's potentially so vast and powerful but I think there are things about the brain that we don't know and we'll never know.

Like many of the young working-class Sheffield artists of the era, he started to educate himself through a systematic exploration of the city library and other municipal resources. Visits to the Graves Gallery on the top floor of the library inspired Adi to start producing his own paintings, sketching copies of the work he saw on display then developing ideas of his own.

'I used to read a lot and go to the library a lot', said Newton. 'I was really into the Theatre of the Absurd, Jarry and the French poets and painters and this led me to Duchamp as he had a big interest in Jarry and pataphysics. In the Graves Gallery upstairs, they had Frank Auerbach and Warhol and Rauschenberg.'

The central library in Sheffield is a pale stone Art Deco fortress on Surrey Street that has served the city as a bulwark against idleness and ignorance since it opened in 1934. To young people like Adi Newton and Paul Bower, it was an everlasting battery that they could draw upon for the knowledge they hadn't found at home or at school.

'Me and Adi would go to the central library coffee bar', said Bower, 'and make a cup of tea last an hour then just go down to the reference library. That's where we were introduced to Soviet Constructivism, Stanislavsky, *Battleship*

Potemkin and all that. Sometimes you'd just get into a chat with some old blokes, usually old communists and they'd tell you how the Labour Party had sold out and that we needed a revolution.'

The prohibitive expense of buying books and records made the lending library an autodidact's paradise. Adi's appetite for outsider art was voracious and he was soon opening doors into the imaginations of Samuel Beckett, Antonin Artaud, Eugene Ionesco and Franz Kafka as well as borrowing avant-garde vinyl from the record library in the same building.

'I always liked early experimental music,' said Newton, 'people like John Cage, David Tudor, Luciano Berio, Earl Browne and all those early electronic composers.'

There is a theory that today's instant access to all music, art and film through streaming or the internet has created a generation of gadflies who are less willing than their predecessors to put time into an appreciation of challenging art. If we imagine Adi as an example of an enthusiast in the 1970s, it may be that he hears one of his tutors at college mention a composer called Xenakis who makes music based on mathematical patterns. Adi might think this sounds interesting and write it down in his notebook. At the weekend, he might catch the bus into town and see if they have any Xenakis records in the lending library. When they say they have but they are currently on loan, Adi might put his name on the waiting list then go to the reference library to seek out more information on this composer. He might find a book that he can't take home but that reveals a few facts about Xenakis that makes him seem even more intriguing (he is a communist who fought in the Lord Byron Brigade for the Greek

Resistance, receiving a shrapnel wound in the face in 1945). Adi might then catch the bus home again, empty-handed but with the romance of Xenakis and some imagined sound-scapes in his head. In a week or two, he might make another bus journey into town and return with the long-anticipated vinyl in his hands, reading the sleeve notes on the bus and puzzling at the cryptic names of the musical pieces. Perhaps, in the feverish wait to hear the music, Adi had already told his pals how cool the composer was and had bought himself a Xenakis-style combat smock and eye patch.

11 Adi Newton in Chris and Veronica's garden in Hanover Square, Broomhall, 1976

If the image of Adi in 1975, lowering the needle onto side one of Xenakis's *Persepolis*, could be placed alongside a contemporary image of someone reading this book, whose only effort has been to skip the ads on a YouTube video before anticipating the same piece of music, who do you think would be more likely to listen beyond the first minute of a piece of music that sounds, admittedly, like a rush-hour gridlock of detuned car horns? The investments of time and imagination bear no comparison.

Adi is definitely an artist who has put the time in. From his formative days in the library and at Meatwhistle, through his time in The Future, Clock DVA and The Anti-Group, he has dedicated himself to a life of uncompromised art and style. When James and I were trying to round up interview-ees for this book, Adi was working on a project in which various composers had been asked to stretch Beethoven's *Ninth Symphony* from its regulation one-hour duration to an aurally challenging twenty-four-hour sonic cycle.

'You've got to do it for yourself,' said Newton, 'I don't really create things for anybody else. I do it to fulfil a need within me and I don't think about it being either experimental or accessible. I don't plan it or control it. It's just always there.'

When Adi turned up at Meatwhistle in 1975, he brought some much-needed intellectual rigour to the knockabout humour that had characterised Musical Vomit. Soon, he was writing plays and absurdist sketches for the others to perform along with a ubiquitous shop-window dummy called Mr Hague who would be dressed in various costumes to suit the script in question. Memorable dramas from this time included the Beckett pastiche *Waiting For Hago* (starring Mr Hague) and the Berlinesque Isherwood parody *The All-Night Cafeteria*.

Studio Electrophonique

Along with many of the Meatwhistle artists, Adi entered this creative world with feelings of liberation and relief. Outsiders from all over the city became collaborators in an instant and talking about art now resulted in new art being created rather than getting your face rubbed in the gravel of a rain-pocked comprehensive school playground.

'Meatwhistle was a really free atmosphere', said Newton. 'Chris, Veronica and Justin were about but they didn't enforce any kind of system on us. They were very anarchic. We were able to pursue our interests. I'd just read Hans Richter's *Dada Art and Anti Art* and it was a revelation because it introduced me to the ideas of artists breaking down normality. Meatwhistle was a resource for bringing people together to try new things. It was protection from the criticism of the outside world.'

While we were trying to make the outside world aware of the stories that orbited Ken's studio in the 1970s and 1980s, James was starting to wonder if the outside world would ever be interested in his new incarnation of Studio Electrophonique. The one vinyl EP he had released was now so rare and sought-after among his select double-decker coachload of fans that he didn't even own a copy of it himself, but wider fame and adulation were still elusive. Then, as if scripted by some benevolent hand, two blessings fell upon us. First, one of James's songs got into the hands of the French pop icon Etienne Daho, and Studio Electrophonique Mk 2 were invited to open for him at the Paris Olympia. Second, I received a reply to one of the many catapulted gobbets of digital groundbait that I had fired into the internet months ago asking for stories from people who may have known Ken Patten.

128

Adolphus rising

As James was sending me pictures of the name of Ken's studio in star-scale red neon outside Paris's most prestigious venue and relating the tale of how his biggest ever gig was almost shut down in a terrorist scare after he Sellotaped some complementary cassette singles to the underside of select seats in the auditorium, I was bleaching the cat-litter tray and wondering if the email I had received the same morning from a curiously named stranger was genuine or a cruel trick from a bored musician in a cheap French hotel.

The message was from Dennis Greatbatch. He claimed to have been a good friend of Ken's and was happy to meet us to share some stories. The final part of the message, however, struck me as either the most fortuitous stroke of investigative luck or, as I feared, James just winding me up. Dennis told me that he still lived locally and had been given lots of the old studio equipment when Ken died. As soon as I received Aeropostale reassurances that James wasn't behind the Greatbatch veil, I contacted Dennis and, to my great joy, he was a real person with a true and wonderful story to tell. As soon as James returned from the continent, we made the short trip to Dronfield, Derbyshire, to hear it.

Dennis was working as a television engineer at the short-lived Sheffield Cablevision station on Matilda Street when he met Ken in 1974. A group of visitors from the Sheffield Amateur Cine Club were being shown around the TV station and Ken was one of them:

I think we'd shown some of the films they'd made on our station and they just wanted to have a look around at what we did and how we did it. I got chatting with Ken about his interests in recording sound and about his own recording studio and he invited me round to have a look. I was only twenty-one when I first went around to his house. You'd open these double doors and he had the most amazing studio in there. There was a black leather chair where he used to sit and, to his left was a Burns guitar and a Fender amplifier. There was an electric piano at the side of that and, on the other side, a whole wall of stuff: his six-way mixer, his tape decks, a Revox machine, a Ferrograph and an Akai machine. I sat down in there and he played me this piece of music he'd made through a beautiful pair of Tannoy speakers. It was superb. There was a thirty-year age gap but we became great friends.

Lorna was a lovely person but she'd got a tough side too. She only tolerated so much from the bands who came in. Someone lit some weed up at one point and I think she soon put a stop to that. They actually used the bedrooms to do some of the recording and there'd be cables running in and out of windows down to the extension where Ken had the studio and I remember once someone had trod dog mess up the stair carpet and she threw the lot of them out and Ken as well.

As Dennis was talking, I could see James looking around for any analogue gear that had been taken out of storage for our delectation. We were in a very neat and well-sponged kitchen, however, and neither of us would have had the guts to ask about it anyway.

Ken used to listen to commercial sounds and think, 'How the bloody hell are they doing that? What can I do to get that sound or even a better one?' Once, I remember he wanted a bass drum sound that wasn't muffled and I told him he needed a compressor. The next thing I knew, he'd got a circuit diagram of a compressor from *Wireless World* and he'd built three of them.

Dennis stood up, closed the door into the lounge and returned. James, momentarily energised, slumped back into his seat at the kitchen table. Dennis's wife was watching *Eastenders* next door and the volume was too loud.

Ken was into all sorts. He was delaying signals going through one tape machine into another then onto a reverb unit then putting them out of phase. I think a lot of these bands that went to Ken's, they did their recording, Ken did his magic and they'd never heard themselves sound as good. He was a magician.

Dennis seemed pleased that someone was taking an interest in Ken's work and even had an inclination that Ken himself might be guiding the whole operation from his black leather chair in the hereafter:

I'm interested in spiritualism and Ken was too. We used to talk about it quite a lot. You know, the afterlife and all that. Now I follow a lady clairvoyant called Pauline Mason and, during a recent session, she gave me a date in 1990 that she said was significant for me then started talking about a small chap who had passed away, a father-figure type. Funnily enough, I'd just come across Ken's old cine camera in the loft and it started me thinking. I went on the internet to see what date he'd died on and, as well as finding out that it was 1990, I came across your request for info about Ken's life. My feeling is that it was orchestrated from beyond. It was meant to be. Anyway, I've got his camera and some other bits out to have a look at.

James was up and pawing at the louvre doors into the dining room before Dennis could get them open. The three items displayed on the sideboard neatly summed up the marvellous incongruity of Ken's creative ambit. We watched in hushed anticipation as Dennis unclasped a black box and removed a pristine cine camera from its snug, felt-lined casing. This was the device that had captured the moments we had seen flicker across the wall of James's attic room. This perfectly preserved machine and a neat pair of pale wooden monitor speakers could have been artefacts gathered to dress the set of a 1950s home; the third item, even today, looked like a dense, advanced herald of the future. It was the original Roland System 100 mixer that Ken had used with The Future, Vice Versa and Pulp. When he plugged it in, the VU meters tremored and the whole unit appeared to breathe out in Def Con green and red. This was the machine that channelled the sound of the Sheffield space age: 'My loft's absolutely chocka but I'm sure there's more stuff of Ken's in there. When I've had a proper look, you can come back and see what's turned up.'

Dennis got to know Ken in the directionless span of time between glam and punk. It could be argued that the young electronic artists of Sheffield yawned at the British punk explosion as they had already assimilated the strains of rebellion they needed from American punk, German *kosmische* music and various European terror groups.

The glam outfits Phil Oakey had worn to work at the university bookshop had certainly lost their sheen as he was now shovelling coal every morning at Thornbury Hospital: 'I was half porter, half boilerman. By 8 o'clock in the morning I had shovelled two tonnes of coal into hoppers, then I'd clean up and work in the operating theatre.'[2]

Oakey was now finding echoes of his beloved science fiction novels in the cosmic symphonies of the German bands who had emerged from the Zodiak Free Arts Lab in Berlin in the late 1960s. Tangerine Dream's *Alpha Centauri* and Klaus Schulze's *Irrlicht* and *Cyborg* albums pioneered the use of synthesisers and sequencers to create futuristic epics that felt completely detached from rock's mothership of guitar, bass and drums. The fact that one of their sci-fi heroes, Michael Moorcock, was also hanging around Ladbroke Grove with Hawkwind and The Pink Fairies and, in fact, wrote the lyrics to Hawkwind's 1975 album *Warrior on the Edge of Time*, meant that both Oakey and Ware felt more affinity for this futuristic vision than the nihilism of punk.

'I felt more comfortable with the fallout of the hippy era', said Ware. 'Punk was exciting but it seemed a bit old hat after the New York Dolls. Punk sounded like pub rock to us. You can't get more punk than Iggy and The Stooges.'

Some members of Cabaret Voltaire were using their summer holidays to sniff the air for intimations of punk. Richard Kirk had left his foundation art course at Psalter Lane and was Interrailing on the cheap. Stephen Mallinder couldn't go because he had a summer job on the Sheffield City Council gardening gangs.

'I remember seeing this guy in a railway station in Rimini', said Kirk. 'He looked like Dalí and he'd got paint on his shirt and it looked like it was deliberate. We used to buy old clothes from junk shops and customise them. We got noticed in Sheffield in that period between glam and punk because of the way we looked.'[3]

The bands at Meatwhistle were still in thrall to glitter, foil and ladies' tights, even with the added effect of Adi Newton's ascetic levels of discipline. Some bands lasted a week or two, some didn't make it past an afternoon at Holly Street. Notable groups from this era include Simon Scott's Kit Kat Club, Totem Pole, Arthur Cravan's Tent Band, Underpants, The Hari Willy Krishna Band and, most memorable of all, a Crosby, Stills and Nash parody band featuring Newton, Gregory and Reddington called Lister, Greg and Red. Their only local hit was a song called 'Sore and Red'.

Meatwhistle was a place where any idea could be tested to assess its tolerance, a place where young people with no musical training could try to create music with a guaranteed squad of enthusiastic teammates. Back in the fold at Holly Street, Ian Craig Marsh had gone down the Chris Watson route and built himself a wooden Dewtron mail order synth from *Practical Electronics*. When he demonstrated this at Meatwhistle, it appeared to be capable of a limited range of noises, one being a motorbike and the other a strange vocoder effect. As Ian had mentioned wanting a keyboard to wire up to the machine, he was delighted when Glenn Gregory found an old rotting harmonium in the backyard of a house where a party was being held. They dragged this instrument to the workhouse and tried to buckle them together in unholy union. Martyn Ware also took his first steps in musical composition while at Meatwhistle, buying a Rolf Harris dual Stylophone and writing his first song, 'Wimpy Bar Magnet', for the current house band, Underpants.

'None of us were musically trained', said Ware. 'None of us believed we would ever be involved in music. Meatwhistle made us believe we were involved in an all-encompassing art project, like Andy Warhol's Factory. All aspects of art were acceptable: film, drama, bands that lasted for one day. Nothing was off-limits.'

When Kirk returned from Europe, Cabaret Voltaire started to consider a first public appearance. The Dada element of confrontational and transgressive performance was an obvious ingredient they aimed to incorporate but they were also taking cues from The Velvet Underground and Doctors of Madness. The latter were a London proto-punk band led by Richard 'Kid' Strange who, like the Velvets, had a taste for dark, masochistic tones and the screech of an electric violin, played in their case by a character in full Skeletor make-up called Urban Blitz. When the Doctors of Madness played at the Sheffield City Hall in February 1976, they opened their set with a reading from William Burroughs' *Naked Lunch* and Richard Kirk was driven into such a frenzy in the front row that he knocked the lead out of Blitz's electric violin.

Chris Watson had run off twenty-five copies of their latest compositions from the loft at Lemont Road and was convinced that Brian Eno would be into it if they could only make a connection. They sent him a copy but never heard back. Undeterred, the trio even caught the train to York where Eno was lecturing as part of his *Art as a Technique for Survival* tour and followed him into the bogs to get to the bottom of it. Eno denied all knowledge so they gave him a replacement copy and let him finish his piss in peace. Watson was furious when he listened to the next Eno album,

Another Green World, some months later: 'That was the album where he started using a lot of drum machines,' said Watson, 'I'm sure he cribbed off our tape.'[4]

Other hapless journeys around the country to prepare the Voltaire battle plan included a train to see Can that sailed straight through the venue's location in Doncaster and took them to York and a later, more successful, trip to see the German band in Bradford where Chris Watson stood stage left and enjoyed a lengthy appreciation of Irwin Schmidt's karate-chop keyboard technique.

'Me and Kirky went to see Hawkwind a few times', said Mallinder. 'Liquid Len was really cool with his visuals. We went to see Tangerine Dream and Gong at the Richmond Free Festival. Anything that had a smattering of electronic stuff was interesting.'

By now, Watson's collection of instruments and electronics was testing the joists in the family home. He had an EMS Synthi suitcase synth with black and blue keys and an inbuilt 256 note sequencer in its lid, a Vox Continental organ with red and black keys and a Farfisa organ with drum pads that they had bought in Johnson's Electrics on London Road.

'This dodgy looking guy with a toupee came up to us in an instrument shop and said "Look lads, I'll sell you one of these. I've got one at home"', said Kirk. 'It turned out the guy was on the cabaret circuit in Sheffield and had been on Opportunity Knocks. He set us on the road with that one. It was forty quid or something.'[5]

They were later amazed to discover that this Farfisa organ that had once belonged to an old Yorkshire showman with a wig and gammy leg was the same model pictured on the back of Kraftwerk's second album. The clarinet that Kirk had bought for £6 because he couldn't afford an oboe like Andy McKay's was going to be part of any imminent stage show, as were the heavily treated vocals of Mallinder. The vocalist had been selected because his voice sounded the least Sheffield of the three members. As most of Cabaret Voltaire's early recordings contain vocals so crushed, decayed and modulated that they could be the alarmed cries of Daleks or buried earthquake victims, this selection process was probably unnecessary.

Cabaret Voltaire's first gig took place at a science disco in the upper refectory of Sheffield University on 13 May 1975. Looking back, the chemistry wasn't there.

'We conned our way on to the bill', said Watson. 'It was an organisation called Science For The People who had a disco every week at Sheffield University, and they were looking for something to liven it up, and I happened to be working with one of the organisers, and he said: "Hey, you're in a group, can you play rock music?" So I said: "Yeah, sure, anything you like," and he said: "Great, we'll get you on half way through the disco."'[6]

Cabaret Voltaire had been advertised as 'rock and electronic music' but their lack of respect for the traditional disco template soon turned the crowd against them.

'No one had really heard of Dada then but, for us, it was a biblical thing,' said Mallinder, 'to fly in the face of convention and fuck people off. Ken Kesey was another influence with his idea of pranksterism. We had a sense of humour and, most of the time, we just wanted to take the piss and annoy people. So, at that first gig, we definitely weren't playing disco or rock, we were playing tape loops of steam hammers and I was shouting through a synthesiser ring modulator. Richard had a rubber suit on that was covered in fairy lights that were plugged into the mains, so he could have blown up at any moment. In the end, the crowd got on stage to throw us off and I was the main focus of their frustration.'

The steam hammers had been recorded in the harbour at Ostend on an Interrailing trip but these weren't the only source of antagonism. A band associate who was a member of the far-left terrorist group The Angry Brigade had given the band a film about chemical warfare and they decided to project that as a backdrop to their debut performance. Kirk had his guitar slung behind his back and, when the audience didn't rise to his improvised clarinet and hammer duet, he threw his guitar into the now simmering crowd. This triggered an invasion which resulted in smashed equipment and a smashed bone in Mallinder's back.

'Richard was using his clarinet as a club,' said Watson, 'the organisers were nearly in tears. They came on stage, shouting: "For fuck's sake, get off, you've ruined our reputation, we're totally discredited." They weren't allowed to use the university for any purpose again.'[7]

'A lot of people who came were our friends', said Kirk. 'We were lucky lots of people we knew were there, otherwise we would have been dead.'[8]

'We ended up in the Northern General with Kirky fucking about pushing me around in a wheelchair', said Mallinder. 'Years later I got shit for this when I was on a TV show in Australia. They were like: "You're hard aren't you, getting beaten up by Friends of the Earth or whoever they were." I said, "You've got to understand, these people were very annoyed."'

Adolphus rising

The band didn't play a second gig until a year later.

On 25 September 1975, Kraftwerk were featured on *Tomorrow's World*, a primetime science show that instantly made these German 'engineer musicians' the topic of excited discussion during the last days of the Meatwhistle workhouse. The funding of the project had run its course and the hardcore group of Meatwhistlers now felt armoured against the world's censure and ready to go out and fend for themselves.

Veronica Wilkinson, who had such a powerful effect on young people in Sheffield during this time, instilling, in young women especially, a belief that they could succeed and be fulfilled without being attached to something devised or led by a man, didn't want to abandon her fledglings abruptly so she made enquiries about finding an alternative space where they could continue to collaborate and dream.

She found an old 'little mesters' workshop above a sandwich shop on the corner of Devonshire Lane and negotiated a cheap monthly rent before leaving Sheffield to pursue her own dream of becoming a painter in a shack by the sea in Cardigan Bay.

The first Meatwhistle pioneer to break out of Sheffield was Glenn Gregory, who caught the train to London on his seventeenth birthday in May 1975 with the ambition of becoming a photographer. A few months later, Adi, Paul Bower and Howard Willey joined him.

'Adi and Howard had a job spraying shop-window mannequins at Robert Brothers department store on The Moor and we found out that they had a branch in London so we just thought, screw it, let's try moving down there', said Bower. 'So we went down and we saw this empty shop on the Caledonian Road and a sign in the butchers next door saying it was to let. We rented it and filled it with tat from the markets. We called it Cravans after the surrealist and boxer, Arthur Cravan, who Adi had a bit of an obsession with.'

'I liked Arthur Cravan', said Newton, 'because he'd organise gatherings, present a lecture then start taking all his clothes off. He was into creating situations with the public. He didn't create visual art but his life was like an art piece. He was quite an obscure character so I was into that as well.'

Cravan, who was married to the poet Mina Loy and once fought heavyweight world champion Jack Johnson in a strange boxing bout that pitted aesthetics against athletics, had disappeared without trace in 1918 after trying to sail single-handed from Mexico to Chile.

'We lasted about six months before we came back to Sheffield', said Bower. 'We were lucky because we could all go back to live with our mums.'

Chapter 11
NEW RUINS

Under the bark of felled trees, I seek the image of things to come, of vigour and, in underground tunnels, the obscurity of iron and coal may already be heavy with life.

Tristan Tzara, 'Note on Poetry'

On New Year's Day 1976, Adi and Mal Veale moved into the old workshop on Devonshire Lane. The workshop was unheated but had a couple of open fireplaces that could be stoked into life if wood could be scavenged from nearby ruins or building sites. There was also a coal bunker next to the sandwich shop that could sometimes be raided for fuel.

In time, Mal came to occupy the 'loft' space, draping silver foil space blankets over the beams and huddling close to the meagre heat of the grate. Ian Craig Marsh descended on the workshop shortly after occupation and commandeered a wood-panelled room to house his growing bank of electronic instruments and devices. The door to this room had a panel of smoked glass so, in true Sheffield noir style, he added the lettering 'Ian C Marsh – Private Investigator'.

'I spent hours working on that office', said Marsh. 'I japanned the furniture and had an artist letter the sign, and then I sat around inside in my pin-striped suit, waiting for cases.'[1]

'The workshop became a place where you could have parties', said Paul Bower. 'Later, it was where we formed our punk band 2.3 and did the work for our fanzine, *Gun Rubber*.'

The parties drew the usual Meatwhistle crowd but the city centre location and the lack of neighbours meant that wild, fringe characters often made an appearance. The mysterious biker, Luger, features prominently in the recollections of both Adi and Paul Bower.

'Luger was a big Hells Angel', said Adi. 'He had long black hair like a Native American Indian. He had no shirt, just a black leather waistcoat and a bare chest covered in tattoos. He was fearsome looking.'

'He was on the run from The Blue Angels in Chesterfield', said Bower. 'Apparently, he had a gun, hence the name. I think he lived in the workshop for a bit then, one day, he just gave Adi a pile of money and a leather jacket and said, "Thanks, man", then left, never to be seen again.'

Other rumours include one that suggests the reason for Luger's sudden departure was a criminal confrontation in which he repelled and 'retired' a police dog.

In March, *The Man Who Fell to Earth* came out in Sheffield cinemas. Starring David Bowie as the pale, lonesome alien Thomas Jerome Newton, it prompted most of Sheffield's young acolytes to attempt the Yorkshire version of Bowie's milk and cocaine diet. When milk and Lemsip weren't enough, however, some, like Adi, went a step further and changed their name.

'I added Newton,' said Adi, 'because of Isaac Newton and Thomas Jerome Newton from *The Man Who Fell to Earth*. The style became like that after too, with the fringe and the duffle coat.'

The Cabs, meanwhile, had convalesced after being roughed up by the eco-warriors of the science faculty and were ready to pre-punk the London bands. The month before The Sex Pistols and The Clash brought punk to Sheffield at The Black Swan on Snig Hill in July 1976, Cabaret Voltaire played their second gig, an early morning happening at the Lord Derby Grammar School in Bury. Bob Dickinson, the musician who had allowed the Cabs access to the university synth, facilitated this unusual treat for the students at what was normally a sleepy morning assembly in Lancashire. The school was Dickinson's alma mater and he was also meant to be playing at the assembly with his ensemble E-music. The piece Cabaret Voltaire were supposed to be presenting was a fifty-minute creation called *Mars 1958*.

'It was nine in the morning,' said Mallinder, 'and we were drunk. I had a silver suit on and Chris had a stocking over his head and these mad shades.'

'The teachers looked very worried', said Kirk. 'My hair was green and we wore bicycle chains. We thought we were the Velvets and, at the same time, we thought we were a terrorist group. I'm sure if we hadn't ended up doing music and the arts, we might have ended up going round blowing buildings up.'[2]

Although the teachers stood aghast against the wall bars, the students seem to respond enthusiastically until a fire alarm sounded and the plug was pulled after four minutes. Apparently, there had been complaints from those doing exams in the sports hall next door.

A few weeks later, as a continuation of their tenuous link with Sheffield University's music faculty, the band were asked to prepare and perform an interpretation of two pieces by the avant-garde French composer Jean-Yves Bosseur at a formal, black-tie affair at the Arts Tower.

The Cabs reworked a piece called 'Exhaust' and collaborated with Bob Dickinson on another called 'Vietsong'. For the latter piece, Richard Kirk had created a cinematic backdrop of lush Vietnamese jungle filmed on Super 8 in his mum's back garden in Pitsmoor. Chris Watson wore his girlfriend's tights over his head, bankrobber-style, and the reaction from the assembled middle-class connoisseurs in Lecture Theatre Seven was cool and disdainful. Bosseur, who had studied with Stockhausen in Cologne in the 1960s, later passed on his compliments to the band but no such praise came their way on the night.

'We played in the bottom part of the Arts Tower', said Mallinder. 'It was proper velvet jackets and wine glasses and we soon got ejected. We just thought they were middle-class tossers. We were nice to them but, when we played, it all went tits up. I think they got us more than we got them. They thought we were agent provocateurs and it was their duty to understand new art that involved young mad people. This was pre-punk but the smell was in the air. It wasn't exactly Paris 1968 but we saw that everything was stale and flat so we were happy to play the revolutionary role.'

These were exciting times but the absurdity of the situation wasn't lost on Cabaret Voltaire. Suddenly, key cultural figures from Europe's avant-garde were contacting a telephone engineer from Totley, a council gardener from

Heeley and a would-be schoolteacher from Pitsmoor to take soundings on the cultural wave of the future.

'In the early days', said Mallinder, 'we did get a hell of a lot of interest from the traditional avant-garde, when we just saw ourselves as jumped-up kids with tape recorders. We had a lot of contact with top French composers who looked up to us. We found it very funny.'[3]

Riding high on a terrifying surge of modulated animal bleats, the Cabs decided to introduce themselves to the mainstream, sending tapes of some new loft compositions to major record labels. These tapes, which included the previously mentioned buzzsaw Beatles cover version 'She Loved You', 'Venusian Animals' and 'The Dada Man' were not snapped up as the next hot commodity in the summer of punk. Only Simon Draper at Virgin Records replied with anything approaching encouragement.

The insular nature of the Cabs' development in the loft at Lemont Road had resulted in something so unique, singular and strange that the band were torn between the desire to become more well known and the desire to protect the secret magic at their core.

'We were a close-knit group,' said Kirk, 'almost like a terrorist cell. We wouldn't let any outsiders in, we were very cagey about letting people into our group, nicking our ideas.'[4]

The Dada urge to discomfit and appal sometimes meant the Cabs were in danger of transgressing into sociologi- cal waters where they couldn't touch the bottom. A final collaboration with Bob Dickinson at Leith Town Hall in August 1976, which the band didn't attend, involved a taped composition and printed handouts based on the contemporary kidnapper and murderer Donald Nielsen, commonly known as the Black Panther. Later, they would write tracks called 'Baader-Meinhof' and 'Do the Mussolini (Headkick)'.

'There was a danger that we slipped into using terrorist imagery with a lack of depth', said Mallinder. 'There was a glamour to it but we weren't "it". A lot of it was just playing with taboos. If people tell me I can't go there, I'm going to go there. With "Baader-Meinhof", the words alone were fearful to people but we thought we had the right to foreground these things that were happening in the world.'

British punk bands and British punk songs exerted minimal force over the young electronic artists in Sheffield but the punk attitude exemplified by bands such as Buzzcocks – to bring out your own record, design your own sleeve art, form a band before you could even play an instrument – was embraced and taken in new directions. More rapt attention was given to American punk releases; Ian Craig Marsh bought the Ramones' debut album on US import in April 1976 and held a reverent listening forum with others at the workshop.

'I don't think the Second World War finished until punk came along', said Phil Oakey. 'Punk changed people's attitudes. They realised they didn't have to do what their parents did.'[5]

Oakey, by Sheffield standards, was quite punk, piercing his own nipples as a farewell, perhaps, to the Second World War. His musical influences, however, were still rooted in the space-synth fantasias of progressive rock, *kosmische* or experimental American sounds such as Frank Zappa's *Hot Rats*.

'It's funny that people call us an eighties group when in fact we were a seventies group', said Oakey. 'Our influences were massively progressive. We liked Genesis.'

Hoping to confirm this fondness for Phil Collins, James and I arranged to meet Martyn Ware at Sheffield station on a sunny afternoon in the middle of a global pandemic. The terms used daily at government podiums were beginning to sound like the names of dance-era Cabaret Voltaire remixes: 'Ramp Up', 'Transmissions from the Second Wave', 'Tighten the Lockdown (Relax the Lockdown)', 'Flatten the Peak'.

We waited in the Micra in an illegal drop-off zone and kept the engine running with one eye on the transport police booth and the other scanning the arrivals for a doom-laden synth slinger from 1980. What we weren't expecting was a cheerful-looking guy in shades, shorts and a Hawaiian shirt covered in fighting fish, carrying a plump decorative cushion in a brown Laura Ashley paper bag.

Trying to hide his disappointment at the vehicle and the amateurs within it, Martyn climbed in and we set off through the city that had shaped his early visions. He hadn't come all the way from London to see us. We didn't have the pull. He was coming to see his older sister who still lived in the city. I parked in the underground car park of my office building on Portobello and, when we emerged into the sunlight next to St George's Church, his 1970s gyroscope started to readjust.

'I'm sure this building is where Western Works used to be.'

We were standing outside Regent Court, the university's Computer Science building, constructed on the sacred site of Cabaret Voltaire's studio lair.

et my bearings in a bit', said Ware. We headed down
Lane to Fagan's pub where Tom, the landlord, had
agreed to let us in to conduct the interview.

On 11 January 1977, John Peel played the new David
Bowie album *Low* in its entirety on his Radio One show.
Martyn, Adi and Ian listened to it in the workshop at
Devonshire Lane.

'*Low* changed our lives', said Ware. 'What Bowie and
Fripp and Eno proved was that people using traditional rock
instruments with electronic manipulation can sound just as
futuristic as people using synths. Like, the drums on *Low*
are just studio drums but they've been put through a time
modulator.'

Between this event and The Future's visit to Ken's studio,
the workshop creatives were involved in a few abortive
musical happenings.

With the dregs of the Meatwhistle spirit, they devised a
group called VDK and The Studs and managed to secure
a slot supporting Manchester punks The Drones at Psalter
Lane art college. True to form, more time was spent devis-
ing clever names and confrontational outfits than on a tight
musical set. Glenn Gregory was the frontman, Voice Dekay,
Martyn Ware was Art Zero, Adi was Eggy Brando and they
were supplemented by two members of the new Sheffield
punk band 2.3 (Paul Bower and Haydn Boyes-Weston) and
two members of Cabaret Voltaire (Richard Kirk and Stephen
Mallinder).

Loose arrangements for songs were discussed over a
few drinks before they took to the stage. Paul Bower chick-
ened out before showtime because he was scared that
some beefy pottery students might take against the act but

sixteen-year-old drummer Boyes-Weston went all out in a boiler suit with 'Cut Student Grants' daubed across the chest. Gregory, meanwhile, took to the stage in a gold Lurex suit. The set included cover versions of Iggy Pop's 'Cock in my Pocket', Lou Reed's 'Vicious', The Kingsmen's 'Louie, Louie' and a final fifteen minutes that started off as a free-form approximation of the *Doctor Who* theme tune then, when the angry manager of The Drones entered stage left and started trying to unplug the band, morphed into a new song called 'The Drones Want to Come on Now'. As they were in the process of being wrestled off stage, Haydn, who worked in a butcher's shop, took a bucket of pigs' ears from behind his drum kit and launched them out over the crowd. The fearless spirit of artistic misrule exhibited at this event tightened the bond between the various characters who would go on to form the most influential bands in Sheffield.

'We had a supergroup before we even had any groups', said Ware.

The workshop's commitment to graft and invention also resulted in the production of Sheffield's first punk fanzine, *Gun Rubber*, with Bower as editor and Newton as anti-editor. The name, whose meaning eludes even the publication's creators, was suggested by Meatwhistle founder Chris Wilkinson as a final provocative arty salvo before he left the group to their own devices. Articles were written under pen names, mainly so their authors' bands and projects could be lauded without sounding too big-headed: Bower was Ronny Clocks, Ware was Art Zero and Adi was Violet Ray, after Sister Ray, Man Ray and also Violet May, the fearsome old lady who ran Sheffield's most famous record shop.

12 Paul Bower, editor of *Gun Rubber* and CAPCOM of the Sheffield space age, 1983

Features of note within the stapled covers included an interview with the Ramones from the fire escape outside The Electric Circus in Manchester in issue five and a letter from Steven Morrissey of Stretford in issue six. It was the design aesthetic, however, that elevated *Gun Rubber* to a higher artistic plane. Adi and Paul had rescued some of their junk shop tat from Cravan's when they returned to Sheffield and among this haul was a collection of vintage S&M postcards. Incorporating these, collage-style, alongside contemporary punk imagery plus the odd bonus shot of Glenn Gregory reclining in a starlet's wig and basque (see issue two) meant that *Gun Rubber* art was even displayed years later at the Tate Gallery, artist unknown. To Adi, especially, punk was just another movement to subvert and satirise:

We went down to see The Stranglers at The Red Cow in London when nobody knew who they were. We used to dress up. I had a black leather jacket from the 1950s with TWAT written in studs on the back. We weren't staunch punks, we made it into more of a satire. Iggy Pop and The Velvet Underground were more of an influence for me. I found a copy of *Raw Power* by chance in a shop. I didn't know who he was but I liked the cover. I wasn't disappointed.

Ware's first performance on stage with a band had triggered a hunger for pop fame. Earlier, in his Meatwhistle days, he had been head-hunted to front the progressive hair rockers Orion at an upcoming Sheffield gig but the opportunity was snatched away when they split before the date arrived. In the adrenaline rush following the VDK and The Studs appearance, he paid for hundreds of stickers to be printed, emblazoned with various band members' names and entirely false claims that their new single, 'Doctor Who', was coming soon.

Ware and Gregory convinced local record shops that their record deal was genuine and the promo stickers were duly displayed. The many leftover stickers were plastered across every lamppost, phone box, litter bin and bus shelter in Sheffield city centre. What an uninformed passer-by or even a clued-up music lover would glean from an encounter with a window full of stickers that simply read 'Eggy Brando' is still unclear. No single was ever recorded.

Studio Electrophonique

The days and nights were full in 1977. In addition to the creation of bands and the publication of fanzines, there was the challenge of hand-tailoring replica James Caan *Rollerball* outfits and learning how to roller skate so the gang could weave enigmatically in and out of the floats during the annual Rag Week parade. When they still weren't ready for bed, horror film marathons were always an option at the Classic Cinema on Fitzalan Square. Pro Pus was a necessity if you aimed to stay awake through five Roger Corman films, watching carefully for the identical, climactic shot of a rooftop collapsing in flames while keeping your eyes peeled for the free cheese and onion sandwiches that were sometimes handed out by the usherettes for sustenance.

Martin Fry of ABC, who had recently arrived from Manchester to study English Literature at Sheffield University, noticed the peculiar cultural rhythms of the natives: 'The scene in Sheffield was always weirder. It was always people who wanted to watch *Eraserhead* in the afternoon on Pond Street.'

'People ask me now about TV programmes that were on in the seventies,' said Bower, 'and I say, "I didn't watch TV. We were out seven days a week."'[6]

In June 1977, a final warm-up gig took place before Martyn, Adi and Ian decided to make a proper go of it with The Future. Adi recalls this event:

We used to have music on all the time when we were at Meatwhistle, stuff like Kraftwerk, and there was even an old Ferrograph tape machine that I had worked out how to use. Ian had started building this big analogue synthesiser and Martyn had bought this Rolf Harris Stylophone with a green electronic eye on it like a theremin and we used to mess about with that. This girl was organising a party at Bar 2 or somewhere and we ended up playing live there. I don't know how it happened. It was pretty spontaneous. It was really improvised with no solid form.

Billed as The Dead Daughters, the performance was only really remarkable in terms of Ian's stage wear which consisted of his full *Rollerball* outfit mismatched with a Spiderman mask. Days of deliberation followed as to the conceptual choices available to the trio regarding their new direction.

'Adi was obsessed with dadaism and surrealism,' said Ware, 'and no one knows where it all came from. I was fascinated. For a bit we were talking seriously about forming a cult based around the year 1000. We started researching it at the central library and everything.'

Eventually, the direction they settled on was north and onwards into the cold, blind future.

'We were convinced we were doing something interesting,' said Newton, 'and, at that time, we felt record companies didn't really know so much about what was going on. So we adopted the position of "This is the future of music. This is the way music is going to go."'

Chapter 12

NO ILLEGAL CONNECTIONS

'New way,' I said, 'What's this about a new way? There's been some very large talk behind my sleeping back and no error.'

Alex DeLarge, *A Clockwork Orange*

The summer The Future arrived in Sheffield, Adi and Martyn became very close. They had never been abroad before so they hatched a plan to catch the train then the ferry to Amsterdam. They ended up sleeping rough in Vondelpark on the first night in the summer heat then sharing a youth hostel dorm with a heroin addict who shot up in the next bunk to the incessant soundtrack of a Blue Cheer cassette. They wandered through the ultraviolet pleasure zone of the red-light district, aghast and guilder-less but did scrape up enough currency between them to watch a screening of Linda Lovelace's *Deep Throat* which Martyn reviewed for *Gun Rubber* upon his return.

The work of The Future was characterised by the electronic instruments the band had recently acquired, an adherence to new conceptual principles regarding the creation of new material and the ingenuity of Ken Patten in marshalling this madness onto tape.

No illegal connections

As the breadwinners of the band, Ware had recently bought a Korg 770S from Musical Sounds on London Road and Marsh had bought a Roland System 100. The main patches that came with the Roland synth seemed to be limited to effects with names like 'extreme applause', 'thunder clap' or 'funky frog'. One line in the instruction booklet stood out to Ware, however, and could have been adopted as a battle cry for all the artists in Sheffield who were saving scarce cash to buy machines that they were determined to master and manipulate. The phrase, in bold, read: 'THERE ARE NO ILLEGAL CONNECTIONS'.[1]

'The ambition was to work to a manifesto', said Ware. 'Once you've established that confidence in yourself and you feel it's reinforced by the people around you, it creates an armour that protects you from criticism. It's irrelevant if you're shit or not, it's just what you have to do to express yourself.'

The first step was to invent a primitive but functional lyric-generating programme on the computers that Ware and Marsh had access to at work.

'We came up with a system for lyrics,' said Newton, 'a word-permutation system in the tradition of Swift's word machine or Dos Passos or William Burroughs or Gysin. We called it CARLOS after a heroine of ours, Wendy Carlos, and it stood for Cyclic and Random Lyric Organisation System.'

With the lyric-spewing computer sorted, it was time to apportion roles in this group of the future. They did consider the automaton approach, naming themselves A, B and C, but couldn't agree about who would be A.

'We thought Adi was fascinating,' said Ware, 'and I wasn't confident enough to be the singer. Even Adi couldn't sing per se but that didn't seem to matter. What we ended up creating with The Future were soundscapes for imaginary films with Adi's inane, quasi-intellectual ramblings over the top in a Sheffield accent.'

The musical soundscapes were inspired by artists such as Bowie, Kraftwerk, Can, Faust, Amon Düül, Roedelius, Eno and whatever new noises they could tease out of the new gear.

Piecing together new tracks at the workshop in Devonshire Lane, they received limited appreciation from their pals.

'Everybody used to laugh at The Future except me', said Phil Oakey. 'They used to practise in a room with 2.3, who were sort of a semi-punk band, and when they'd walk past with their synthesisers, it was all, "Going to play your Tangerine Dream music then?" I thought it was great.'[2]

'We had the bedroom-type of set-up down at Devonshire Lane,' said Ware, 'but we needed something more so we put an ad in the *Sheffield Star* and it was Ken who responded. He said he had a four-track reel-to-reel and that we could record at his place. I think we pushed the boat out and got a taxi and, when we got there, we were thinking: "This doesn't look like a recording studio", and, when he showed us into the front room, it was all chintz and voluminous armchairs. There was a coffee table in the middle of this deep plush carpet with a four-track machine on it. I was thinking, "This is far too comfortable for recording something as avant-garde as this".'

'It was in the middle of Handsworth somewhere', said Newton. 'It wasn't at all a hip studio. It was just this guy's house and he was very normal. It was a bit like Magritte. I don't know if he knew what we were doing or if he understood it but he knew we had to lay it down and he knew how to get it onto tape.'

One of the songs The Future recorded with Ken was 'Looking for the Black Haired Girls'. Based on a suggestion by Ian and a backing track built on female screams and simulated sirens, it was a disturbing, in-role stream of consciousness from the perspective of David Berkowitz, the murderer known as the Son of Sam who had recently terrorised New York City.

'I do remember Ken looking confused a lot of the time', said Ware. 'He clearly knew his stuff in terms of recording but I'm not sure he could process some of the concepts we were bringing along. He was a sound enthusiast and I think this gave him an agnostic approach to whatever he was recording. We were just chuffed to be working with a four-track. We were like "Fucking hell, this is like The Beach Boys!".'

Other tracks, such as 'Blank Clocks' and 'Cairo', relied on J. G. Ballard narratives to get them off the ground and CARLOS to sustain the abstract mood. 'Cairo' starts with a Roland System 100-conjured desert storm utilising the 'Resonant Wind' patch then breaks into some ersatz Eastern pipes reminiscent of the intro to Roxy Music's 'Ladytron'. Adi, the Ballard of Burncross, closes the track with a clipped northern ode to 'this Venus of the dunes, virgin of the time slopes', stealing a paragraph from 'You: Coma: Marilyn Monroe', a 1966 short story included in *The Atrocity Exhibition*.

'I was really influenced by Ballard', said Newton. 'All the stuff about the astronauts and how space affected them and the dark, hidden nature of NASA; Werner Von Braun and the Nazi scientists at White Sands. It's a strange, dark history.'

The tracks recorded at Ken's provide an accurate snapshot of the band's cultural swag bag: 'Dada Dada Duchamp Vortex', 'Future Religion' and 'Pulse Lovers' were the other tracks recorded during these sessions.

Having a professionally produced tape in their hands and feeling like the meteor-proof rocket ship of the future, the band decided it was time to land a major record deal.

'I started thinking about the best way to get our music to record companies', said Ware. 'I got a book from the reference library that had all the addresses of the major labels and I designed and printed a dot-matrix invitation at work. It said, "Welcome to The Future – this is a once in a lifetime chance to hear blah blah blah". Just bullshit basically. We didn't think we'd get a response at all but, in fact, we sent out fifteen invitations and we got twelve responses saying they wanted to meet us. It was so exciting. None of us had ever been to London. All we had was the tape we had made at Ken's but, suddenly, we felt like we were Kraftwerk. Nowadays, you wouldn't even get one meeting.'

'We didn't want to send the tape down,' said Newton, 'so we sent a letter saying we were going to be in London and we were available to do meetings and audition the tape. It was pretty arrogant.'

The romance of this story drops a sob through the spine; three lads from Sheffield, armed with a tape recorded in a council house by a middle-aged ex-RAF man, getting on a train to London for the first time, being ushered into the gilded anterooms of major record companies, feeling like every move was the right move and every day was the last day before take-off.

No illegal connections

'We had a map spread out on the train table,' said Ware, 'plotting all the meetings and the tube journeys, and we made them all on time to be fair. We had five or six on the first day and the executives were all of the same opinion. We'd play the tape for about a minute and they'd stop us and say, "Can we move on to the next one?" and, after listening to a few, they'd shake their heads and say, "It's not really for us, this, lads. You really need to write some songs".'

The mood at the end of the first day was further deflated by a tape mishap. Adi had been responsible for running off a few copies from Ken's master tape but one of them had Elvis on the other side and, when it was played in the board room, the sounds of the King singing 'In the Ghetto' bled through backwards into the already crowded maelstrom of sounds. Luckily, they had a spare and, after a night at the 'Sheffield Embassy' (Glenn Gregory's basement flat in Ladbroke Grove) they girded their electronic loins for another day of confused rejection.

'I think we were too early with it', said Newton. 'Electronic music hadn't really entered the consciousness of people when we went to London.'

The only labels who were kind or encouraging were Island and Virgin who, at least, gave them some time, advice and a quick guided tour around the dream factory.

'They basically said to us, "You're not ready, go back and knock those songs into shape", said Ware, "Add a few top-line melodies, make the lyrics more digestible". So, when we got back, me and Ian had a meeting and said, "It looks like we're going to have to get a real lead singer if we want to do anything with this stuff. We might have to break it to Adi that he's not the man for the job".'

Adi was aware of the band's different tastes but he was not anticipating the end of The Future.

'My ideas and Martyn's ideas were very different', said Newton. 'He was a huge fan of pop music, things like Hot Chocolate. Which is ok, it's fine. But I wanted to do something more aggressive in a way; action and raw energy.'

A whiff of encouragement from the pop machine drove Ware and Marsh to a quick, calculated act of severance. They piled all Adi's gear outside the door of the rehearsal room at the Devonshire Lane workshop and left him a note saying they were waiting for him in the pub.

'We were in The Raven,' said Ware, 'and we'd brought along one of our pals, Mark Civico, who was a bit of a bruiser in case Adi decided to attack us.'

Adi read the note with a sinking feeling of betrayal and disappointment.

'I thought it was surreptitious, the way it was done', said Newton. 'We could have spoken directly to each other. We'd been working as a band and we'd gone through all these experiences. So that's what initially upset me about it, but I was fine afterwards.'

'He understood the reasons,' said Ware, 'but I think at that point he said, "If you're getting rid of me, you can't be called The Future". So, out of respect, we abandoned that name and started looking for another lead singer.'

An archaeological excavation of the blast craters of the Sheffield space age would uncover, at this juncture, a secondary detonation that altered the landscape in two distinct ways. Ware went on to pursue the pop dream and was enmeshed in all its attendant commercial and artistic demands, while Newton redoubled his resolve to follow his muse into more dimly lit, untrodden back alleys of inspiration.

'I had to do my own thing', said Newton. 'You just can't compromise. Even if it means being outside and not getting all the great big backing and the finances and the push.'

In October 1977, Ron Wright and a few of his student pals at Sheffield University started NowSoc (or The Now Society) as a way of promoting punk and post-punk bands at the student union instead of accepting the same carousel of established bands doing the rounds.[3] Their first events were 'bring your own record' discos in the table tennis room but the band that launched NowSoc's live campaign were Paul Bower's 2.3, who played the first band night in Bar 2.

As part of a long subversive class war that goes on to this day, Bower attempted to charge students more than workers or the unwaged to gain entry and was largely successful, asking 90p for normal folk and £1.50 for pampered students.

Over the next year or two, NowSoc became a vital resource for bringing non-student artists and enthusiasts into contact with a ready-made audience of influential, switched-on students. The Human League, Cabaret Voltaire, Vice Versa, I'm So Hollow, They Must Be Russians, Graph, Artery and others all built up a following at NowSoc and it was also a place where embryonic local bands could see exciting artists from out of town such as The Teardrop Explodes, The Mekons or Throbbing Gristle. Bar 2 was tatty and claustrophobic with torn, faux-leather bench seats and a low ceiling, but it had a good jukebox and, if you were skint, you could listen to the full seven-minute version of 'Riders on the Storm' by The Doors for 10p.

The year ended with another gesture of working-class solidarity as Cabaret Voltaire played a benefit gig at The Penthouse for the striking workers at Batchelors Foods. The bean and pea factory in Hillsborough was a lifeline for many of the young artists in Sheffield in the 1970s and 1980s. During the harvest season, a couple of months' work could be picked up processing vegetables in a cannery so glamorous it had once been visited by Bela Lugosi while he was touring his stage production of *Dracula*. This part-time opportunity enabled young bohemians to save enough cash to fund their artistic dreams for a few months or just give them the space to lie fallow, muse and develop their attitude. It was hard work though, especially on the wire-meshed roasting beds where hot air was pumped in and workers were given salt tablets to replace lost sweat. As a concession to this torture, there was a communal ladle standing in a huge metal urn full of weak orange drink which shrivelled employees were welcome to help themselves to.

Conditions like this were, perhaps, one reason why one-armed shop steward Vin Knight organised the strike of 1977, leading 1,200 workers out for nine weeks in a bid for pay more commensurate with the rigours of life on the production line. The benefit gig resulted in Cabaret Voltaire's first write up in the *NME*, an oblique assessment by Andy Gill that probably didn't help any readers who were unversed in French or modern art: 'Their aesthetic appears to be composed of equal parts minimalism and abstract impressionism with a few objets trouvés thrown in.'[4]

Adi Newton, momentarily adrift, borrowed some money from his parents to buy an EMS Synthi suitcase synth that would enable him to continue his experiments in sound alone:

No illegal connections

After The Future I bought a synthesiser without a keyboard. I wanted something I could treat tapes and vocals through and input guitar or organ or whatever. I had to get a loan off my parents. I had to sort of beg them to get me this EMS but they were great, my parents, they helped me a lot.

As the year closed, Adi was introduced to Stephen 'Judd' Turner, a local lad who Cabaret Voltaire knew from their soul boy days. The Cabs introduced Judd to Adi one night in The Raven.

'Judd was quite unique,' said Stephen Mallinder, 'because he'd come from the Northern Soul scene, which happened at about the same time as punk. We related to Judd because he was part of that working-class scene and he didn't come from a musical background. He was a proper Sheffield kid.'

Judd grew up in Burngreave and trained as a metal moulder after leaving school. His speciality was making fake 50p pieces from old bits of cutlery so he could buy cigarettes from vending machines and sell them on to students. Judd and Adi quickly became a double act.

'We became like instant buddies', said Newton. 'Our friendship was instinctual; lots of energy and conversations and ideas. Having a laugh as well.'

Within a year, Adi and Judd would be playing live together as Clock DVA.

Chapter 13
FAST PRODUCTS

We would rather be ruined than changed
We would rather die in our dread
Than climb the Cross of the mount
And see our illusions die.

W. H. Auden, The Age of Anxiety[1]

Jarvis Cocker got his first guitar for Christmas in 1976. In early 1978, he formed his first band, Arabicus Pulp, at City School with his friend Peter Dalton. A few years above him at the same school, Mark White had learned a few chords on a more pliant guitar and had served his time in a school rock band specialising in Free and Lynyrd Skynyrd cover versions. The band were called Van Demon. It may have been Van Diemen, as a nod to all things Tasmanian but, sadly, the band never became established enough to write their name on a poster or a record sleeve and Mark White can't remember either way. He was a punk now, anyway, and was on the lookout for collaborators in the spikier corners of Sheffield.

Ware and Marsh, meanwhile, had taken possession of the Devonshire Lane workshop and were quick to decide on a new name for their band. Their Meatwhistle pal, David Oxley, had recently brought in a board game for them to play.

'It was a strategy game called *Starforce*,' said Ware, 'and it was so tedious that no one could even play it. The rule book was massive and it had all these different scenarios you could choose like 'The Rise of The Human League' and 'The Triumph of the Pan-Sentient Hegemony'. We went for the first one. The message was that we were humanising electronics.'

Glenn Gregory would have been first choice as a new lead singer but he was now working for *Sounds* as a photographer and singing in a band called 57 Men who would later become Wang Chung. The next most likely candidate was Phil Oakey, Martyn's old pal from King Edwards, who had recently adopted a traffic-stopping haircut.

'It was a great haircut', said Ware. 'He almost looked like some sort of transexual.'

The famous lopsided haircut was supposedly conceived when Oakey spotted a girl on the bus with this striking look. He claims that he sat beside her, asked her where she'd had it done then went to the same place and had the exact same cut. Another theory suggests he was trying to emulate the charismatic playboy Jerry Cornelius from Michael Moorcock's recent sci-fi quartet. In an early piece in the music press, Oakey greeted journalist Giovanni Dadomo by saying, 'You look like Jerry Cornelius'.

'Phil used to work in a bookshop and has seriously considered adopting the Cornelius persona himself', wrote Dadomo. 'He even owns the out-of-print anthology of Cornelius stories, the lucky bleeder.'[2]

In the first book of the series, *The Final Programme*, techno-magician Miss Brunner attempts to create the perfect human specimen by merging her own body with Jerry's. The glorious hermaphrodite that emerges from the machinery is so awe-inspiring that the world cowers before it. The 1973 film version is a camp cult classic involving nuns playing fruit machines, needle-gun battles, human pinball and Jon Finch as the louche, Withnail-esque antihero in black nail varnish, swigging Bell's whisky as he drives through blasted British landscapes strafed by psychedelic light flares and synapse-searing synthesisers. The film also included a cast list tailor-made for the target demographic in Sheffield, a group Oakey would term 'the alienated synthesists'. Two of Kubrick's favourites also made an appearance: Patrick Magee, who had played the writer in *A Clockwork Orange*, and Sterling Hayden, who had starred in both *Dr Strangelove* and *The Killing*.

Oakey's attraction to Cornelius made sense; Moorcock described his creation as a character whose 'nature was the industrial city, his idea of paradise was an urban utopia'.[3] Oakey felt the same.

'I am a townie,' he said, 'I gravitate towards concrete.'[4]

When Martyn made the trip to Phil's flat, no one was home, so he left a note saying, 'We've got something we want to talk to you about'.

'I was really excited', said Oakey. 'I thought it was a party or a holiday or something.'[5]

The next trip out on the bus was more successful. Ware, as always, played the role of true believer.

'The day Martyn asked me to join the band,' said Oakey, 'he came around to my flat and he had two records under his arm, one was *Trans Europe Express* and one was 'I Feel Love'. He said, "Look, we can do this". I think that was his actual phrase.'[6]

Phil was invited down to the workshop where he was reacquainted with Ian Craig Marsh.

'I didn't know Philip at all,' said Marsh, 'I'd just met him a couple of times and thought he was totally obnoxious. I thought he was an A1 git.'[7]

They had met once during the Meatwhistle performance of *Marat/Sade* in 1973, when Marsh had an alarm clock in his pocket, and on a second occasion when the synth player's look was even more outlandish.

'I was looking fairly absurd in a pair of women's tights as a top just dragged over my head and ripped,' said Marsh. 'I also had a 13–amp plug around my neck and a baked bean can on my head. Phil came up to me and said: "What happens if I plug you into the mains? Does your head light up?".'[8]

'The only time I remembered meeting Ian was when we both went for the same job at this computer place', said Oakey. 'He came in dressed totally in black with gloves and an umbrella on a sunny day.'[9]

Oakey was given a cassette full of music and challenged to add to it.

'It was like an audition really', said Ware. 'We gave him a cassette of what we'd done, said, "Take it away, write some lyrics and see if you can come up with a melody for the top line".'

Oakey went home and wrote the lyrics and melody to 'Being Boiled', a cryptic attack on parental attitudes, employing a cock-eyed religious analogy concerning the use of infant silkworms to make socks.

'I got some religions mixed up', said Oakey. 'I thought Hinduism and Buddhism were the same thing.'[10]

When he returned to the workshop to present the song, Ware and Marsh were astounded at the originality and imaginative freedom at work before them.

'Within two lines he'd got the job', said Ware.

It wasn't just the startling originality of the lyrics that made this track the first heavy-gauge salvo of the synth wars. The composition of the music was a feat of craftmanship worthy of the little mesters who had turned out their own masterpieces in steel in the same cramped workshop. Martyn Ware recalls the process.

We didn't jam. We were like a Cro-Magnon version of what everyone can now do in their bedroom. It was just me and Ian and the ubiquitous purple fruit trays on the walls. All we had was a SM58 microphone, my Korg monophonic synth, Ian's Roland 100 modular synth and that was it. Everything was recorded straight into the tape recorder. We recorded the rhythm for 'Being Boiled' on the System 100, which Ian was the master of. We thought it sounded a bit like Parliament or Funkadelic. Then we put down a rising chord sequence that was later nicked by Visage for 'Fade to Grey'. So we'd got the rhythm and that monophonic bass line and we had to bounce them from track to track so we could fit the lead melody line on there and that Morse code beat. People tend to prefer the original version from the workshop to the one we did later in a big studio on a 24–track machine. They like the patina of degradation.

Ever the hustler, Ware used every opportunity to tell the world about his new band. An unexpected chance for self-promotion came in January 1978 when Ware and Bower queued up all night outside the Gaumont cinema to claim their seats for the first Sheffield screening of *Star Wars*.

Me and Martyn went to my mum's and she made us some sandwiches and we queued up all night. It started raining but we were alright because we were just under the canopy. Someone from the newspaper came up and interviewed Martyn and he told this guy how much he liked sci-fi and anything futuristic. Then he told the reporter that he'd started a band called The Human League and they were going to make a single. The reporter just laughed.

The band's first mention in the press, therefore, was in the *Sheffield Telegraph* on 29 January 1978 with Martyn responding to a question about the sacrifice he was making for art and science fiction: 'A member of the local pop group The Human League said standing in the cold was just part of the masochism of living in Sheffield.'[11]

The fact that The Human League could even consider the prospect of a record being released was, again, the work of Paul Bower. 2.3 was the first Sheffield band of the punk and post-punk era to release a proper record. Their first and only single, 'All Time Low', was funded and released by Bob Last's Fast Product label. Last, a lapsed architecture student who had dropped out of university after being told off for being too postmodern, was based in Edinburgh. He was inspired to start his own independent record label after reading *The Military Thoughts of Mao Zedong* and being gifted a copy of *Spiral Scratch* by Buzzcocks. After his own single was pressed, Bower sent a demo tape of 'Being Boiled' to Fast Product for their consideration.

In the seventh and final issue of *Gun Rubber*, Paul Bower even did his best to sign off with a promotional prediction for his pals' success in the decade to come: 'The Human League will challenge a lot of your ideas about how a rock band should look and sound. They are involved in making disco music for the 80s.'[12]

The new band, keen to polish their statue before anyone else had even thought to cast one, wrote a manifesto full of the vaulting ambition necessary for lift-off:

In the summer of 1977, The Human League was formed due to the members finding no conventional channels for their immense talents. None of The Human League have any orthodox musical training but prefer to regard composition as an extension of logic, inspiration and luck. Therefore, unlike conventional musicians, their influences are not so obvious. Interested in combining the best of both worlds, The Human League would like to positively affect the future by close attention to the present, allying technology with humanity and humour. They have been described as 'later 20th century boys' and 'intelligent, innovatory and immodest'.

Less interested in global pop domination but keen to develop beyond the constrictions of Chris Watson's parents' loft, Cabaret Voltaire were looking for a new place to rehearse. Paul Bower, of course, was on hand to plot the next step in Sheffield's cultural evolution. He was looking for a place where 2.3 could practise and was drawn to a factory on Portobello that had a familiar aura:

I went to the factory at Western Works because I'd heard there were some rooms upstairs to rent and, when this guy showed me around, I thought, 'I've been here before'. When I was younger, I'd been cajoled into coming to a Young Socialist's meeting without realising it was actually The Workers' Revolutionary Party, which was quite weird and culty. They used to tell kids it was going to be a disco and, when they'd got them inside, they'd lecture them for two hours about the gold standard and the evils of capitalism. And this was the same room. The small room that Cabaret Voltaire ended up taking over, which was the old office, had all these Trotskyist Constructivist posters on the wall. People look at pictures of the Cabs in there and think they must have put them up but they were already there. I'm not sure of Mal's politics but I do know that Richard was an anarcho-syndicalist.

'My father, at one point, was a member of the Communist Party and I was a member of the Young Communist League', said Richard Kirk. 'For a little while, I wore the badge when I went to school.'[13]

Having a post-industrial HQ full of insurrectional posters in the epicentre of the city's musical explosion burnished the Cabs already radioactive halo of danger and dash. They did little to dispel this, squinting their eyes to imagine Western Works as their own version of a New York loft space, an immersive environment where both sonic and visual confrontations could be plotted. The streets around the Western Works entrance and the church opposite were the city's main red-light area in the 1970s and 1980s and, if the Cabs were arriving or leaving during dismal weather, there were usually a couple of damp sex workers sheltering in

13 Cabaret Voltaire rehearse at Western Works, 1979

the factory entrance. There was even a rumour that the factory on the floor below was engaged in fabricating portable nuclear shelters. This, it seems, was untrue.

'The floor below made women's nighties,' said Mallinder, 'which used to really worry us as they were highly flammable.'

'Having our own space was important', said Kirk. 'It was a bit like Andy Warhol's Factory on a fifty pence budget. A clubhouse, almost. Somewhere to meet where we could have a spliff, listen to music then make music of our own.'[14]

The Cabs worked hard to maintain their reputation as untouchable, disciplined contrarians with the stainless style to repel all local challengers. They would often stride into rough city centre boozers and order Babycham all round just to feel the ripples of impending doom shiver around them. In nightclubs they would ask for Pernod while others swilled Wards Bitter, although this had a practical purpose as you could see if Pernod had been watered down unlike other adulterated spirits. To younger bands and aspiring musicians coming up on the rails of the tap rooms of The Beehive, The Hallamshire or The Raven, the charge emanating from the Pernod/Babycham booth was palpable.

'The younger bands would've been shit-scared of us', said Mallinder. 'We were older and we thought we were cool. We'd always done things like going to London to buy our clothes so we were definitely slick fuckers.'

Shortly after Phil's successful audition to join The Human League, they managed to secure a booking to play in the refectory at Psalter Lane art college. They had quickly worked up original tracks such as 'Dance Like a Star', 'Circus of Death' and 'Blind Youth' as well as arranging a stark, moody cover version of 'You've Lost That Loving Feeling' by The Righteous Brothers. There were concerns, however, about their presentation and stagecraft. The gig took place on 16 February 1978.

'It was our first gig that wasn't just messing about like with VDK and The Studs or the Meatwhistle bands', said Ware. 'We just had dining tables with the synths on them and a tape recorder in the middle. At the back we had a few detuned tellies to make it look futuristic and Phil was at the front clinging to the microphone for dear life.'

'I've probably never been as scared in my life,' said Oakey, 'I still can't believe I did it. I couldn't remember the words. On "The Path of Least Resistance" I just sang the same line over and over. I was in a complete panic.'[15]

Paul Bower, of course, was there to usher this event into existence:

14 The Human League, 1978

I think there were about sixty or seventy people there. Phil had his lopsided haircut, Martyn had his silver jacket on, Ian had his emotionless Ron Mael face on behind the keyboard. They didn't have slides behind them at this point and I was stood at the back by the sound guy trying to convince him to keep turning the volume of the tape up. Then, about halfway through a forty-minute set, Phil just walked off stage and came straight through the audience to where I was standing. He said, 'Hi Paul. How's it going?' and I said, 'Yeah, it's going great Phil but I think it's traditional for the lead singer to stay on stage for the whole show'. He just went, 'Oh right, great', and dawdled back to the front.

'I was so nervous', said Ware, 'that, when I came off stage, my mouth was full of blood because I'd been biting the inside of my cheek from the effort of focusing on playing the songs.'

The electronic gear was from the age preceding presets, so every single dial had to be reset at the start of each track. Hand-prepared matrix sheets had to be consulted on stage so that the correct configurations could be synchronised between songs.

'I remember after the show,' said Bower, 'the manager of this local group called The Push, who were meant to be Sheffield's answer to The Boomtown Rats, came up to me and said, "Sure Paul, it's very arty, it's very Berlin, but they'll never sell any records".'

Unlikely as it may seem, my mum and dad were at that gig. They weren't cosmonauts of the cutting edge: my dad was a chargehand at Presto Tools and my mum worked at the Co-op Bank on West Street. In February 1978, I was five years old and remember clearly that the musical affiliations my dad held were more loyal to the Mojave Desert than the electronic wastelands of central Sheffield. The tapes on rotation in the car were *Hotel California* by The Eagles, *A Farewell to Kings* by Rush, Cheap Trick's first album and Meat Loaf's *Bat Out of Hell*. He was disproportionately impressed by guitar solos and, as a result, Rick Nielsen's five-necked instrument was a high point that still hasn't been surpassed and certainly wouldn't have been threatened by three jokers in a school canteen with a tape recorder.

My dad had collected Bowie knives as a kid and was bereft when my grandma found them one day and threw them away. As a consequence, he has spent the rest of his life scouring antique shops, flea markets and car boot sales trying to discover lost treasure from the past. After meeting some Victorian-bottle hunters at an antique fair at Sheffield City Hall in the mid-1970s, my dad got to know artist David Walker Barker, then a student at the Psalter Lane art college, and Dick Cowell, who was a lecturer there. Along with my dad's pal Mick Heaton, who played football for Sheffield United, they soon became addicted to the illicit thrill of driving out to ancient condemned rubbish dumps beside railway lines or motorway embankments in glamour spots such as Barnsley, Darwen and Huddersfield to dig vast, unstable tunnels in search of Victorian Codd bottles with their marble stoppers still intact.

Heaton, who went on to be first-team coach at Everton under Howard Kendall when they won the old first division in the 1980s, had started bottle digging because he couldn't sleep at night due to the stress of wondering whether he would be picked on a Saturday.[16] This worked as therapy for a time but, soon, he couldn't sleep at night due the nagging suspicion that someone else was digging in his tunnel on some distant, wind-picked rail siding. Aside from the obvious danger of a tunnel collapsing and being entombed in Victorian refuse, they often had to dodge the police and were twice apprehended in their pursuits: once because they were digging on the site of an old hospital where human bodies were buried and once when they were suspected of being members of the IRA on a bomb-planting mission at a Lancashire sewage works.

As their friendship grew, Dick and my dad started to socialise. Dick and his wife, Gillian, were the first bohemians I ever encountered. Our maisonette in Lowedges was neat but it was built to council scale and equipped with features that were purely functional. Dick and Gillian's house in

Nether Edge was a lofty, high-ceilinged pleasure palace full of artfully chosen pop culture antiques and the alien smells of simmering pulses and joss sticks. They had stripped varnished floorboards, a vast, battered leather couch and a fur rug. They had a juke box, a pinball machine and a Jennings Indian-head fruit machine. It was like stepping into the Lennons' Kenwood mansion. This unlikely social connection is the reason my mum and dad ended up at the first gig by The Human League at Psalter Lane refectory. To this day, my dad still rates it below Cheap Trick live at the Nelson Mandela building in 1983.

From 1977 to 1978, a fanzine was doing the rounds in Sheffield that counterbalanced *Gun Rubber*'s mood of portentous subversion with a more frothy and positive attitude. Stephen Singleton, working from a nerve centre below 44 Bowood Road, began to produce *Steve's Paper* as an attempt to jolt Sheffield out of its provincial stupor:

The fanzine started as a bit of a joke because there was already a fanzine around in Sheffield called *Gun Rubber* which was a punk fanzine. They were a bit older than me and I thought they were really cool. I was about seventeen and I loved punk music so I'd go down to London on Saturdays and walk up and down the King's Road. There were loads of people making fanzines down there like *Sniffin' Glue* and *48 Thrills* so mine just started out as a sheet of paper telling people what was going on in Sheffield, a bit like people would write on Facebook now. It was just me, finding old shops in town that sold deadstock fifties jeans or winklepicker shoes or plastic sandals, finding new record shops and telling people about gigs that were coming up at the university.

Stephen's youth and bright-eyed enthusiasm set him apart from the electronic experimentalists of the city who were often quick to dismiss his evocations of Sheffield's flimsy punk wonderland. Features in *Steve's Paper* included essentials about where to find the best haircut in town or how to clean grime from a silver jacket.

'We used to take the piss out of Steve a lot and be snotty about his fanzine,' said *Gun Rubber* editor, Paul Bower, 'but we were wrong.'

Despite his age and inexperience, Stephen proved to be a canny, tenacious, independent operator, offering himself up as the crucial missing link between the bewildered world of adult commerce and the money burning holes in the pockets of Sheffield youths:

Eventually, I started to sell advertising space. I'd go to the Top Rank club with my fanzine and they'd give me £50 to advertise on the back page. I was on about £16 a week working at H. L. Brown's the jewellers on Fargate. It got to the point where I was getting £150 for advertising on each issue, and that would take me weeks to earn in my normal job.

It was while hawking his fanzine at the Top Rank club on Arundel Gate that Stephen first met Mark White, his future collaborator with Vice Versa and ABC. For White, who was still a sixth-form student at City School, the meeting was timely and alive with the spirit of new possibility. White, in an unusually perceptive moment of teenage realisation, had recently paused to consider the unrelenting kaleidoscope of pop movements that had acted upon him, carrying him through a Sheffield adolescence buoyed by the swell of glam, drawn deeper by the undertow of punk, now dashed on the rocks of new wave: 'I said to myself at the age of sixteen, Mark, it's never going to be this good again.'

Jarvis Cocker recalls this time of melancholia and indolence as a knock-kneed observer from a few years below:

I remember walking past the sixth-form block and hearing 'Warm Leatherette' by The Normal. It seemed to be on every time you walked past at break time. It was Mark White playing it. He was about three years older than me so I hardly knew him.[17]

'Actually,' said White, 'I think I was playing "United" by Throbbing Gristle.'

Imbued with the conviction that he must start a band but with no real idea of how to go about it, White approached Singleton and asked about putting an advert in his fanzine to attract suitable candidates.

'I met Stephen when I was sixteen', said White. 'It was a Sunday night at the Top Rank Suite and he was selling his fanzine inside. I said, "I'm thinking of starting a punk band", and, to Steve's infinite credit, he said, "I'll be in your band", and I just went, "Oh, OK", and that was that.'

Keen to emphasise the cultural necessity of their early efforts, the duo called themselves Vital Outlet. White's experience with Van Demon meant that he had grasped the rudiments of the guitar but, after a few punky practice sessions at Mark's house, the idea wore thin.

During this period, Singleton's friend from High Storrs School, David Sydenham, was staying at Bowood Road after being kicked out by his parents. As a condition of his tenancy, Stephen insisted that he learn how to play an instrument so that he could assist with musical experiments in the cellar. Singleton's friend, Gordon Butler, had made him an oscillator and this was the machine at the heart of their new collaboration. After a few sessions, the pair invited Mark White along to augment the sound. White's initial visit to the Bowood Road cellar introduced him to the possibilities offered by electronics.

'I got off the bus on my way to Stephen's,' said White, 'and you could hear the noise from his basement 300 yards away. It was very experimental bleeps and boinks like a mad professor running riot and testing a synthesiser. Eternal gratitude to his mum, Carol, for putting up with it.'

The ideas blossomed and soon the trio started to amass a cellarful of electronics. White recalls these early days:

I'd realised quite early on that I needed to earn some money to buy musical equipment because it was fiercely expensive. I became a trolley boy at the Asda in Handsworth. Soon, we had a Korg MS20, a Korg M500 and a Mini Pops beat box. Getting anything to sync was a nightmare. I'd worked out you could process the drum machine through the MS20 to get a really big and modern kick and snare sound. After that it was just jamming; you try this, I'll try that and then we'll launch it on the public whether they're ready or not, whether we're ready or not. That was the punk spirit.

During the first weeks in the cellar, original and experimental was the only way to go.

'We started writing our own songs because we couldn't do cover versions', said Singleton. 'We didn't have a great deal of ability at that point.'

'Camille', one of the songs recorded at Ken Patten's in 1979 for their Music 4 EP, was an atmospheric rendering of a storm warning.

'"Camille" had dialogue we'd taped off the TV', said Singleton. 'It was something that was on late at night about disasters and hurricanes with this old guy narrating it. We called it that because the programme was about Hurricane Camille. We'd go to jumble sales and buy old tape record-ers and it was like, yes! I've got a new piece of artillery. We used to take cassettes apart and make little tape loops like samples.'

In March 1978, The Human League recruited Adrian Wright as a fourth member to address the issue of their inert stage show. Wright was a film studies student at Psalter Lane who worked as an ice-cream man on the side. He had attended their first gig at the college refectory and thought they were terrible. Ian Craig Marsh had heard about Wright's vast and eclectic collection of slides and approached him with a view to providing suitably kitsch and apocalyptic imagery as a projected backdrop for future gigs.

Wright had spent his childhood and adolescence obses-sively collecting toys, action figures, American TV annuals, Gerry Anderson ephemera and Hollywood gossip maga-zines. The slides he kept catalogued neatly in ring bind-ers were an often bewildering juxtaposition of bubble-gum culture, space age fantasy and cold war reality. A typical sequence of slides floating behind the band at an early gig might have comprised shots of *Batman*, Lauren Bacall, B-52 bomber planes, John Wayne, a lunar lander, Janet Leigh, Thunderbird 2, *Lolita* and a helicopter gunship. The logic was questionable but the effect was instant.

'As soon as we started doing shows with Adrian,' said Oakey, 'with pictures of people's heads blowing up or Jesus crying, the gigs started to go well.'[18]

By the spring of 1978, Martyn Ware's dream of releasing a single was close to a reality. Bob Last liked the sound of the 'Being Boiled' workshop demo and wanted to bring it out on his Fast Product label.

'We quite liked the demo,' said Ware, 'but the idea of putting a record out was like saying: "We're going to fly to Venus". We had 100 per cent artistic ambition and 0 per cent commercial ambition. If Bob had replied saying: "It's alright but can you put some guitars on it?", we'd have said, "Absolutely not".'

The Human League's lofty artistic notions were hinted at in the spoken-word introduction to 'Dance Like a Star':

This is a song for all you bigheads out there who think disco music is lower than the irrelevant musical gibberish and tired platitudes that you try to impress your parents with. We're The Human League, we're much cleverer than you and this is called 'Dance Like a Star'.

Even new boy Adrian Wright was quick to adopt this sussed, irreverent attitude to the lowly consumer: 'I think it's the fact that we metaphorically smoke Havanas and our audiences metaphorically smoke Tom Thumbs. And that's it really.'[19]

Last wanted to release something that was 'self-consciously postmodern' so, in the true spirit of Sheffield DIY, Ware decided that he would design the sleeve himself. The result was a pink consumerist collage in the style of The Independent Group, signed 'Electronically Yours': 'I went to

Andrews art shop on West Street, bought loads of Letraset and made the cover. The whole single cost £2.50 to make and that was for the art materials.'

The single was released in April and received independent music's equivalent of a papal blessing when John Peel played it on his Radio 1 evening show. Readings from deep space detected chatter from major labels coalescing around the sound of the future but one canny punk had obviously been flicking through The Human League's record collection. John Lydon, reviewing 'Being Boiled' in the *NME*, dismissed the next big thing in two words: 'trendy hippies'.

The rise of The Human League was also punctured but only partially deflated by a gig at the university that served to remind Martyn Ware that not everyone was ready for tomorrow's sound.

We did a gig at Bar 2 which David Bower had organised for a trade union branch party. We were halfway through 'You've Lost That Lovin' Feeling' and, to be honest, we weren't going down a storm. These blokes would've been happier with The Barron Knights. One guy must have thought, "Right, I've had enough of this shit", and he just stepped up onto the stage, took the mic off Phil and said: "Right, we're going to have a beer race". He didn't even have the decency to let us finish the song. Phil was dumbfounded, Ian never said anything but I was fucking livid. These trade unionists were soon all lined up drinking pints and sticking the empty pint pots on their heads and I was stood there on stage thinking: "Fucking Philistines".

Even the other bands in Sheffield weren't universally aware of The Human League's ascent into the cultural stratosphere.

Stephen Singleton, whose fanzine claimed to test the pop pulse of Sheffield, hadn't even heard of them when Vice Versa were offered a support slot at a NowSoc gig in July 1978. The event, billed as a 'What, No Drummers?' night, was offered to Singleton as a chance to road-test some early compositions but he initially refused as he thought The Human League sounded like a political movement akin to The Anti-Nazi League or Socialist Worker.

After the gig, however, Singleton was impressed, especially by Ian Craig Marsh's on-stage Perspex shed that he had built partly to protect his expensive gear from missiles and spilled pints and partly to create an exclusion zone for concentration and relaxation. He'd even got a small TV in there.

'I asked him what the TV was for', said Singleton. 'He said, "It's just a normal television. I don't have a lot to do during the show so if I get bored I just watch *Coronation Street* or whatever."'[20]

Cabaret Voltaire marched into the summer of 1978 unalloyed and free from the taint of the pop machine. They played a gig at The Limit on West Street on 15 August that exemplified their willingness to walk the tightrope between arty provocation and being kicked to death.

The Cabs were supporting a Sheffield band called Molodoy who were not only named in honour of Anthony Burgess's *A Clockwork Orange* but also dressed as Droogs on stage, complete with boiler suits, bowler hats and the single painted eye. Due to the fact that Molodoy had original songs with titles such as 'Children of the Third Reich', they attracted an extreme and volatile crowd.

'When Cabaret Voltaire opened for Molodoy at The Limit,' said Paul Bower, 'Richard Kirk called me over and showed me a crowbar he'd brought with him. The Cabs were planning to open with one of their more hardcore, experimental sets, and Molodoy attracted a bit of a National Front skinhead crowd. He said: "I'm not going to start anything Paul but, if there's any trouble ...".'

Roger Quail, a teenager from Firth Park who would later play drums with Adi and Judd in Clock DVA, remembers the fever-dream mood evoked by the sound of the Cabs: 'Snow on a TV screen in an empty room. Diseased sounds blip from speaker to speaker like tsetse flies.'[21]

The bootboys were not impressed and their patience was tested even further when the three members of Cabaret Voltaire walked off the stage with their music still playing, ordered pints from the bar and stood there drinking them in a gesture of artistic detachment that registered among the bristly crowd as a massive piss-take.

The Limit, which became a vital meeting ground for young artists and enthusiasts from all over South Yorkshire and hosted bands like U2 and Simple Minds in their post-punk apprenticeships, was still clinging on to its rock roots in the summer of 1978.[22] They still closed each night with The Eagles' 'Take It to the Limit' and, on 11 September, they hosted a gig of legendary incongruity when the silver foil moon unit of The Human League played on the same bill as Def Leppard, local rockers fronted by Stephen Singleton's old school pal Joe Elliott sweating meaningfully on the subterranean stage with a rough-hewn wooden crucifix banging against his bare chest.

Across town, Joe Elliott's future bandmate, Rick Allen, was sitting at the electronic drum kit in Ken and Lorna's bedroom waiting for the nod from downstairs. Richard, as he was known in 1978, was the fourteen-year-old drummer for The Johnny Kalendar Band, and the tracks being recorded at Studio Electrophonique were three cover versions of originals by Styx, Argent and Doris Day. Within a year, Rick would successfully audition for a place in Def Leppard while lead singer Johnny, who was originally Johnny Coggin from Crookesmoor, would go on to enjoy a lifetime residency at various Benidorm bars.

After the test flight of 'Being Boiled' and their teething problems on the trade unionist circuit, The Human League finally achieved the escape velocity necessary to fly into the clear air beyond Sheffield when Virgin Records offered them a multi-album deal. Martyn Ware remembers this phantom launch:

When we signed for Virgin on Richard Branson's houseboat in Little Venice, it seemed very glamorous but then we real-ised we could only afford to pay ourselves thirty quid a week until we sold some records. This was like an 80 per cent pay cut for me as a computer operator. My mum was going, "Oh, Martyn, what are you giving that up for? You could have a career for life there", and I had to say, "Mum, I've got to have a try or we'll never know will we?" She came around when we'd had a few hits. She used to drag the postman into the flat at Broomhall to look at the gold discs on the wall.

At the same time, Cabaret Voltaire were looking for a record deal. Stephen Mallinder recalls the plan:

The *NME* and *Sounds* were really important to us. We picked up on journalists who might be interested in what we were doing. Like Andy Gill, who wrote for the *NME* but was from Sheffield. Andy was great, a bit hippyish but we'd all go round his flat for a spliff and he'd hold court about new music. I think that's where I heard The Residents for the first time. Anyway, we picked up on the fact that journalists published their top ten playlists and that, sometimes, these included demo tapes as well as records. So we sent a tape to Jon Savage and he included it in his playlist then came up to Sheffield to do an interview. He was the one who mentioned us to Rough Trade.

The Rough Trade deal to release the Cabs' 'Extended Play' single in October came with a small advance that enabled them to buy a four-track Revox machine for their Western Works headquarters. The Virgin deal for The Human League came with a slightly larger advance that enabled them to move out of the workshop on Devonshire Lane. After finding then being evicted from a great rehearsal spot below Cole Brothers on Cambridge Street, Ian told the band about an abandoned vets surgery he'd spotted on West Bar. It was the former premises of Leslie Walker, Fletcher and Saxton Veterinary Surgeons and, of its five floors, only one was vaguely habitable. There were no lights or power in the rest of the building and it was infested with rats.

When music journalist Giovanni Dadomo visited, he painted a sensory image of the band 'on the second floor of a small, rust-covered factory building in the appealingly named Love Street. Intoxicating smell of yeast from a nearby brewery. Like snorting Hovis.'[23]

'When we got our first proper studio,' said Ware, 'it was this derelict vets' surgery with old cages and needles scattered about. It was vile but we rented it for peanuts. Ian's dad was a builder and he helped us fix it up. We painted it orange because there was no natural light. We blacked out the windows so, from the outside, it still looked abandoned. We had a Soundcraft 32-into-8 mixing desk, and an Ampex one-inch eight-track tape recorder but only six tracks worked. Even with six tracks we felt like The Beatles. We had some compressors and a spring reverb and our synths, of course. The studio led into a kitchen that was full of empty milk bottles. We used the kitchen as a vocal booth and the recorded vocals always sounded amazing. I think it was because the glass bottles gave the room a bright, brittle sound. Completely accidental of course. We decided to call it Monumental Studios even though it was a shit hole.'

On 15 November 1978, Phil Oakey worked his final shift shovelling coal at Thornbury Hospital. The trials of an embryonic pop idol who still has to navigate everyday life in a northern city were hinted at in an early mention of The Human League in the *NME*:

On the top of a bus in Sheffield, he is merely a tall bloke with a very silly haircut. On the stage, he is a friendly emissary from some wonderland of cultural deviance.[24]

Chapter 14

NOTES FROM A CONDEMNED TERRACE

It is just in this same cold, loathsome semi-mania, this same half-belief in oneself, this same poison of unsatisfied wishes that there lies the essence of the strange delight I have spoken of.

Fyodor Dostoevsky, *Notes from Underground*

The winter of 1978 was bleak and very long. Snow was general all over the north. It was falling softly like kisses upon the grey suds of the Don and thickening the cold iron ribs of riverside factory gantries. It was falling too upon the pale dome of the Abbeydale Picture House and crowding the corners of leaded lights in the shivering workshop windowpanes on Snuff Mill Lane. It lay thickly drifted on the municipal City Road grave where Cyril Griffin lay buried and, in the quiet, it fell faintly through the universe, ushering in a decade of discontent and dread. It would fall until March 1979.[1] Thatcher would be here in the thaw.

Just before Christmas, Adi and Judd took Clock DVA on the road for the first time. They had already attracted banning orders from various Sheffield venues. Their August gig at The

Penthouse ended with Adi plucking a tube of fluorescent strip lighting from its housing, waving it about like a pissed Jedi then smashing it to pieces on the lip of the stage as a reaction to a complacent audience. The rest of the band followed suit and were soon surrounded by broken glass and irate bouncers who were, suddenly, anything but complacent. Their debut at NowSoc a few months later also resulted in audience bewilderment and a ban after several televisions were bludgeoned into shards and splinters during a strobe-induced climactic freakout. This was all part of Adi's masterplan:

I like confrontation. To confront people's ideas with art, music and theatre. Taking them into a space they've never been in before and exposing them to something new. Sometimes, methods have to be extreme. The idea of destruction and annihilation was punk but it went back to early rock'n'roll with riots and kids smashing up theatres. At that first gig, I don't think the crowd knew what was happening. It was pretty impromptu but it got quite riotous.

The very first tape made by Adi and Judd set out their stall as purveyors of witty, transgressive material that, at times, made Cabaret Voltaire sound like Leo Sayer. It contained a track called 'Texas Mk2' which was sound clips from the film *The Texas Chainsaw Massacre* treated through Adi's EMS Synthi to make them even more disturbing. It also featured, for balance, a version of The Ronettes' 'Then He Kissed Me' retooled as 'Then He Shot Me'.

Exiles in their own land, they were now unloading their van in the teeth of a snowstorm at a club in Halifax owned by celebrity wrestler Big Daddy. The crowd were a typical club audience, expecting the pop hits of yesterday and today to get them in the mood for Christmas. A few minutes into Clock DVA's set, the mood began to curdle. The audience had quickly sized the band up as seven-stone students with weak wrists and no bollocks. They had certainly underestimated Judd.

'Judd was small and thin', said Paul Bower. 'He had cheekbones you could cut paper with but he could look after himself. We weren't fighters but, if anyone had a go at me or Adi, Judd just smacked 'em.'

The band were prepared to ride out and even revel in the hostility but, when a pint of ale was upended on one of the synths, the music died and Judd waded into the crowd, chopping at all comers with his bass guitar. Without Big Daddy for back up, the crowd shrank in terror and soon the band were back in the wintry car park, stacking soggy synths and blood-stained, skull-sprained guitars into the back of the van. Squinting out a clear path home through the white-out in the comfortless confines of a cold pan-elled van put the band in mind of Napoleon's retreat from Moscow. Eventually, they slid into the turbulent wake of a snow plough and made it home in the early hours.

Martin Fry arrived in Sheffield at the height of punk. He was born in Stretford, Manchester and grew up in subur-ban Bramhall before moving across the Pennines to study English Literature at Sheffield University. His dad was an engineer at Carborundum Tools in Old Trafford. His inter-est in music had been fortified by teenage expeditions to mid-week clubs in his hometown, listening to Rose Royce and Chic and becoming hooked on the liberating communal experience of a packed dance floor.

'I remember hearing Sly and the Family Stone's "Family Affair",' said Fry, 'and it just ignited everybody. That really left a mark on me. The main obsession was trying to unite people on the dance floor.'

Fry attended The Sex Pistols' gig at Manchester's Lesser Free Trade Hall in 1976 and this fused two distinct musical worlds in his psyche, the soulful world of yesterday's glamour and romance and the urgent world of today's frustration and rage.

'That was a Road-to-Damascus moment for me', said Fry. 'This was the first indication that someone like me could be in a band. I'd never seen anything that confrontational. It was fantastic. I painted my shoes green but I didn't do the hair.'[2]

When the long winter of 1978 descended on Sheffield, Fry had detached himself from the traditional patterns of undergraduate life and was fully embedded in the dank concrete shadows of the city's artistic underclass. He had started his own fanzine, *Modern Drugs*, mainly as a way of gaining free entry to clubs such as The Limit:

I loved Burroughs because of Bowie. Jack Kerouac, Hermann Hesse, J. G. Ballard, Jean-Paul Sartre … the stuff you read when you're an isolated teenager in suburbia. I was opinionated. I wanted to have my say. The idea was that music and art are the modern drugs.[3]

He had also opted into a social experiment organised by the university whereby a handful of adventurous students were transplanted from standard accommodation in the leafy enclaves of Ranmoor and Broomhill and introduced to life on the barricades of Hyde Park flats. Fry cut a simultaneously imposing yet bedraggled figure on the streets of Sheffield that winter. As a penniless student with a headful of Kerouac, Burroughs and Trocchi, he was able to justify his cheerless existence as an essential bohemian phase that would breed great art. To others, however, he appeared to be a diffident, voyeuristic presence, marching about at high speed in his only set of clothes, clutching a carrier bag full of notes for future fanzine features.

Around this time, Fry met another Sheffield University student who didn't appear to fit the academic mould and who would go on to exert significant influence on the launch of the Sheffield space age. John Blyther had arrived in the city from Droitwich to study architecture in 1978 but had spent most of his first year DJing for his mates in the cavernous Victorian basement beneath his student digs on Oakholme Road. He became known, and is still known in Sheffield folklore, as Disco John:

All the potential troublemakers had been stuck in this annex of Stephenson Hall and we started having punk/funk discos in the basement, playing War, Galaxy, Peter Brown and Donna Summer with some punk tunes thrown in. I also started going to see bands at NowSoc. At the end of the first year, me and my mate got thrown off the degree course so I dyed my hair pink and went on tour with The Slits and The Clash, hitchhiking around the country. When I came back to Sheffield, I got a job washing dishes at The Beauchief Hotel. Martin was living on Hyde Park flats and we knew each other from seeing bands. He always wore the same full-length leather coat. He looked like Bowie from the *Low* era but a bit ratty.

Fry developed a vicarious fascination with Clock DVA. To him, they were genuine artists committed to a life of untrammelled self-expression, untainted by the succour of public acceptance or commercial success. The concomitant dangers of such a lifestyle, however, were not so attractive. Fry was forced into doing grim part-time jobs around Sheffield including one that involved working in a cutlery factory with Judd, sweeping up swarf cuttings.

'Some of it was terrible', said Fry. 'Crap drugs and no money but Sheffield was a great place to be a bohemian. Ten pence would get you across the whole city on the bus. You knew that punk rock was finished and the future was coming.'

Judd's old friends in Cabaret Voltaire were also aware of the darker side to this bohemian pose and the roots of its growth.

'The Northern Soul movement collapsed in on itself and became a heroin movement', said Stephen Mallinder. 'Judd had a problem with heroin. The soul movement had been built around uppers and speed and all-dayers and, as people got older, heroin seemed to be an antidote to that.'

In May 1979, Judd overdosed on heroin but survived. Despite the associated dangers that surrounded Clock DVA, outsiders such as Martin Fry and Disco John learned a lot from the artistic discipline they displayed under pressure.

'Adi was a true artist', said John. 'He loved objects. Even the clothes he wore. We all used to wear second-hand clothes and he had this beautiful suit that must have been a vet's suit as it had buttons all the way up one arm so you could undo them and see to a cow. He loved macabre details like that.'

'Adi was a real catalyst for me', said Fry. 'I asked him what he was going to do for the rest of his life and he said "I'm going to do this. I'm going to make music." I realised there and then that it was an option. It just takes someone to say that to you.'[4]

'Martin was a big fan of Clock DVA', said Newton. 'He wrote nice things about us in *Modern Drugs* and I got him that big leather coat from a charity shop. It was a full-length brown military motorcycle coat from the First World War. I was always collecting stuff from when we had the junk shop in London. We used to wear all sorts. We used to wear plus-fours and tweeds from the 1930s. Charity shops were much better in those days because young people didn't really go in them.'

The incipient glory of The Human League had revealed cracks in the scene the young artists had built up around West Street and Devonshire Lane. Although their first royalty cheque for 'Being Boiled' only amounted to £120 between them and Phil Oakey had recently been forced to do a runner from his flat on Commonside for non-payment of rent, the media perception of the band magnified their status.

Their first tour ended in February 1979 at The Nashville Rooms in London where they were granted a backstage audience with David Bowie, who declared that watching The Human League 'was like watching 1980'. In March, Paul Morley travelled to Sheffield to gather material for an *NME* cover story that would appear at the end of the month, depicting the band in poses of Siberian austerity in the still-snowbound gritscapes of the city.

'I have seen the future of rock'n'roll,' said Morley, 'and there's not a guitar in sight.'[5]

Instead, Morley wanted readers to 'imagine the feeling you get from all these people and corporates: the Maels, Bolan, Bowie, Lou Reed, Zappa, *The Goodies*, Robert Fripp, early Eno, Neil Innes, Sweet, *Space: 1999*, Rezillos, Andy Warhol, Alice Cooper, Hanna-Barbera, Roy Wood. Now mash it all together and think of a sound that doesn't flow, dawdle, float, but thumps, cracks, insists. You're now close to an impression of The Human League.'[6]

Sheffield bohemia began to settle into a shifting hierarchy centred around the pubs on West Street. Old first-division bands like Cabaret Voltaire, The Human League and Clock DVA would hold court in The Beehive, whereas younger, second-division bands would congregate a few doors down in The Hallamshire, plotting acts of regicide and mutiny. The spirit of shared artistic endeavour was draining away and new plans and manifestos were guarded more closely.

'Sheffield was full of bitching and rivalry', said Phil Oakey. 'I had contempt for all the other bands except for Cabaret Voltaire.'[7]

'There were a lot of different gangs,' said Martin Fry, 'and everybody would sit at separate tables in The Beehive. Nobody swapped plectrums.'[8]

'Everything changed when the *NME* and *Sounds* and *Melody Maker* started to take an interest in what was happening in Sheffield', said Adi Newton. 'Then, when record companies started being interested in putting records out, everything became focused on that. Everyone became more protective of their own thing. Before that, there was more solidarity and it was more of a social scene. Music suddenly became competitive and commercialised and exploited. The bands that went along with that found out later on that the reason they started doing what they were doing wasn't there anymore. It became like work for them. Fashion almost became the main focus.'

By mid-1979, Vice Versa had a handful of completed tracks that they wanted to record professionally. The lingering punk spirit was still alive in the cellar at Bowood Road and, with the help of Stephen's mum, Carol, they planned to mount a self-sufficient media blitz.

'Buzzcocks had made a record and financed it themselves', said Singleton. 'All you had to do was make the record, get it played on the radio and you were away. So we found out about Ken through his advert in the *Sheffield Star*, phoned him up and booked in. We were saying to him on the phone, "We're not like other bands, we've got a drum machine and a synthesiser", and he was like, "I've done synthie bands before. Oh yes, I can record synthies."'

James and I made an arrangement to visit Stephen to talk to him about his memories of Ken and Studio Electrophonique. It was during the festive netherworld between Christmas and New Year and we took him a stack of vintage David Bowie magazines as an offering. He lives in a minor steel baron's Victorian villa close to the Botanical Gardens and not far from the basement where Disco John was given his name. The scale of the house reminded us of our own diminutive-council-house origins and our knock on the iron-studded oaken door was timorous and weak.

Stephen was very kind to us. He showed us into the kitchen and made us brews in matching Brontë sister mugs. His own sister, Sarah, said hello then retreated to a distant room and we were left to question Stephen beneath a large Warhol print, accompanied by the blips and gurgles of an industrial fish tank percolating beside us. Both Stephen and his sister have a youthful bloom that is at once infectious and endearing. Stephen told us he had received a Marc Bolan box set for Christmas and was still jolted by the emotive voltage emitted by these recordings fifty years after they first entered his system.

'What kind of gear did you have when you first went to Ken's?' asked James.

We had a Watkins Copicat, a drum machine, a homemade synth and a homemade oscillator, a Korg synth, a bass guitar and an H&H amp that had a mad fuzz sound. We took all that to Ken's and recorded all the songs for the *Music 4* EP. We'd got it all mapped out before we went in there because we were thinking: 'This is costing us a fortune, this.' I had it all written down, when to knock the switch off on the drum machine and when to knock it back on. I was like a virtuoso on that drum machine just to save time and money.

Stephen remembered Ken being puzzled by Vice Versa's unconventional attitude to instrumentation:

I'd gone to the studio with my bass guitar and I'd taken three of the strings off and he was going, 'Why have you only got one string on your bass guitar?' and I said, 'Well, I only use this string on this song and if I just touch the other strings it makes this horrible buzzing noise.' To me, that was lateral thinking: take off the strings I don't need if it meant getting a cleaner sound.

We'd heard rumours of the trace levels of hospitality on offer to recording artists at Ken's and this was confirmed by Stephen and Mark.

'All we had was a glass of water and Ken got tea and biscuits', said Singleton. 'I used to draw pictures of Ken in my notebook while I was there of him saying: "Tea and biscuits for me, water for you".'

'His wife used to bring us in cups of water,' said White, 'I think on the last day, Ken said: "Lorna, cups of tea for the lads, please". We'd finally made it in Ken's world.'

When the four tracks for the EP were finished, Ken helped the band press 1,000 vinyl copies through a connection he had with Pye Records while Stephen designed the fold-out sleeve. Ken also took this opportunity to enter the Vice

15 ABC perform their showcase at Penny's nightclub in Sheffield October, 1981; Disco John can be glimpsed in the DJ booth

Versa track 'Riot Squad' into the 1979 British amateur tape-recording contest, progressing through the domestic rounds into the international finals in Switzerland. His early glories in the world of experimental tape composition had been with the escapist exotica of John Marsden's Maile Hawaiians in 1973. When Ken tested the pulse of Sheffield in 1979, the throb was one of synthetic suspicion and state savagery and he was left unplaced and bauble-less in Basel.

It was at this point that the cottage industry at Bowood Road went into overdrive.

'Me and Mark both really liked art', said Singleton. 'If we were doing a gig, it was like, great, now we can do a poster. We were into making collages from magazines and newspapers. Anything we could incorporate, we would use. Just like any instrument we could get hold of, we'd play with. I think we ended up with 996 copies of the record to sell so we sent one to the *NME* and one to John Peel and I think mums and dads and grandmas and grandpas got one and Rare and Racy took about ten. So we still had about 947 left and it was like, hmm, what now? At first my mum would help out because it was hard for us as kids to go down to Rough Trade and talk to people who were in their thirties. It was like trying to argue with your dad. So we'd just send Mum down and say: "Tell them we want so much money for each single we sell and we're not accepting any less." She was like a barrier between us and the distribution people. People at Rough Trade were like "Oh, hello, Carol. Have a sit down." She worked at Trusthouse Forte Hotels as her normal job but she was good to have on our side. It was good to have someone involved who wasn't thinking what they could make out of you.'

After ABC signed a major record deal with Phonogram, Carol became the head of the official fan club.

Not long after releasing the *Music 4* EP, David Sydenham left Vice Versa. He was going through a bad spell personally and his enthusiasm and commitment paled in comparison to that displayed by White and Singleton so they made plans to continue as a duo. The formally stated ambition in their 1979 manifesto was for Vice Versa to dispense with the stale encumbrances of the traditional rock group in transit. Predating Heaven 17's yuppie satire by a few years, Vice Versa imagined a future where they would travel the world by plane and train, carrying all their electronic gear about their person:

The use of prepared tape montages and pre-sound in performance allows space to exploit kinetics and transmit electronic dance beat music. The aim: to provide a soundtrack to the second industrial revolution. The method: extending the miniaturisation policy to ultimately become the first attaché case commuter band.

Keen to feature this up-and-coming local band in his fanzine, Martin Fry made contact and asked if he could conduct an interview for the next issue of *Modern Drugs*. Arriving at 44 Bowood Road in his mildewed Prussian leather greatcoat, Fry had a presence that intrigued White and Singleton. 'I thought he was the tallest person I had ever seen,' said Singleton.[9]

'Martin was interviewing us in the living room,' said White, 'and it was going really well and then, in this weird psychic moment, me and Stephen just looked at each other and one of us felt empowered to ask him if he wanted to join the band for the next gig, which was in Middlesbrough in ten days' time. We really wanted it to be a three-pronged attack.'

Fry appreciated the offer but wasn't sure what he could bring to the project musically. He was keen, however, to throw himself into the electronic age.

'He said, "Well, I don't play any instruments", said White, 'and we said, "That doesn't matter. We've got a basic synth. Just make noises on that whenever you feel motivated and do a bit of whooping."'

Disco John remembers the moment of his friend's fearless step.

'Martin wasn't really musical. With Vice Versa, he just played an oscillator which was just one knob that changed the frequency or the tone. It was just a mono note in the background and whether it was the right note was hit or miss. But he had bravado and he had balls. And who knew? Because he was quite private and unassuming in real life.'

Ten days after this bond was made, the band were on the train to Middlesbrough to support Cowboys International at the Rock Garden. The band's efforts on stage drew anger, ridicule and the odd missile but Fry was sure from the first cautious oscillation that he had found his place in the world.

'They set me up in the corner', said Fry, 'I just made bleeps and noises on this oscillator. It was a skinhead audience, and the bottles rained down, but I loved it.'[10]

As well as adding the essential third prong, Fry's inclusion added an unforeseen benefit. White and Singleton, with their impish, bird-boned appearance were regularly stiffed or duped at the point of requesting their fee after gigs in hard-nosed venues. When Fry approached the Middlesbrough promoters after the Rock Garden gig looking like a proto-version of Rutger Hauer in *Blade Runner*, they were paid the full £70 with no quibbles.

Two events occurred in late 1979 that adjusted the musical course of Vice Versa, setting them on a heading that would take them from the icy waters of electronica to the tropical pop lagoon where ABC would languish, becalmed, a few years later.

First, Martin moved into Disco John's Dickensian slum in Crookes.

'Barber Crescent was a condemned row of houses owned by a moneylender', said John. 'We lived in the end terrace and the whole place was rotten. If anyone's girlfriend came round in heels, they'd go straight through the floorboards and get stuck. We could never afford to have the heating on and, when we moved out, it snowed and the weight of it just collapsed the damp timbers in the roof. The front room used to be my mate's bedroom so, when he'd gone, we blacked out the windows with a mattress and stuck all Vice Versa's musical equipment in there. It was like a black hole but, because the terrace was condemned, there were no neighbours so the noise didn't matter.'

'The houses were black from years of soot,' said White, 'I think the whole row was due for demolition.'

That this site of grimness and squalor became the crucible that delivered the gold lamé ingot of ABC is another unlikely romantic fable to emerge from this era.

'They rehearsed in that front room for fifteen months solid,' said John, 'two or three days a week while we were living there. It was fascinating. Me and Martin used to sit and theorise about being the perfect frontman and developing a persona or an alter ego.'

The musical direction they plotted during this intensive period of regeneration was also heavily influenced by an experience shared by White and Singleton on 30 September 1979 when they bought tickets to go to see the early performance by Chic at the Sheffield City Hall.

'It was that good,' said White, 'we went straight back out to buy a ticket for the evening performance as well. For the second show, we were both ready for it and we were up and dancing pretty quick. We were up in the aisle giving it some disco and Nile Rodgers said: "These guys have got the right idea. C'mon Sheffield!"'

'Nile Rogers shook our hands,' said Singleton, 'and it was like a baton being passed. We were touched by the hand of Chic. They wanted to be the black Roxy Music and, from that moment, we wanted to be the white Chic.'

The north of England has an uncomplicated love of Black American music. All the artists from the Sheffield space age, even those whose embrace of experimental electronica left little trace of this influence in their own work, have professed an often unfashionable passion for soul, Motown, disco and funk.

Martin Fry was outside Mr Kite's Wine Bar on Division Street with Judd when he first met Martyn Ware. Ware was carrying a twelve-inch copy of Sylvester's 'Mighty Real' and remembers, today, the influence of Black music:

If you went out at the weekend to Penny's, it was quite common to have a couple of hours of music where Black imports would be mixed with electronic music or glam and this was quite particular to Sheffield. In Broomhall, where I used to live, they used to have an amazing blues club in someone's basement. It was a fiver to get in and you got a free joint on entry. When you're seventeen and this is three minutes' walk from your front door, it's the best thing ever. We bought the *NME* and *Sounds* and *Melody Maker* and religiously followed what the taste makers would say but, after a while, we detected a pejorative attitude towards Black music, a snooty attitude that suggested Black artists weren't as credible as White artists. It used to really get on our tits, to be honest, when we were starting out with The Human League. We'd say to anyone who would listen: 'We love disco, Giorgio Moroder is fantastic, Donna Summer is amazing, Michael Jackson is making some of the most future-facing albums that have ever been created.'

To Stephen Mallinder, whose heart first opened to the sound of soul at the Ark club in Crookesmoor, the connection was not just about the music. 'Being into Black music in Sheffield was a class thing,' he said, 'Detroit and Tamla Motown was music that we didn't think about in terms of colour, we thought about it in terms of class. These people represented something closer to us than Emerson, Lake & Palmer.'

Mark White offers up the theory that certain cities are twinned by a psychic link or a common wavelength: 'There is an odd connection between the north of England and Black America. We always got it. Sometimes way ahead. Sheffield and Detroit. Manchester and Chicago. We were always tuned into it.'

Sociologically, a similarity can be drawn between Sheffield and Detroit: two super-industrial cities in decline where the working-class labour force was suddenly surplus to requirements in a rusting, seized-up urban landscape.

'It just seemed normal to me that there were closed-down steel works everywhere', said Mark White. 'You either react to that by being escapist or you react to the grittiness by being gritty like the Cabs. We just wanted to shut our eyes, click our heels and pretend we were in Hollywood or Vegas. We felt so far away from London that it kept all the riff-raff out. We all had our own thing. When the New Romantic thing started in London, we couldn't give a shit.'

To Martin Fry, the escapism of the weekend had its roots in northern working-class literature and film: 'It was the *Saturday Night and Sunday Morning* thing. In a big city like Sheffield, a lot of the time you felt invisible. Saturday night was your chance to be noticed.'

Mark White's claim that everyone had their 'own thing' threw up some unholy unions. Jarvis Cocker developed a Barry White fixation, culminating in the glorious kitchen-sink eroticism of 'Sheffield Sex City' in 1992, described in the sleeve notes as 'a tour round the fleshpots of Sheffield in a T-reg Chevette'. The Human League Mk II also owed a debt to the walrus of love, with their League Unlimited Orchestra mimicking the name of Barry's backing musicians. Adi Newton bought a live James Brown album from a charity shop and gave it to Martin Fry and, suddenly, among the huddled masses of Barber Crescent listening to Richard Searling's *Soul Service* on Radio Hallam, it wasn't beyond the scope of their dreams to imagine themselves as the drum-tight soul boys of the 1980s. When the idea came to add a spoken-word interlude in the middle of the hit single 'The Look of Love' a year or so later ('My friends say, Martin, one day you'll find true love ...') the idea was stolen from James Brown's stark junky monologue 'King Heroin'. When imagination is all you can afford, where else can you live?

The last record released by The Human League on Bob Last's Fast Product label was *The Dignity of Labour* EP in April 1979. If 'Being Boiled' wasn't consciously postmodern enough to suit Last's initial motivation for setting up the label, this record certainly was. It comprised four instrumental tracks all called *The Dignity of Labour* and came with a bonus flexi disc which thrilled listeners whose fondest dream was a floppy record that featured the band members and Last discussing the merits and drawbacks of including a flexi disc with their new EP.

In the *NME*, the band justified the release by saying, 'We never get the chance to play instrumentals on stage mainly because we don't want to bore our audiences to death. So, we thought we'd bore them on record.'[11]

The cover depicted the Russian cosmonaut Yuri Gagarin striding solemn and solitary across a parade square in the Soviet Union. The artwork was the natural result of a general fascination some young artists had developed with the exoticism of eastern Europe.

'There was a transgressive interest in what was going on behind the iron curtain', said Martyn Ware. 'Their art was great, they had theremins, Russian literature was amazing. It was the exotic nature of it. Nothing to do with politics really. It was a curiosity to know about this secret place. That's why we went around with NATO jackets and Russian hats.'

An examination of a cross-section of records from the serious young men of 1979 and 1980 does reveal a preoccupation with communist or fascist military art and design.

If it weren't for this artistic phase, a possible parallel universe might exist where Bob Last decided to sign Joy Division instead of The Human League. According to Last, an offer was on the cards but he was troubled by their use of imagery that had right-wing antecedents. Joy Division, he decided, were all about 'looking into the darkness', and he wanted 'difficult pop' that 'gets rid of the fear of pleasure'.

The title of The Human League's latest piece of 'difficult pop' was stolen from a passage in *A Clockwork Orange* that described a mural in Alex's block of flats. The Soviet-style painting featured noble labourers 'stern in the dignity of labour at work bench and machine'. All the touchstones of space age dystopia were present and correct but the record failed to set fire to the atmosphere and the band moved into Monumental Studio with their better songs to record their first album for Virgin Records. Phil Oakey didn't have to move far, as he had been sleeping rough in the studio since absconding from his flat.

Cabaret Voltaire were also finding, perhaps to their pleasure, that their early releases on Rough Trade were not being understood or embraced by the wider world. The *Sounds* review of their single 'Nag Nag Nag' in June 1979 dismissed it as 'flat as a witch's tit. It's dull, unusable and quaint but it does have a good title. Probably about a horse.'[12] They too were about to spend the summer preparing a debut album, *Mix Up*, which featured 2.3's Haydn Boyes-Weston on drums and would be released in October.

If Western Works was the foundry that forged the first dark smeltings of dystopia in 1979, just down the hill on West Bar, Monumental Studios was programmed to project a more optimistic view.

'Ours was a darker vision', said Stephen Mallinder. 'If The Human League were utopian, we were probably classed as Yorkshire dystopian. We projected warning signs inspired by films such as *The War Game* and the darker side of the Cold War. There was a Ballardian sense of dystopia through things like *Crash* and *The Atrocity Exhibition*. We didn't want to glamourise it but we saw something in the shiny future that had a darkness beneath. We saw the injustices. We were fearful of power and paranoid about power out of control.'

On 3 September 1979, recordings made at Ken Patten's Studio Electrophonique were played on John Peel's Radio One show for the first but not the last time. Peel played 'New Girls/Neutrons' from Vice Versa's *Music 4* EP and, in an instant, the vinyl supply chain blockage at Bowood Road was eased.

'When John Peel started playing our record, Rough Trade rang us up and said, "We want them all"', said Stephen Singleton. 'We thought it would be a good idea to have a sleeve that folded in a mystical way and we had been sat in Bowood Road folding 1,000 of them. Then John Peel played it and it sold out and we thought,"Oh fucking hell no, another 1,000 to fold".'

Back in Stephen's kitchen, James and I edged forwards over the cold dregs in our matching mugs. These are the portions of the artist's chronology that we feed on like parasites. The damburst of self-expression and validation before spirits are drowned or contaminated by compromise.

'What was better,' I asked, 'the anticipation of the glory or the glory itself?'

Stephen smiled, took his glasses from the top of his head and rested them on the table.

'Well, you reach a moment and then it's downhill from there, isn't it?', he said. 'The best thing was being creative and making the music. Back then, everyone had their own peculiar, homemade image. It hadn't come from stylists wheeling in clothes on a video shoot. We were our own art directors and we did it all ourselves, which is what made it honest and genuine.'

In the autumn of 1979, Disco John and Martin Fry were keen to stave off the dread of another ice-glazed winter in the monoxide mansions of Barber Crescent by seeking out a venue in Sheffield that could make use of John's vast record collection and provide an outlet for the emerging bands from the city who inhabited the sonic spectrum somewhere between the illumination of The Human League and the night-glare of Cabaret Voltaire. John remembers:

In the summer before I came to Sheffield, I worked in a factory and I'd bought all this DJ gear from a guy on the factory floor. I used to go and see bands a lot at The Hallamshire and I had all this DJ equipment, so I was on the lookout for a new place where we could put bands on and play music. Me and Martin went down together to look at the George IV pub for the first time. The venue was upstairs and it was quite a big room. There was a picture of Jim Reeves on the wall and timber beams, but we felt like it could be our space. I'd play Bowie stuff like 'Sound and Vision' or early electro stuff like Fad Gadget or Kraftwerk. If you had to go to a nightclub anywhere else in town, you had to wear a shirt and tie. We had more freedom at the Blitz.

The Blitz at the George IV pub on Infirmary Road launched on 27 November 1979 with a performance by local band

Notes from a condemned terrace

I'm So Hollow. The pub fronted onto the gargantuan granite slab of Kelvin flats, a crooked brutalist barrier just down the hill from the Arts Tower. The upstairs room was decorated in a jaunty stagecoach theme with a mirrored wall behind the low stage and portraits, not only of Jim Reeves, but of other country elders such as Don Williams and Charlie Rich, beaming down in avuncular approval from the walls.

Although John was helped in his endeavours by Russ and Martin Russian from the band They Must Be Russians, the Blitz was a one-man labour of love for the short time it existed:

I'd hire a taxi in the morning to come to Barber Crescent, load up the disco equipment, drive down to the George IV and carry all the stuff up the stairs myself. I would have arranged the band's bookings myself, drawn the posters myself, walked around town sticking them up, designed the ticket, DJed when the band wasn't on then packed everything up myself and get another taxi back up the hill to Crookes. And that was my day off from washing pots at The Beauchief Hotel.

The Blitz, like The Limit, provided a safe space where artistic enthusiasts could dress up, dress down and generally express themselves on a Tuesday night in Sheffield in a tolerant zone that melded the concrete and rust of Kelvin with the gingham and prairies of Kansas. The poster for the opening night promised a 'Nouvelle Musik Disco' and twinned a cut-out picture of Stephen Mallinder in full cry at the microphone with a line drawing of a ravaged, skeletal corpse.

As the 1970s ended, there were a few Sheffield bands ascending the launch tower and pulling at the hatch to gain entry to the capsule. They would have to wait until the dawn of the 1980s for the countdown to begin. In December 1979, Clock DVA drummer Roger Quail spotted Stephen Singleton in the queue outside Virgin Records on The Moor. They were both hoping to be one of the lucky five customers who would receive a free Talking Heads *Fear of Music* sweatshirt with their purchase of the album. Stephen snagged one, Roger missed out.[13]

The decade ended with the same tragic, cosmic melody that had signalled its arrival, ringing through front rooms across the country. Just before midnight on New Year's Eve 1979, in the moments before the future arrived in Sheffield, David Bowie sang 'Space Oddity' on Kenny Everett's TV special. Performing unadorned in a plain white shirt from an outsize padded cell, Bowie ended the song with the line 'Planet Earth is blue and there's nothing I can do' and looked pleadingly into the camera as it closed in on his mismatched eyes. A drum like a failing heartbeat slowed to a stop and the decade was over.

Chapter 15
DREAMS OF LEAVING

Every act is a cerebral revolver shot.
        Tristan Tzara, Dada Festival, Salle Gaveau, Paris, 1920

From the outset, the 1980s in the north felt like a decade to survive rather than enjoy. The first hit sound of the year was the Ripper tape sent to Assistant Chief Constable George Oldfield and played around Yorkshire, Cabaret Voltaire-style, on loudspeakers attached to patrolling police vans. Fear stalked the northern conurbations. I remember my dad feeling the need to meet my mum at the bus stop when she came home from work in the dark because her walk back to the house took her through a tree-lined alleyway next to the Territorial Army barracks. When my mum dismissed this as unnecessary, he said to her, 'Anybody could be hanging around in them trees', and, in my seven-year-old imagination, I pictured the torn bodies of women turning in the high branches as my mum hurried by with her handbag clutched tight and her heels loud on the flagstones.

In January 1980, industrial unions in the UK clashed with Margaret Thatcher for the first time when 100,000 steelworkers went on strike for better pay. The new Tory government's intransigent, divisive stance against nation-alised industries was established early in the decade as an iron-clad template for fiercer battles to come.

Presentiments of doom were also being detected on a global scale as the Soviet invasion of Afghanistan prompted US sanctions and the announcement of the Carter Doctrine on 23 January, assuring the world of the president's intention to respond with extreme prejudice to any Soviet aggression towards American allies in the Middle East.

Keen to distance itself from the prevailing ideologies on both sides of the Atlantic, Sheffield decided that it would secede from the union and become the People's Republic of South Yorkshire. Led by Labour councillor David Blunkett from 1980 until 1987, Sheffield City Council declared itself a nuclear-free demilitarised zone, flew the red flag above the town hall on May Day and signed an unofficial peace treaty with the city of Donetsk in Soviet Ukraine. In the decade's first month, another local band with a J. G. Ballard fixa-tion, The Comsat Angels, released 'Independence Day' as a single from their debut album.

Expanding their empire as the new decade began, Vice Versa released the second EP from the Neutron Records bunker on Bowood Road in February 1980. Entitled *1980 – the First Fifteen Minutes*, it was promoted as 'Your Survival Guide for the 80s' and featured one track each from four Sheffield bands: Vice Versa, Clock DVA, I'm So Hollow and Stunt Kites. At this time, those in correspondence with the Neutron nerve centre were receiving regular futuristic info-morsels from the label. Catalogue number NT002 had followed the inaugural *Music 4* EP and included no music, just a 'data pack' containing Xeroxed collage art, a manifesto (Tract One) and some celluloid eye protection, all dispatched in a plastic sleeve to your letterbox for £1.50 plus 20p post and packaging.

Having honed their origami skills with the first EP, the second was even more ambitious: a six-page, seven-inch sleeve that folded like an Ordnance Survey map. The tracks and the art that accompanied them were a snapshot of the times. Clock DVA illustrated their song, 'Brigade', with an image of noble male and female freedom fighters superimposed over an abstract religious collage. I'm So Hollow kept it simple with a contemplative thought bubble for 'I Don't Know' and Vice Versa went all out as hosts and chief harbingers of doom with mushroom clouds, armed spies, chemical chain reactions, dead bodies and Soviet palaces to kick off the 80s disco with their track 'Genetic Warfare'. The Stunt Kites let the side down with a ragged piece of punk imagery for 'Beautiful People' that wouldn't have made the cut at Seditionary in 1976. The cover featured a Ken Patten lookalike with a pomaded side parting and glasses, businesslike in a shirt and tie before a wall of tape machines, possibly in a nuclear bunker rather than a downstairs extension on Handsworth Grange Crescent.

On 1 April 1980, Disco John hosted a ZE Records night at the Blitz on Infirmary Road. The time for mutant disco had arrived in Sheffield. ZE Records was founded in New York in 1978 by Michel Esteban and Michael Zilkha, whose dad owned Mothercare. By 1980, John Peel was calling it 'the best independent record label in the world'.[1] Through Esteban's girlfriend, and future *Vogue* editor, Anna Wintour, they secured a licensing deal with Chris Blackwell at Island

Records and were soon showcasing new tracks by artists such as James White and The Blacks, Was (Not Was) and Kid Creole and The Coconuts at the ultra-hip Paradise Garage in New York. Disco John's early entry into this scene had an inevitable impact on his housemate Martin Fry, who was soon in thrall to this accessible yet artful new pop movement.

April 1980 was a crucial month for Vice Versa. They had released a cassette-only album on Neutron called *8 Aspects* and then made their first European trip as a band to support Young Marble Giants, who were just about to eclipse Vice Versa in the apocalypse stakes with their *Final Day* EP. The trip to Rotterdam had been arranged by Fry's old friend from Manchester, Mike Pickering, who had helped him with the *Modern Drugs* fanzine and was now a DJ and promoter. During the trip, Pickering took the band to a record shop called Backstreet and this led to an invitation to record a one-off single for the shop's independent record label of the same name.

The record was called 'Stilyagi', an ode to the nobility and savagery of the Russian Teddy Boy. The B-side was called 'Eyes of Christ'. Although this new release still carried all the heavy electronic ballast and bombast of the grey-overcoat brigade, a random moment of spontaneity and creativity in a Rotterdam studio unlocked a new, more radiant, future for the band.

'During rehearsals,' said Mark White, 'I remembered something I'd read about David Bowie when he was record-ing *Lodger*. He made everyone swap instruments and play something they weren't used to. I suggested we should try this out and I think I ended up on percussion and I handed the microphone to Martin.'

'Martin was a huge fan of the writers Samuel Beckett and Truman Capote,' said Stephen Singleton, 'and he started rapping and singing about these guys, making us all laugh with his ideas like "funky Beckett, he was dancing in the library" or "Rotterdam, pots of jam, leg of lamb". Me and Mark were in hysterics. Martin was ad-libbing and howling and yelping like James Brown.'[2]

'We had absolutely no idea that he could even warble', said White. 'He sounded like David Bowie on *Young Americans*. I just resigned on the spot. I laid down my microphone.'

In the excitement that followed, Vice Versa made plans to launch this as an offshoot project called 'ABC – The Radical Dance Faction' with Fry on vocals.

'For a while,' said White, 'we thought we might be able to run two bands in parallel paths; keep doing Vice Versa then, on the side, Project ABC.'

Metaphorically casting their greatcoats into frigid waters from the upper deck of a North Sea ferry, Vice Versa returned from Holland blowing whistles and wearing DayGlo cycling shirts. It appeared that their portentous vision of the 1980s had only lasted for the first fifteen minutes and now the outlook was sunny with a hint of horn section. Vice Versa were, perhaps, the most nimble and intuitive of the Sheffield bands of the era, taking as their credo a line from one of their own songs, 'Artists at War'. One of the only distinguishable lyrics on this track from the *8 Aspects* cassette is the repeated imperative 'always forward', a maxim they followed in the months that followed in the cloacal confines of Barber Crescent.

Disco John, who lived in the house where this transformation took place, remembers the audacity of their labours:

ABC cut their first demo with the engineer Martin Griffin and that, for me, is how they should have stayed, attempting to be like James White and The Blacks. Martin had created an alter ego called James Romance and the plan was to be that character on stage. In these rehearsals, they were attempting to be like Chic and James Brown. Obviously they weren't as good but they had a go.

Although they had mentally committed to a sleek, exotic vision for their future art, the prosaic grimness of their everyday lives, described by Stephen Singleton, often threatened to hobble these plans.

We were all really poor. Martin and I were working at Batchelors Foods so that we'd have a little stash of money to spend on the band. We were really disciplined and sensible. We didn't go and get drunk in the pub. It was like a career path we were forging and, if it meant doing horrible jobs, we'd do it. When we weren't working, we'd just sit in the house on Barber Crescent trying to write songs, starting from scratch and somehow getting these songs out. We were self-taught, learning as we went along. We had a vision and we wanted big success. We saw what other bands from Sheffield were doing, like The Human League. They had a major record deal and that's what we wanted. We wanted to make a hit record so we thought, let's do it, let's go for it.

'Stephen was very motivated', said Martin Fry. 'It was him against the world. He was like an embryonic Brian Jones. Mark was very resolute and analytical. He would never back down. They were both hard to please or impress. If you had ten ideas, they'd pick you up on seven of them and maybe the other three would sift through.'

By May 1980, The Human League were already promoting their second Virgin album, *Travelogue*. Although the band did have a major record deal, they were still recording in the perpetual night of their derelict studio in West Bar.

One of Virgin's house engineers, Richard Mainwaring, had been given orders to leave The Manor, a stately twenty-four-track residential studio near Oxford and to report immediately for missionary duty at the bleak outpost on Love Street. His acclimatisation to the Spartan standard was brutal:

There was no landline in the studio and, late one evening, I was asked to take a call at the minicab office across the street. There was no electricity in the building apart from the studio itself and, as I stumbled down the stairs to the totally dark ground floor, I met with an extremely bright torch beam. I was so shocked by the light in my eyes that I fell back against the wall and slid to the ground unable to utter a word. The torch belonged to some police officers who were investigating why someone was creeping about in a disused building. Luckily, Martyn heard the commotion from upstairs and came down to explain.

The idea of composing miniature soundtracks for imaginary films that Ware had pioneered at Ken Patten's studio in 1977 was still with him in 1980 but, increasingly, the pop machine was eager for a hit single.

Virgin lit the blue touchpaper on a few damp fireworks like 'Empire State Human', a needless, neutered version of 'Being Boiled', and even a pop single called 'I Don't Depend on You' written and performed by The Human League but attributed to an imaginary band called The Men. Sadly, nothing took flight or exploded with anything that might inspire the awe or wonder required of the pop sensations of the future.

Their first album, *Reproduction*, hadn't sold as many copies as the label had hoped and reviews like Andy Gill's in the *NME* suggested that the band had been superseded by more savvy pop operators:

Every TV appearance Gary Numan makes must be like a dagger to the heart of The Human League, every radio play a bit more salt in the wound. And they've only got themselves to blame for not striking while the iron was hot. Instead of dithering around with the unnecessary, pretentious *Dignity of Labour* or the half-assed 'The Men' debacle, they should have gone all out for the killer single, the *TOTP* appearance and the teeny mags … Pop music should be fizzy, sweet and bad for your health; *Reproduction* is as flat, neutral and unappetising as a glass of Coke that's been standing for too long.[3]

The *Holiday '80* EP, released one month before the second album, included 'Marianne', a masterful pop palimpsest that Brian Wilson might have composed if he'd been born in High Green rather than Hawthorne, but it also included covers of old Gary Glitter and Iggy Pop tunes and a dial-in instrumental from The Future's recycle bin called 'Dancevision'. On 8 May 1980, The Human League's original line-up appeared on *Top of the Pops* for the first and only time, miming to a cover of Glitter's 'Rock'N'Roll'. The establishing shot of Ian's Roland System 100 was impressive and Martyn did his best to galvanise the band, patrolling the stage behind Phil in a shirt and tie, clapping, fist-pumping and generally looking like a middle manager trying to coax the work experience lads into a bit of office horseplay on their first day. Phil, of course, looked astonishing, but the vintage of the song was jarring and it kept the band in low gear, troubling Bob Last and the Virgin executives who were biting their nails behind the camera rostrum on the studio floor. They were even overshadowed by the presenter, Peter Powell, who summed up their performance as 'synthesised rock'n'roll' and, on an elevated plinth above the stage wearing a turquoise test pilot's all-in-one jump suit, looked like the one most likely to take flight into the future.

Jarvis Cocker admired the futuristic trajectory of The Human League but also appreciated the fact that they still operated locally and had to negotiate the same streets as the Earth people of Sheffield.

'I went out and bought the *Travelogue* album pretty much as soon as it came out,' said Cocker, 'Sheffield has always had a preoccupation with the future and escapism and stuff like that, coupled with a very down-to-earth, kitchen-sink mentality as well, so you kind of got the idea of spacemen who've still got to put the rubbish out.'[4]

Jarvis's school band, Pulp, were making their first tentative steps from the lunar module in the summer of 1980, appearing ninth on a ten-band bill at the Bouquet of Steel festival at The Leadmill on 16 August. They had recently retired the more flavoursome name Arabicus Pulp, as no one was familiar with the misspelled coffee bean reference Jarvis had added after thinking it sounded cool in an economics lesson. Pulp appeared on stage at

3:20pm, thrashed out a few covers by The Troggs and The Monkees, performed an original piece called 'Message to the Martians', then had time to go home to Intake for their tea before returning to see the headliners, Artery, later the same evening.

The covers of the first two Human League albums did not feature pictures of the band. *Reproduction* was suggestive of new life in a disco petri dish with naked newborns wailing beneath a busy glass dancefloor, while *Travelogue* presented the public with a blurry, blown-up still from *National Geographic* magazine showing a figure in silhouette being pulled through icy wastes by a team of dogs.

'The record label were screaming at us for a title and a cover', said Martyn Ware. 'I found this photograph that I thought was evocative and the name *Travelogue* suggested wanting to get out of Sheffield, like a kind of mind-travel.'[5]

Someone with too much time on their hands might trace some kind of prophetic arc in this diptych of album art: the first image suggestive of the delight in discovering that electricity and imagination could give birth to new artistic movements; the second having connotations of the last journey of Victor Frankenstein, all Weltschmerz and Romantic misery, disillusioned with his noble project and heading north to kill his creation.

The band were torn between an ingrained Sheffield urge to poke a stick into the spokes of the pop wheel of fortune and a genuine desire for chart success.

'We were obsessed with not making the new songs sound smooth like on the first album', said Martyn Ware. 'We thought we'd overload every channel on the desk and make a racket that sounded like synth-punk.'[6]

Dreams of leaving

The record received mixed reviews in the music press. Some, like Dave McCullough, sensed a split personality within the group:

This is an irritating album. Mostly, it's prostitutional, dreadful or averagely condescending and then, suddenly, quite unexpectedly, the wacky yik yak subsides and they break gently into something called 'Dreams of Leaving', an evocative anthem which I can't stop myself returning to. 'Dreams of Leaving' is astonishing, original and totally captivating … the opening two tracks on the second side are almost as good.[7]

Their only *Top of the Pops* appearance did little to elevate the band's chart position and, by 19 May, they were back on the road with Clock DVA as support, playing in Manchester the day after Ian Curtis committed suicide.

Cabaret Voltaire had a close relationship with Factory Records, appearing on the Fac1 poster for the Russell Club in Hulme and contributing two tracks to the label's first vinyl release, *A Factory Sample*, in 1979. Joy Division also appeared on the record and the two bands had a certain bond. After Ian's death, Stephen Mallinder remembers the Cabs' offer of a haven where the members of the Manchester band could absorb their loss and reset:

We'd played with Joy Division a lot and we'd been to Ian's funeral. The rest of the band wanted to carry on but they didn't want to record in a studio where people would be asking questions. We invited them to come over to Western Works for the weekend to play their new stuff. They demoed the tracks that ended up on the first New Order album with everyone taking turns doing the vocals. Steve, Hooky, Bernard, me and Rob Gretton all had a go. I think Bernard got the job because he was the least shit.

During a break in the selection process, the combined forces of the Yorks/Lancs dystopioso were smoking weed when a uniformed police officer strolled through the door. The Manchester contingent went rigid with fear and paranoia but the Cabs greeted the policeman warmly and handed him the spliff. It was a pal of theirs who often popped in when his city centre shift ended.

In August 1980, Clock DVA and Vice Versa played together at The Moonlight Club in London. The bands travelled to gigs together in a van, often driven by Judd who only had a provisional licence and who could only be kept awake on late night return legs by having Clock DVA drummer Roger Quail at his shoulder, prompting him with topics of the day until they reached the Tinsley cooling towers, the unofficial gateway to the People's Republic.

The gig was reviewed in the *NME* by Paul Morley, with customary insight:

Clock DVA retch out fierce, grating sounds to demonstrate the confusion in their souls. They play part-free miniaturist crisis-funk, the discomforting sound of structures collapsing, tensions accumulating and rhythms nagging. They use lead sax, played by A. Beard, that prefers to torture than to soothe. The trio [Vice Versa] pounce around the tiny stage like demented puppets, eyes-a-popping, limbs-a-thrashing, occasionally tending to their keyboards on sticks, shouting out surprised vocals, harmonising with wicked spirit, singing songs about signs and signals, cult and culture, glossy mythologies from geneticism to Mary Quant cosmetics. This way they construct a suitably violent, panicky sound: harshly percussive, deliriously fluid, smashing and clashing, a heady anti-muzak.[8]

On the return journey from The Moonlight Club, Quail remembers a stop-off at Toddington services where they enjoyed their usual: beans on toast and a few games on the Space Invaders machine. He also remembers this as the night when ABC performed in a semi-public fashion for the first time. Eager to try out their smooth new direction, the Vice Versa lads stopped Clock DVA in the car park of the service station in the early hours and performed one of the routines they had been honing in the black hole of Barber Crescent. It was an a cappella version of Smokey Robinson's 'Tracks of My Tears', complete with backing vocals and a coordinated dance routine of shuffles, dips and finger clicking. Clock DVA were unimpressed.[9]

The two bands appeared together again in September at the Futurama festival at the Queens Hall in Leeds. This would be Vice Versa's last ever gig. Highlights of the festival were televised on BBC 2 and featured an impressive sixth-form moustache from Mark White, an ill-advised cream acrylic roll neck from Martin Fry, some junior saxophone bleats from Stephen Singleton and, most impressively, Adi Newton fronting Clock DVA wearing a clergyman's cassock. Vice Versa were featured performing 'Democratic Dancebeat', singing of 'industrial music from back-to-backs' while sounding a bit like a Sheffield version of The B-52's.

Clock DVA performed '4 Hours', a song that, for many, defined Sheffield music before the pop lift-off of 1981.

Adi, on a festival bill that included singers such as Ian McCulloch, Mick Hucknall, Siouxsie Sioux and Alison Statton, sounded like the voice most likely to accompany a decade of nuclear terror, economic collapse and existential dread. The martial beat he smashed out on the tambourine stand with a single drumstick pre-empted Gang of Four by two years and REM by eight.

Shredding the Vice Versa manifesto, Singleton, White and Fry pledged to devote a cold winter on Barber Crescent to the success of Project ABC. They swiftly recruited a teenage rhythm section from Dronfield – Mark Lickley on bass and Dave Robinson on drums – and played their first gig on a quiet mid-week night at Psalter Lane art college.

Rumours of this transformation of a band who had previously adhered to rigid electronic modes and manifestos may have nudged Martyn Ware closer to the precipice over which The Human League were about to fall. Tensions had been rising between Martyn and Phil for some time about the direction of the band and the wisdom of staying true to electronic artistic edicts issued in obscurity in 1977. For some, such as Paul Bower, it was a clash that could have been predicted: 'Two of the most charismatic, annoying, talented, fractious, big-headed people that you could ever have the pleasure of meeting were in one band.'[10]

An additional strain was applied when Gary Numan picked up on The Human League's frequency and had two No 1 singles with 'Are "Friends" Electric' and 'Cars'.

'Until then', said Ware, 'it had been a good laugh and arty and everything, but that was the point that broke the morale of the band. All we could see stretching out into the future was being mentioned as influential when, in reality, we were really poor. That was the engine that drove the split, really.'[11]

'It didn't feel to me like it could go on,' said Last. 'Bands have extraordinarily complex dynamics and there were lots of tensions. I was actually worried that we were going to get dropped.'

The band were unhappy that they were becoming known as a covers band and this frustration increased when Virgin issued 'Only After Dark' as a single without the band's consent. Behind the scenes, manager Bob Last was in talks with Virgin's head of A&R, Simon Draper, both of them keen to salvage something profitable from the wreckage they could foresee around the next hairpin bend. An *NME* article in July 1980 by Charles Shaar Murray described the band having a lengthy argument over a missing set of *Empire Strikes Back* transfers that had come free with a magazine.

'My take', said Last, 'was that I'd got so fed up of them bickering that I thought they were going to just possibly split apart completely. So I was just putting jigsaw pieces together in my head to see what would work.'[12]

The end, when it came, had echoes of the ousting of Adi Newton when The Future split and the boot was on the other foot.

'I just turned up at the studio one day,' said Ware, 'and they said, "We're throwing you out of the group, Martyn", and I said, "I don't think so, it's my group". I was extremely upset at the time because we were very close as a band and Phil had been my best friend for years before that.'

Ian, who had been uncomfortable with the plotting all along, saw how upset Martyn was and decided, on the spot, to stand beside him.

'If Martyn's thrown out,' he said, 'I'm out too.'

Last and Draper came up with the idea of the British Electric Foundation, a faux-corporate umbrella company that would badge Martyn and Ian's new, as yet unnamed, musical project and the work of other artists they may wish to produce or collaborate with.

Bob Last's time spent reading *The Military Thoughts of Mao Zedong* paid dividends during these carefully plotted manoeuvres as his exploitation of the fault-lines in one stalled and fractured band resulted in him becoming the manager of two new bands, both with Virgin record deals. After the initial anger and shock felt by some members of the band about this corporate fait accompli, equilibriums settled and Ware and Marsh made their own move which would reap unforeseen profits in perpetuity. They were unhappy that Last's managerial surgery assumed that the Phil Oakey pop rocket would launch under the banner of The Human League. In order for this concession to be agreed upon, Ware and Marsh were promised a percentage of the sales of Oakey's next album. That album would be *Dare* and it would sell almost two million copies worldwide.

Coincidentally, Glenn Gregory was in Sheffield on the day The Human League split up, on duty for *Sounds* to take pictures of Joe Jackson at Sheffield City Hall. Contacted by a seething Martyn Ware, he agreed to meet his friend in The Red Lion, just yards away from the place they first met at the Meatwhistle workhouse on Holly Street. As the pints of Wards Best Bitter were drained, the Joe Jackson gig was forgotten and a new plan was hatched to defeat The Human League Mk II in the brewing Sheffield synth wars of 1981. Martyn asked Glenn to be the singer in the group that would become Heaven 17 and, within ten days, they had written '(We Don't Need This) Fascist Groove Thang'.

'It was like proposing to somebody when you already know they're going to say yes', said Ware.[13]

'I don't think I even thought about it longer than the time it took me to say yes', said Gregory.[14]

With alley cat cunning, Cabaret Voltaire slipped into the void vacated by The Human League and managed to snag their first *NME* cover in November 1980, accompanied by a long interview conducted by Paul Morley. They had continued to operate with their customary mischief and misanthropy in the first months of the new decade, releasing 'Three Mantras', 'the world's longest single', which was as long as an album but priced like a single as an apology for the fact that it only contained two mantras.[15] The Eastern Mantra had one insistent lyric, repeated for twenty minutes against a backdrop of more authentic Eastern samples and a bed of rudimentary percussion; it was the phrase 'The Human League' spoken in reverse then played backwards, David Lynch-style.

The band had waited in the rain outside Sheffield station for famed *NME* photographer Pennie Smith to arrive on the train from London for the cover shoot. She arrived, asked Richard to stand next to a puddle, took his picture then got straight back on the train to go home. The cover shot encapsulated the prevailing mood in Sheffield before the Hollywood heatwave of *The Lexicon of Love* and the Vogue-ish vignettes of *Dare*. Escapism would triumph over fatalism, dreams over reality but, for now, 1980 was all about monochrome shadows, dark puddles and heavy raincoats.

Paul Morley introduced the article with a passage that novelist David Peace probably stored away for future reference in his Ossett bedroom:

Catch a train into the dark depths of the North again. Flee the wonderland ... As the train rolls into ghostly Sheffield, a profound greyness descends. Grey – the colour of The City, the colour of depression. Imagine a musical soundtrack for a November Sheffield, for a decaying symbol of crumbling capitalism, for the lonely hearts and lost hopes of the city-dwellers, for reason ... imagine the turbulent, tense, obsessive Cabaret Voltaire sound. An integration and aggregation of stern rhythm, rigid sound, unexpected noises, ghostly bumps, news reels, snatches of conversation, screams, wails, unspecified signals ... a sound of our times. The sound for our times.[16]

Clock DVA drummer Roger Quail remembers his bandmate Judd summing up Sheffield in 1980 as 'a one-eyed raincoat town' when he bumped into him outside W. Hartley Seed's bookshop on West Street; the inference being that the streets were full of serious young musicians with dead infantrymen's coats and Antonin Artaud fringes.[17] Roger was on his way to a job interview and was eyeing up a Zola novel he couldn't afford after months on the dole. Judd offered to go in and nick it for him at half the cover price.

'In some ways it was just an innocent reflection of the times', said Richard Kirk. 'No different to The Beach Boys singing about surfing and the good times in California. But there was no surf to ride in Sheffield, just post-war desolation, unemployment and ugly urban landscapes.'[18]

Dreams of leaving

It had been a cold year in the north. Adi Newton, keen to keep all his artistic muscles supple as the Polymath of Parson Cross, had commenced work on a Ballardian novel called *Invisible Suns*.

'I never finished it', said Newton. 'I was always into literature and experimental drama from the Meatwhistle days. I used to read Camus, Jarry and the pre-dadaists and pre-symbolists but also modern playwrights like Beckett and Ionesco. *Invisible Suns* was more like a series of Ballardian scenes, that kind of imagery. Not a narrative as such, just a series of impressions.'

As 1980 came to an end, the launch of The Human League appeared to have failed and the other cadets in the Sheffield space programme were still toiling in unpromising conditions in condemned terraces and derelict factories. Perhaps Adi's aborted literary concept contained a critical truth: that visionary artists persevere and prosper in the most adverse circumstances, warmed by suns invisible to the rest of us.

Chapter 16
THE WALL IN THE HEAD

A young man of 23 who scanned the universe with the most beautiful gaze I have ever known has mysteriously departed from us. It is easy for a critic to say that this was the result of boredom.

André Breton on the death of Jacques Vache, 1918

The story of how The Human League reassembled their troops for the 1981 campaign has been told many times. After the split, the band's commitment to a pre-booked European tour meant that Oakey and Wright had less than two weeks to recruit someone who could emulate Ware's high backing vocals. Prowling Sheffield with his girlfriend on the lookout for likely candidates, he saw two sixth formers from Frecheville, Susanne Sulley and Joanne Catherall, dancing at The Crazy Daisy and convinced them that they should join the band. Ian Burden from local band Graph and Jo Callis from The Rezillos would also join later in the race to release a new album before Ware and Gregory's new band, Heaven 17.

Bob Last, in the manner of an exasperated father trying to appease his errant children, came to an arrangement where both bands could record new material at Monumental Studios in Sheffield without coming to blows. The Human League were allowed access in the daytime from 10am until 10pm and Heaven 17 would occupy the building for the 10pm–10am nightshift.

On 2 January 1981, Peter Sutcliffe was arrested in his car on Melbourne Avenue in Broomhall, just yards from Oakey and Ware's old school. He was found with a sex worker called Olivia Reivers and detained for driving a vehicle with stolen number plates. He later confessed to being the Yorkshire Ripper and was convicted of the murder of thirteen women.

Shutting out the sickness in his suburban Shangri-La, Ken Patten continued to record every band that answered his ads in the local press. He was getting a lot of interest from young bands and one group, The Naughtiest Girl Was a Monitor, passed on his contact details to Jarvis Cocker:

We were all still at school at that time. We didn't really know anything at all about anything. We'd managed to vaguely befriend some bands who were older than us and more worldly and one of these bands was The Naughtiest Girl Was a Monitor. I'd got to know them because I used to work on a fish stall in the Castle Market and there was a guy who worked in a butchers called Mark Sole and he was their bass player. When we were talking one day on our lunch break about our bands, he said, 'You need to meet The Colonel'. They used to call Ken The Colonel, after General Patton from the Second World War. I'd heard the single that The Naughtiest Girl Was a Monitor had recorded there and it was alright. One of the songs was called 'West Street' and

Studio Electrophonique

I knew West Street; it was the only street I could illegally drink in.

Jarvis and Peter Dalton were the only surviving members of the original band and they had recently been joined by schoolmates Wayne Furniss on drums and Jamie Pinchbeck on bass guitar. Jarvis raised the subject of recording with Ken and, after saving up the required fee, they were soon making the short journey from Intake to Handsworth:

It wasn't really that far away from where I lived. Handsworth was walking distance. As we approached, it gradually dawned on me that the studio wasn't a studio as I had imagined in my teenage mind. It wasn't a big, purpose-built facility with a giant mixing desk. It was just his house. A pretty normal house on a super-normal street in Handsworth, which is a very ordinary suburb of Sheffield. But we just thought, whatever, you know. He's a grown up, he knows what he's doing.

Although the dawning disappointment of this distinctly domestic setting may have punctured the spirit of the young band, Ken's ingenious use of electronics within this homely environment soon reinflated them with adolescent wonder and awe:

When we turned up, Ken was a bit bemused. I don't think he'd realised how young we were; I was the oldest and I was only seventeen. We soon realised that one of the main recording areas was going to be the bedroom and that's where the drums were set up. He'd told us not to bring any drums because he'd built his own Simmons-style electronic drum pads to avoid his wife or his neighbours complaining about the noise. So Wayne, our drummer, was up there with his headphones on and we were downstairs but, through some creative use of wiring, he could hear us. The thing that really impressed us though was, when Ken turned on this little black and white TV, we could see Wayne upstairs on the telly. This was (a) for communication but also (b) on the insistence of his wife to make sure people didn't misbehave in their bedroom, which is fair enough I guess. There may even have been some kind of plastic covering on the bed to make sure you didn't soil it in any way.

Ken had been recording in his house since the 1950s and, as the bands got younger, the generation gap yawned wider than ever.

'I remember he wore glasses and used Brylcream', said Cocker. 'You saw loads of blokes who looked like Ken in Sheffield at that time. He was just a normal middle-aged guy. Some people got into gardening or making elaborate topiary and it just happened to be that Ken was into sound technology.'

The startling youthfulness of the band must have awoken a nurturing instinct in the Pattens. An ember of warmth was even revived in Lorna's bosom when the drummer, Wayne, mentioned feeling the beginnings of a cold. Ken's wife had a reputation among visiting bands as the disapproving spectre in the shadows of Studio Electrophonique, but in this instance she was attentive, administering a robust dose of smelling salts in a matronly fashion until the drummer almost vomited over the protective sheeting on the marital bed.

Studio Electrophonique

Ken was patient with us. He encouraged us, which was a good thing because we were very naïve and not very technically proficient. It was the start of a learning process. We were used to just hearing all the instruments at once at rehearsals like a big modge but Ken separated all the parts and that was new to us. I was always trying to put loads of effects on things to mask the fact that we couldn't play in time but Ken insisted that we kept trying to play it properly so we wouldn't have to do that. He wasn't just saying, 'These kids have come, I'll just take their fifteen quid and it doesn't matter what it sounds like'. He had a pride in what he was doing and wanted to do the best he could for you. We learned from that. We learned that we had to listen to each other instead of just going, 'Can you turn my bit up please?' He was very kind to us. A lovely bloke.

Pulp recorded four songs at Studio Electrophonique in the summer of 1981: 'What Do You Say?', 'Please Don't Worry', 'Wishful Thinking' and 'Turkey Mambo Momma'. As was his custom, Ken ran them off a cassette of their work along with the reel-to-reel master tape and said that they were welcome to return or make use of his other, auxiliary, services in the future.

'He must have liked us a bit,' said Cocker, 'because I remember, as we were leaving, he pointed at this caravan on the drive and said, "If you ever want a live recording, there you go – mobile". Like he could turn up, in just a normal caravan, and run a few wires through the window of the venue. We never went back to make use of that particular service but maybe others did.'

After orchestrating sessions that launched the careers of future members of The Human League, ABC, Clock DVA and Heaven 17, Ken was now handing Jarvis the cassette that would direct the steerage of his artistic life:

When I think back on it now, it was a key moment in the development of my musical career because the tape we made at Ken's, I ran off a few copies and made a hand-drawn sleeve and I took one of the tapes down to The John Peel Roadshow at Sheffield Polytechnic. I hung around after he'd finished and collared him when he was leaving the venue and gave him this cassette. He said he'd listen to it on the way home and he actually did. This led to Pulp getting their very first Peel Session which was long before we ever had a record contract. We were all still at school and John Peel was like the Holy Grail. It was like, 'Whoah! We're going to heaven!' all from the cassette we recorded with Ken. I'll always be grateful to him for that.

In the autumn of 1981, years of labour in the workshops and basements of the grey 1970s finally bore bright and glorious fruit in Sheffield. Heaven 17 released *Penthouse and Pavement* in September, The Human League released *Dare* in October, ABC were recording *The Lexicon of Love* in London with Trevor Horn and even the eternal outsiders, Clock DVA, had just signed a major deal with Polydor Records after their first album, *Thirst*, was hailed by Dave McCullough in *Sounds* as 'the best album I have heard since *Dragnet* or *Unknown Pleasures*'.[1] The longed-for age of bounty and opportunity had arrived but was not to be entirely without blight.

On 26 September 1981, Stephen 'Judd' Turner was found dead in his bedroom in Broomhall flats. He had overdosed some days before.

After critical recognition for the first album, Adi Newton had changed the line-up of Clock DVA, dispensing with the services of all existing members, including Judd.

'Judd was into heroin and it got hold of him', said Newton. 'Part of the problem was that it wasn't pure. People like William Burroughs could afford pure medicinal heroin from a doctor and you can do it for life if you're getting top grade medical stuff. It wasn't like that in Sheffield. It was rough stuff cut with all kinds of shit and that's how people died. I was never into it.'

The barb of addiction was so far into Judd in 1981 that, upon receiving his complimentary vinyl copies of his own work on *Thirst* and the single '4 Hours', he immediately took them up to Record Collector at Broomhill to exchange them for ready cash. This type of behaviour was seen as a distraction that threatened the upward trajectory of the band. Adi managed to galvanise Judd into one final artistic contribution, persuading him to play bass on a track they worked on for Martyn, Ian and Glenn as part of the embryonic British Electric Foundation project. The track, ominously entitled 'Uptown Apocalypse', was to feature on the cassette-only release *Music for Stowaways*.[2]

'Adi had moved on and chucked Judd out of the band', said Paul Bower. 'People say that's what killed him but that's not true. Loads of people have been kicked out of bands. Weirdly though, on the weekend that he died, everyone seemed to be out of town. If he'd expressed to us that he was going through difficult times, we would have stayed with him.'

After Judd's death, rumours began to circulate that he had overdosed deliberately or been killed after receiving a 'hot shot': a super-strong dose of heroin maliciously dispatched by a drug dealer as a warning to other addicts that they needed to pay promptly for the goods provided. Neither of these rumours were true.

'Judd had stopped taking heroin for a while', said Newton. 'When he started again, they put him on this methadone, like a linctus, to wean himself off it. Drinking that killed him. It was accidental.'

Many of Judd's friends were unable to face the bleakness and desolation of the funeral at City Road cemetery. Judd had been brought up by his grandma in difficult circumstances and the squalid nature of his premature death felt like a tableau of sickness and waste rather than the romantic last flaming of a riotous youth.

16 Clock DVA bass player Stephen 'Judd' Turner, 1979

'I didn't go to the funeral,' said Newton, 'I couldn't face it. I was living on Bates Street in Walkley and I kept expecting to see him riding up the road on his motorbike.'

Roger Quail, who had bonded with Judd as two halves of the Clock DVA rhythm section, only found out about his friend's death days later at a rehearsal for his new band, The Box, as his parents didn't have a phone at their home in Firth Park. On the day of the funeral, he got as far as the cemetery gates but could go no further. Instead, he sat on a bench in the October sun and remembered his pal.

'I remembered how Judd loved the art of Francis Bacon and Val Denham,' said Quail, 'I remembered how he loved the song "Pini Pini" by Arto Lindsay and Neto. He loved the song "Drugs" by Talking Heads. In fact, Judd loved drugs in general but I never thought they would kill him. I remembered seeing him walking up West Street not long before, having a laugh with Bono and the lads from U2. He was an avowed non-musician but he'd come up with some unique and innovative bass lines like the one on "Impressions of African Winter" which he'd played with a timpani mallet. I remembered watching him on stage as he stared out the audience in the strobe light.'[3]

'I still owe Judd a fiver', said Paul Bower. 'He lent me a fiver just before he died because some of us wanted to get dressed up and go to Sinatra's cocktail bar which had just opened in town.'

As with Ian Curtis, who died the year before Judd, it is easy to bury young dead artists with romantic ballast they may not have recognised in themselves. Judd was a friendly, non-judgemental lad with a generous spirit. He was also brave and fearless when it came to sticking up for himself and protecting his more foppish pals. To Adi, he was more like a glimmer twin, a life force who lived his art without pretension.

'He was like a brother to me', said Newton. 'We were constant companions for a long time. I think of him as a Neal Cassady figure. Kerouac was fairly straightforward, Cassady was more interesting. Judd had that same abundance of energy. I've never really got over his death. His image is always with me, fixed in time.'

When stainless steel is made, the durable sheen of beauty and perfection can blind one to the strain, muck and wreckage that is essential to its creation. Judd was the first collateral casualty of the sonic boom in the Sheffield music industry.

'When Judd died', said Martin Fry, 'that was sort of the end of an era for me. Something had to change, It was too mad.'[4]

Until now, Sheffield bands had experimented with music and imagery that gargled the grey dread and decay that loomed over them in their everyday life with the alien glamour of experimental art, portentous science fiction and enigmatic terror factions. In September 1981, Cabaret Voltaire released their album, *Red Mecca*, a masterpiece that Andy Gill described as 'the most complete and chilling musical representation of eighties' Britain yet produced'.[5] The album had been created amid a summer of domestic riots and international hysteria.

'People say The Specials "Ghost Town" was the soundtrack to the unrest of that year,' said Richard Kirk, 'but a lot of people think that *Red Mecca* was the sound of that feeling too. The insurrection on the streets found its way into the music. You took some heart in the fact that people were kicking back against the system and were prepared to take on the police. We weren't paranoid, this stuff was really happening.'[6]

With unerring prescience, the Cabs were sounding a subsonic siren that would rumble through the decade, sending a blast wave through the landscape that would merge eventually with the police cavalry charge at the Battle of Orgreave.

'It wasn't so much that we were dark and foreboding', said Stephen Mallinder. 'We were distrustful of power.'

'The whole Afghanistan situation was kicking off,' said Kirk, 'Iran had the American hostages. It's not called *Red Mecca* by coincidence. We weren't referencing the fucking Mecca ballroom in Nottingham.'[7]

For Chris Watson, this was the last record he would make with Cabaret Voltaire. He took up an offer from Tyne Tees television to train as a TV sound engineer and left Sheffield.

Since early 1981, ABC had made it their mission to attract heavyweight record company attention and had already presented their new vision at a couple of London gigs, one at the A-Z Club and one at Legends. Many who were familiar with their previous incarnation as Vice Versa couldn't comprehend the artistic leap into Hollywood hyper-space that appeared to have been made overnight.

'The ABC showcase in London was amazing', said Martyn Ware. 'I thought it was the best thing I'd ever seen. They appeared to emerge fully formed from the chrysalis. This amazing exotic creature. The songs were brilliant, the arrangements were brilliant, they looked fantastic.'

'People make a very incorrect leap of logic', said Mark White, 'when they think Martin came along like some sainted being and changed everything. It was the same creative process at work in Vice Versa and ABC so, for us, there was no great interregnum where things suddenly changed. We co-wrote everything but, with ABC, we started to write in a certain way so that everything would focus on one person. We wanted people to fixate on the singer who would remain in role and the band would assume a supporting role.'

In the weeks before they signed a major deal with Phonogram, they were witness to bizarre scenes on the cobbled street outside Barber Crescent. One day, sitting in the mouldering kitchenette with Disco John, they watched as a limousine containing Muff Winwood and Dave Betteridge from CBS Records coasted to a halt, presumably wondering how they had managed to take a wrong turn into 1892.

Taking a reading from the constellations above Crookes, the band decided the time was right for a Sheffield showcase. Disco John, determined to flood Sheffield with the sunlit optimism of his growing collection of ZE Records imports, provided the perfect setting, a nightclub buried beneath a brutalist multi-storey car park on Eyre Street. Here, a mid-week groover could expect to walk in from Sheffield's icy clasp and be seduced by 'Wordy Rappinghood' by The Tom Tom Club, 'Me No Pop I' by Coati Mundi or 'She's a Bad Mama Jama' by Carl Carlton.[8] The showcase took place on the first Monday of October 1981.

I'd started a dance night at Penny's on a Monday night to compete with The Limit, I called it Tropical Heatwave and had this idea to have the chirp of crickets playing constantly in the background. ABC had been in their bunker practising for so long that they thought they were ready to showcase their set.

Martin had the lamé suit made to mimic James Chance and Elvis, I put on a Hawaiian shirt to complete the illusion. The whole point was escapism. Music and fashion were so important to us because there wasn't much space for creativity elsewhere. Back then, you'd go to clubs and there'd be twenty lads dressed up to look like Bryan Ferry.

'We'd got our full showbiz kit on', said Mark White. 'Lamé jackets, I think Martin had his black spangly jacket on. We were really into James Brown's cape routine when he pretends to be overcome and is helped offstage under a cape so our idea was that Martin would finish the set by storming off stage and straight out of the door of the venue. So he did, and people were like, "What the fuck's all this about? What's happened?". I think he actually walked home with his spangly jacket on.'

The audience, even friends from local bands, were unaware of the months of preparation that had polished the performance and stood amazed at the tight new songs and the showmanship on display. They were also treated to a platter of fresh fruit on each table to add to the tropical vibe.

Despite Disco John's best efforts to suspend the realities of Sheffield life for one night only and transport revellers from a concrete void to an island paradise, that Monday evening on Eyre Street ended on a more typically depressing note:

The owner of Mr Kite's wine bar had nicked the owner of The Limit's girlfriend, and The Limit were annoyed about us starting a Monday night disco at Penny's to rival theirs. So the owner of The Limit came down with about ten of his bouncers looking for his ex and wanting to start some trouble. The night ended with a scrap in the multi-storey car park and the assistant manager of Penny's ended up smashing the owner of The Limit across the legs with an iron bar.

The band had already written songs such as 'Tears Are Not Enough' and 'Poison Arrow' and were keen to find a producer who could capture the stainless gloss they were after. High on the wish list was American producer Alex Sadkin, who had masterminded 'Pull Up to the Bumper' by Grace Jones but, after hearing Trevor Horn's production on Dollar's 'Hand Held in Black and White' single, they decided to send their demo to him instead. According to Martin Fry, the mission statement for the first album was 'to make a record for an imaginary girl in Barnsley who doesn't buy records'.[9] The band were aware, however, that the time for deliberating and theorising was short and that, down the road, Martyn Ware and Glenn Gregory were nipping at their heels with a similar philosophy.

'I was appalled', said Mark White, 'when I learned on the Sheffield grapevine that Heaven 17 had got a new bass player and were writing new stuff. I was like, "For fuck's sake, we can't let them beat us to it".'

ABC met Horn at a pizza parlour on London's Queensway. Fry was puzzled when he saw the producer had a wrestling magazine in his bag but was prepared to overlook this.

Trevor took us seriously', said Fry. 'When I grew up, nobody listened to me. That's why I had to create a world of my own. We told him our whole manifesto of why we weren't going to be like Haircut 100 and all the other bands. The songs weren't punk songs, they were overblown, romantic

17 Stephen Singleton, Mark White and David Sydenham recording Vice Versa's Music 4 EP at Ken's studio, 1979

and commercial. We had this slogan: 'change is our stability'. We wanted polish.'[10]

Although *The Lexicon of Love* album was to evoke associations of cinematic glamour and romance, the practical realities of its creation were more humdrum and squalid. It was made in Horn's Sarm East studio underneath a haberdasher's on Brick Lane which, in 1981, was a depopulated urban slum patrolled by begrimed tramps and pockmarked with rubble-strewn bombsites. Despite the name change, the DNA of Dickensian degradation seemed to have hitched a ride in the escape hatch that took ABC out of Sheffield. The boys were undaunted, however, and would not allow the mission to be knocked off course.

'People would have a vision of the world as being very cold and robotic', Fry continued. 'Gary Numan was brilliant but you got a lot of people copying him in groups in Sheffield. They were writing songs about electric pylons and trying to be very modern. I thought I'd put it on its head. Music should be emotional and romantic and bombastic.'[11]

Escaping from a city in peacetime seems like a straightforward concept but the reality is more difficult. In *Estates*, Lynsey Hanley's study of working-class ties that bind, she refers to the psychological restraints encountered by the inhabitants of Communist East Berlin after the wall came down in 1989. For many of these people, the sudden freedom to express their thoughts and desires and the liberty to travel without the shackles of the state anchoring them in place was paralysing and they simply carried on as before, unable to see beyond 'die Mauer im kopf' or 'The Wall in the head'. Hanley claims that a similar feeling was bred into young people who grew up on council estates in the 1970s and 1980s; the feeling that the world of art and music and literature and success was to be enjoyed elsewhere by superior beings who existed beyond the confines of the toytown tracts they had been raised in. According to Hanley, only individuals with the lucky combination of ability, initiative and cheek have a chance to escape to the world beyond the wall.[12]

Richard Hoggart noted from personal experience that working-class life was comforting but stifling and repetitive. An immersion in popular culture, however, can illuminate routes through the wire if you can soak up the knowledge quickly enough and find a band of comrades to plot your escape with.[13]

'We didn't want to just be playing in the George IV pub in Sheffield to a group of people who loved what we did', said Martin Fry. 'We wanted to make records that could travel around the world.'

By the end of 1981, Ken Patten had produced several vinyl releases by local bands. The Switch recorded their *Coming Home* EP in 1978 at Studio Electrophonique and The Naughtiest Girl Was a Monitor, De Tian and New Model Soldier also had records pressed bearing Ken's name. Pulp were next in line to have their work immortalised on vinyl when their November Peel Session attracted the attention of a local record label.

'After the Peel Session', said Cocker, 'we were approached by some guy who was doing a compilation album of independent bands. It was called *Your Secret's Safe With Us* which was a very appropriate title as nobody bought it. They were so tight they couldn't afford to put us in a studio so they just used one of the tracks from Ken's and that was the very first recorded output from Pulp; a track called 'What Do You Say?'.'

The compilation album which gave the world the first Pulp recording may not have hit the charts but the teenage band did make the cover of the *Sheffield Star* after their trip to Radio One in November 1981, even though this local publicity was tainted by the prevailing dread of nuclear annihilation.

The wall in the head

In the week when Jarvis and the lads were pictured in an awkward front room pose on the front page, the local paper had commissioned local Armageddon correspondent and restaurant critic, Martin Dawes, to write terrifying daily speculations on the effects of an imminent nuclear blast on the city. The hypothetical bomb, which was predicted to detonate 1,000ft above the Tinsley Viaduct, vaporised a few lorry drivers then lay waste to the rest of the region, mainly terrorising the fictional Benson family, who lived at Hunters Bar. Little Peter Benson rushed out just before the blast to rescue his pet rabbit and was later found dead with a broken back. His dad, Jim, went to his aid but subsequently succumbed after exposure to massive doses of radiation.

The daily features included charts of every Sheffield neighbourhood, listing local populations and the estimations of both instant and lingering deaths. Teatime readers were told that, in the lawless aftermath of the attack, 'people murdered for food', 'funeral pyres were constructed in Endcliffe Park' and 'when the morphine ran out, there was always the bullet'. The final Friday night dispatch from hell, to be read, I imagine, just before readers got dressed up for a night at Penny's Tropical Heatwave, reminded Sheffield that 'cases of genetic handicap will appear in the children and grandchildren of men whose sexual organs have been irradiated … Our descendants will curse us'.[14] Barry Hines, who was to write the screenplay for *Threads*, a film about a nuclear attack on Sheffield that was shown to schoolchildren like me on wheeled-in tellies across the city in 1984 and left psychic wounds that have still not healed, must have pasted these daily horror-scopes in his scrapbook for future reference.

Studio Electrophonique

In Sheffield's nuclear winter, it took a special type of person to be able to squint out the first glimmerings of a golden pop dawn. Against his wishes, Phil Oakey was persuaded by Virgin and his bandmates to release 'Don't You Want Me' as a Christmas single. It went to number one in Britain and America, selling almost two million copies. I contributed to this success as a nine-year-old first-time buyer, selecting it from the rotating singles rack in Woolworths on The Moor and rushing home to play it on my parents' music centre. Perversely, as the world sang along to the song's chorus at Christmas discos around the world, I became obsessed with the mordant B-side, 'Seconds', which detailed the assassination of John F. Kennedy.

ABC, meanwhile, were enduring their last few months of obscurity, their faith in the manifesto unwavering as the band drove home from London listening to the monitor mix of 'Poison Arrow' on the van's cassette player. The van broke down in the snow just outside Chesterfield but the music continued and the band were warmed by the prospect of its inevitable success.

'It all happened insanely quickly', said Mark White. 'It's very hard for a young man with a working-class upbringing to suddenly be the toast of London. It fucks with your brain. I was only nineteen when we signed a deal. Everybody had got big plans and just about everybody you bumped into had just been on *Top of the Pops* or was in a band. It was a golden era but we didn't know it.'

Chapter 17
BURIED DREAMS

Leave everything, leave Dada, leave your wife, leave
    your mistress
Leave your hopes and your fears
Sow your children in the corner of a wood
Leave the substance for the shadow
Set out on the road.
                        André Breton, *Surrealist Manifesto*, 1924

When the new breed of Sheffield pop stars moved to London, Disco John was left behind. It had become increasingly difficult to summon up the vision of a paradise isle when the world outside the disco doors was so stale and unprofitable. This anchored feeling of desertion and decline was given a surreal stamp of confirmation when an unexpected guest dropped in one night in 1982:

One Wednesday night, there was a big commotion at Penny's and it turned out that Yosser Hughes from *Boys from the Blackstuff* was there. I don't know much about method acting but he was in character as Yosser all night with people following him about. There was definitely a *Boys from the Blackstuff* feel about Sheffield at that time, with industry closing and people banging their heads against walls in despair. Joining a band seemed like a good plan. It was always my dream but I was a shy lad and it never happened and I had to work. Maybe it would have been better not to work and just to focus, like Adi did, on nothing but art.

Taking this visitation as a sign to stay nimble and one step ahead of impending doom, Disco John fumigated the crickets from the Tropical Heatwave and moved his operation to Romeo and Juliet's nightclub on Bank Street. His new Wednesday night slot was called Atmosphere and was billed as Sheffield's first videotheque.

In typical Sheffield DIY style, this videotheque consisted of twelve old wooden Rediffusion tellies piled on top of each other, all playing a version of 'Careering' by Public Image Limited that Disco John had taped off *The Old Grey Whistle Test*.[1]

Others who seemed to have missed the pop evacuation from Sheffield found themselves scratching out a meagre existence in the shadowlands between lost industry and desperate bohemia. Jarvis Cocker had rapidly descended from the provincial high profile of a Peel Session and a picture on the front of the *Sheffield Star* to an informal tenancy in a derelict factory just off The Wicker. Rejecting a place at university with the romantic notion that he could sustain his ailing band on willpower and inspiration drawn largely from local jumble sales, he had been invited to live at the factory by his friend and bandmate Tim Allcard, who was the caretaker of the premises.

Buried dreams

The semi-derelict rooms of the factory had been repurposed for various local pastimes and now included the headquarters of two rival table tennis clubs, Wicker Boys and St Albion, who would stoke the feud by taking shits outside their rival's door. These days were remembered wistfully by Jarvis in 'The Last Day of the Miners' Strike' by Pulp: 'Well, by 1985, I was as cold as cold could be but no one was working underground to dig me out and set me free.'[2]

David Sydenham, whom Martin Fry had replaced in Vice Versa, was an old friend of Tim's. Struggling with alcohol addiction, David was invited to join them at the factory as a lodger on the condition that he didn't allow his drinking to cause a problem. Jarvis recalled David as a shy, model housemate who wore false teeth and spoke with a lisp. He had lost all his teeth after a two-packs-a-day Polo mint habit before they went sugar free. David lived with them for three months before moving on and not once had his behaviour been unusual or problematic.

After he'd gone, Tim and Jarvis started to find empty Bell's whisky miniatures everywhere in the factory. Hundreds of bottles turned up in the most obscure places: under floorboards, beneath cupboard units, inside the cisterns of toilets. For months afterwards, new caches of empties revealed themselves all over the building.[3]

Jarvis fell out of a window above Sven's sex shop onto the pavement on Division Street in November 1985, breaking his ankle, wrist and pelvis, and almost contracted pneumonia. After his recuperation, he was warned by his doctor that a return to the dank confines of the factory could kill him, so he went back to live with his mum.

As the people who actually had to live in Sheffield grew more and more dissatisfied with the scraps of excitement they had to survive on, distant factions from the other side of the world began to view it as a place of unimpeachable, impenetrable style.

In 1984, the record I listened to the most was *The Very Best of The Beach Boys Volume Two* and the most glamorous thing I had any proximity to was my mate's mum's VW Polo, which had recently been enhanced with the personalised number plate PAM 84. In the boxy bedrooms of council maisonettes and in the spore-filled fug of comprehensive school changing rooms, we dreamed of life in a John Hughes brat pack movie.

Conversely, John Hughes was dreaming of life above a women's nightie factory at Western Works and the bedroom of his most iconic teen creation, Ferris Bueller, featured a giant promotional poster for Cabaret Voltaire's *Micro-Phonies* album. John Bender, the untamed outsider played by Judd Nelson in Hughes' *The Breakfast Club*, bore more than a passing resemblance to Stephen Mallinder circa 1979, a look that could be summed up as 'Jackson Browne meets Dracula on a long walk from Stalingrad to Heeley Bottom'.

That year also saw the release of a compilation album helmed by Ken Patten and recorded in the midst of the miners' strike. The coking plant at Orgreave was less than half a mile away from Ken's front door and, as the striking miners were routed in the fields and gardens and alleyways around Handsworth and the kingdom cracked open in discord, Ken was secure in his own kingdom, taming the guitar frenzy of Bangkok Shock, polishing the slick funk of The Rhythm Brothers and weaponising the infectious electro-pop of Cry For Reality.

The album, *Flightpath One*, was funded by the contributing bands but masterminded by Ken in the spirit of independence and fatherly benevolence.

'There's plenty of marvellous bands in and around Sheffield,' said Ken, 'and I thought doing an album would give as many of them as possible the chance to be on vinyl. I worked it all out and, at a cost of £93 to each band, they would each get eighty-three records with all recording time free of charge.'[4]

Martin Lilleker wrote a full-page spread about the album in the *Sheffield Telegraph*. Beneath the headline 'Patten's Platter', he detailed the concept of the album and asked Ken how he still found the energy to promote new bands at the age of sixty.

'I'm a frustrated guitar player really', said Ken. 'I was born twenty years too early. When I am in the studio, I imagine it's me playing all the instruments. My favourite music is whatever I'm recording at the time.'[5]

Perhaps local success was more nourishing than global success after all. After ABC's second album, *Beauty Stab*, Stephen Singleton left the band he had helped to create and, in 1985, Bob Last found himself at the end of his rather long tether at the Sunset Marquis Hotel in Los Angeles.

Phil Oakey had woken his manager at an unreasonable hour to complain about a lease car he was unhappy with back in Sheffield. Bob drove to Burbank Airport, hooked his beige and orange first-generation Epson laptop up to the payphone with an acoustic coupler and conveyed a primitive email of resignation to The Human League, detailing his displeasure and sorrow at the pettiness of their dealings.

In 1986, I came home from school, made myself a Findus Crispy Pancake and sat down in front of John Craven's *Newsround* to watch the live *Challenger* space shuttle launch turn into the *Challenger* space shuttle disaster. The day when we would swap the maisonettes of Lowedges for the domed colonies of the moon looked further away than it had in 1969. It is at this point that I imagine Jarvis Cocker started to consider learning how to ride a bike after all.

Later the same year, Cabaret Voltaire were driven from their lair at Western Works. Over the years, they had amassed a battery of expensive electronic and analogue equipment but they had always felt safe in the knowledge that their base was inviolable, chained and padlocked as it was at street level and at the entrance to the inner sanctum above the nightie factory. One day, however, they arrived to discover that thieves had gained entry to their rehearsal room from above and had, somehow, hauled their heavy gear across the rooftops of Portobello. The office of The Workers' Revolutionary Party was abandoned once more, and the building was later demolished.

Ken carried on recording throughout the 1980s, although his health was deteriorating and he was on medication for a weak heart. His friend Dennis Greatbatch didn't visit often in later years but the two were still in touch about technical matters:

When our kids came along, we didn't see Ken and Lorna so often. I'd started working for Yorkshire Television and I remember Ken ringing me up and saying he was having real trouble with his TEAC machine. I told him to bring it round to mine but, when he arrived, he was huffing and puffing and he looked very old. It's a fairly heavy machine but he was struggling with it and he looked grey in the face. He just didn't look like the Ken I knew. That was the last time I saw him.

When James and I made our last visit to Michele, we returned the Heron Foods carrier bag full of her dad's film reels and took her a copy of James's first album, *Buxton Palace Hotel*, on CD. She had a one-bedroom first-floor flat in Coppin Square not far from her ex-husband's house in Parson Cross. The enclosed corporation stairwell had a familiar sensory effect on me, the cold trapped air carrying the smell of old piss and poured concrete, the electronic rim-shot slap of every mounted step. Michele let us in and received James's present with dramatic gratitude.

'Oooh, Buxton Palace Hotel,' she said, 'And Buxton, of course, is where mum and dad went on their honeymoon. So there you go.'

We told Michele that we'd found Dennis and that he'd told us about receiving some of her dad's old gear after his death. Michele remembered Dennis fondly but sagged at the mention of her dad's last days. She opened the curtains and pawed at some fluff on the sill:

Dad was acting quite strangely towards the end. Two days before he had a massive heart attack, he said to my mother, 'I've decided I'm going to sell all my musical instruments and implements. I'm going to get rid. I don't want them anymore. We'll make the studio into a proper dining room.' So he put all his things up for sale in the paper and then he died, two days later. He was only sixty-six, the same age as I am now.

He'd been diagnosed with a heart condition so he was used to taking pills and whatnot but, towards the end, when he really started to feel unwell, he went to the doctors and actually had a heart attack in the surgery. They rushed him to the hospital and he was in there for a few days and then he had another one and died. When we got there he was already gone. He'd just put down the book he'd been reading and then he was gone. A Western it was. He'd recorded me playing 'Satin Doll' on the recorder when I was five years old and that's what they played at the funeral. My dad had made a tape a few years before with his guitar, my recorder and a big orchestra in the background and that was the music that was playing in the background as we all walked into the chapel of rest. After that, people kept ringing up about the advert my dad had put in the paper and my mum had to say, 'I'm sorry, but Mr Patten has passed away, but if you're interested, you can come and collect whatever you want'. So, before we knew it, the studio was empty, just like my mum's life was empty.

Dennis got in touch and invited us round. He said he'd found some more bits and bobs that had belonged to Ken. We made another trip to Dronfield and Dennis met us at the door. He allowed us to admire his black Porsche then led us into a garage that was cleaner and tidier than any room in any house I have ever lived in:

So just after Ken had passed, I got a call from Lorna and she said, 'Dennis, I want you to take all this stuff of Ken's', so I said, 'What do you want me to do? Do you want me to sell it?', and she said, 'No. I just want it gone', so I went up there with a transit van. She wanted it all cleared out so I took the tape machines, the Revox, the TEAC, a couple of sound mixers and all the rest. A lot of it eventually went to various colleges and schools but I've held on to a few bits here.

Dennis stooped to reach under a workbench. James's eyes dilated as Dennis started to stack hardware on the bench above: the things we'd already seen like the Roland System 100 mixer and the monitor speakers but also other devices that he named with a technician's relish:

So there you have a working H&H echo unit with the tape loop inside there, and this is actually a Ferguson VHS recorder that Ken used purely because it's got great audio.

James started to examine the echo unit with a dazed reverence that made Dennis smile:

Now, last time, I felt a bit daft saying to you that I think Ken was orchestrating all this from wherever he is but I think it's true. It was meant to be. And I know Ken would like his gear to be put to some use instead of just sitting in my loft for thirty-odd years. So I'd like to loan it to you if you want it, seeing as you've taken on the studio name.

James placed his hands flat on the worktop for grounding purposes.
    'That's unbelievable. Are you sure?'
    'Yes. I've been thinking about it since you last came. And it's a permanent loan, so I don't want them back. I want you to look after them for Ken.'

Placing treasure that we thought was lost forever in the boot of the Micra should have been the satisfactory capstone of our quest but, as James stood with one hand on the raised boot lid and one troubling his mop of hair, the sad sediment of inadequacy had already been stirred in his heart.

'I'm going to have to do justice to all this now, you know', he said.

'Can't you just see it as a magical bonus?' I said. 'Look at that.' I ran my hand across the tobacco-stained trim on the echo unit. 'Look at the Ken Patina on that.'

'I feel like it's a burden.'

'Bloody hell. What's up with you? Just make sure it's all stowed securely, will you. And give Dennis a wave before you get in.'

I started the car up and heard James slam the lid on his cursed inheritance. Scanning pure good fortune for hairline cracks was an inbuilt flaw of ours that tended to ruin any natural blessings that came our way.

Ken's gear now resides in a secret location. It is in perfect working order and James, the new face of Studio Electrophonique, is currently apprenticed to the spirit of Ken, mastering the machines that have fallen, by some miracle, into his custodial lap.

When I wander around Sheffield today, it is hard to pick up a trace of the futuristic fever that gripped the city in the 1970s or to locate the markers laid down by yesterday's visionaries. The brutalist battlements of Kelvin and Broomhall were razed, ousting Mr and Mrs Ware from their happy perch at 17 High Victoria, and, in their place, the most witless and dreary toytown houses have been thrown

18 James Leesley on stage at the Paris Olympia, reviving the sound of Studio Electrophonique

up, a tribute to nothing more than the gods of UPVC windows and Juliet balconies. No one can argue that the modernist housing campaigns of the 1960s were perfect in their execution, but at least they represented an unshackled imagination and a heroic sense of scale.

Hyde Park Block B had its last hurrah when it was chosen to host athletes visiting for the 1991 World Student Games, the biggest sporting event ever held in Britain at the time. The games were unceremoniously declared open by Britain's first astronaut, Helen Sharman, who attended the same school as me and briefly gave the natives a fume of belief that an intergalactic future was still on the cards. All optimism was crushed, however, before the first event could even take place, when Helen stumbled on her jog around the Don Valley Bowl to light the flame at the opening ceremony, spilling the hot coals of hope all over the red carpet before limping on into the night.

'They'd brought the flame all the way from Japan or somewhere,' said Jarvis Cocker, 'and she only had to run the last 100 yards along a red carpet. Anyway, she got hold of it, ran for a bit then fell over and it went out. They still lit the flame, though, but only for ten minutes at the start of the games and at the end because British Gas wouldn't sponsor it all. That's the sort of thing that happened in Sheffield.'[6]

During the brief week of civic pride that preceded the opening ceremony, a week of royal visits and daily pull-out souvenir brochures in the *Sheffield Star*, a story about the powerful reverberations of the city's music was hidden on an inside page. Under the headline 'Murdering Cannibal Listened to City Band', the story was a report from the trial of Jeffrey Dahmer in Milwaukee. Court transcripts had revealed that Dahmer, accused of killing, dismembering and, in some cases, eating seventeen young men had, at the time of his arrest, been listening to *Buried Dreams* by Clock DVA.

'Individuals are individuals,' said Adi Newton, 'I can't control what an individual listens to. *Buried Dreams* was more psychological than violent so I didn't really know what to think when I found out. It must have contained something that connected directly to his particular psychology. Just before *Buried Dreams*, I started reading about various serial killers through history and it is fascinating but, when it comes to it happening in real life, that's a different thing. It's easy to romanticise these things, like people do with artists who had mental problems. Like with Van Gogh and Artaud. They were both ill and trying to express pain and feelings and sensitivity but it wasn't romantic for them. They were suffering.'

Buried dreams

Among other things, the album *Buried Dreams* delved into the story of Elizabeth Báthory, a Hungarian noblewoman accused of murdering hundreds of peasant girls at the dawn of the seventeenth century, bathing in their blood and taking on the title La Comtesse de Sang.

'Adi was really pleased', said Martin Fry. 'It was inevitable that DVA would become a serial killer's favourite band.'[7]

A local bus company in Sheffield has launched a heritage music campaign that celebrates certain influential local bands by plastering double-decker buses with sleeve art from seminal albums. Often, as I wait for the ninety-seven on Arundel Gate, beneath the tall apartment block that has now surpassed the Arts Tower as the city's highest building, a bus will creak to a halt before me and the faux-yuppie trio of Ware, Gregory and Marsh will smirk down from the side of the *Penthouse and Pavement* number twenty to Hemsworth. Or a limited-stop Richard Hawley bus to Barnsley will pull out rudely in front of a hesitant Pulp *Different Class* hybrid on its way to Catcliffe. Today's pedestrians, far removed from the space age of the city's past, dab at smartphones, groggy under the Wi-Fi cosh of modern life, paying scant attention to the glossy graphics that slide by above them. Disappointingly, there is no *Buried Dreams* bus dedicated solely to the Burncross route.

Some of the pop stars of the Sheffield space age still live in the city but, like the astronauts who walked on the lunar surface or who travelled alone, slingshot-style, around the dark side of the moon, they are spooked and dislocated by the decompression they have experienced since returning to Earth. Perhaps their perspective has been permanently distended by the rare altitudes their music rocketed them towards. Perhaps, like the astronauts, it's hard to find fresh excitement in the deracinated drudge when the excitement you have tasted up there cannot be readily articulated or shared with mortal beings. Perhaps I am just annoyed that even the hand-delivery of two charmingly constructed J. G. Ballard postcards only raised a polite rejection from the Oakey mansion on Banner Cross.

Previously, when asked why he had chosen to remain in Sheffield, Oakey said he liked to be 'a big fish in a small pond'.

'We wouldn't stick out very much in London, would we?', he said. 'I never felt adequate against the people who were running the business. That happens to a lot of people who are from the provinces. I don't really know how to use my knife and fork properly so I hide away here.'[8]

When we visited Stephen Singleton, he tried to explain the chimerical nature of sudden fame: 'You get to a point and you think, "Wow, it doesn't get any better than this!" And no, it doesn't.'

Oddly, the two characters who grubbed out an existence in the most squalid lodgings Sheffield had to offer in the late 1970s are now residing in the most exotic locations. Martin Fry has a property at Gibbs Glade in Barbados and Disco John has, against the odds, made his tropical heatwave a reality, living in Bali for the past twenty-five years. Martyn Ware has swapped Broomhall flats for an apartment in Venice and, when Stephen Mallinder and Adi Newton last met up for a pint, they were rioting on Sunset Strip.

Mark White laments the loss of the spirit he felt among Ken and the bands of Sheffield past:

Buried dreams

I remember it was like everybody had a piece of the jigsaw puzzle and we were all putting it together. At that time, it felt like a community endeavour, a joint cultural mission. That, I think, has rather gone. Later, we called our London studio 'Studio Electrophonique South' in honour of the great man.

The space age optimism that prevailed against a backdrop of grey mundanity is now in short supply.

'We are going backwards in time', said Martyn Ware. 'It's like that Philip K. Dick book *Counter-Clock World*. I sound like an old twat but I genuinely think that, because there's less optimism in the world, people are less willing to take risks. We are in a retrograde phase of human development.'

'The way the future panned out was very different to the way I imagined it back then', said Adi Newton. 'It was all about outer space then but now the focus is coming round to inner space; how we cope with the dilemmas of being human in a future with things like AI. We're living in a dystopia now for sure; under absolute control via monitoring and credit control and phones that can listen to you. Conventional functions are all wrapped up and integrated virtually in devices and, if they ever go down, you're absolutely fucked.'

If anyone is allowed an obscure artistic analogy to close the story, it is Adi, who related a story about a visit to the Museo del Prado in Madrid where he came face to face with Diego Velazquez's painting *Las Meninas*. When an era is experienced in blurred, chaotic close-up, only distance can give it the focus and appreciation it deserves.

'The scale of that painting is vast. It must be like twenty feet across. It has a room all to itself. When you're up close to it, it looks like someone's just slapped paint on with a great big brush, just big slashes of paint and bits of bare canvas that aren't even covered. But, when you move out, at a distance, everything comes into perfect depth and focus. No one knows how he did it. The rawness of it up close and the perfection of the image from a distance.'

Ordinary people like us need to remember that art is not some far-off place. Dada and surrealism are rightly held aloft today as movements of high-concept art but they were – like Meatwhistle, *Gun Rubber* and the work of the bands that forged the golden age of Sheffield music – just young people pissing about with ideas that would alarm and bewilder the cultural guardians of the day. It may be bold to claim that more lasting and worthwhile art came out of Sheffield in 1981 than emerged from Zurich in 1916, but it's probably true. At the time, however, it was difficult to make even close family see the validity of a life in art.

'My mum didn't really get my music, or she said she didn't get it', said Stephen Mallinder. 'She was always like, "You've got a degree. Why the fuck are you doing music?" Once I'd brought a few records out, she was really proud of me, though. When she died and we cleared the house, we found copies of all my records on vinyl.'

'My dad was a miner', said Ivor Hillman of My Pierrot Dolls. 'He worked down the pit all his life so it must have been tough for him having a son flouncing about in frilly trousers and red hair and blue hair and green hair. Funny thing was, he used to look like he wore make-up, but it was just the coal dust from the pit that looked like mascara. He used to make me leave the house ten minutes before him so we weren't seen together, and I suppose he must have got some stick off his pals but I think they knew to only push him so far. I don't really know if he was proud of my individuality, because he never said owt.'

Ken, as a surrogate father, played his part in nurturing this local outpouring of ideas, providing, as he did, a laboratory of sound and a paternal house engineer who could coax raw visions onto one-inch tape. Glamour and beauty won't settle on your shoulders in a city like Sheffield, it needs to be conjured out of pure imagination and graft. Studio Electrophonique is a name that evokes a slick, polished exoticism that only ever existed in one man's mind and was at odds with the realities of his life and the lives of the young people of the city. It was a name that almost died without fanfare but, like all great artistic statements, it left enough of a trace for others to follow. It survives today on the outer ring road of art which, as we all know, is the only place to be.

ACKNOWLEDGEMENTS

I am grateful to Martyn Ware for sharing his stories and for allowing me to mine his vast digital seam of *Electronically Yours* podcasts for source material; uncited quotes are from my own interviews or from Martyn's podcasts. Roger Quail was also generous in allowing me to use details from his forensically detailed music podcast *My Life in the Mosh of Ghosts*. Others kind enough to talk to me about their experiences and to seek out details, photos and revelations included Michele Patten, Stephen Singleton, Mark White, Stephen Mallinder, Adi Newton, Paul Bower, Glenn Gregory, Jarvis Cocker, John Marsden, Dennis Greatbatch, John Blyther, Ivor Hillman, Rob Coupe, John Mayfield, Michael Day, Roger De Wolf, Kitty Parker and Jon Downing. A debt of gratitude is also owed to the British Pop Archive team at Manchester University Press and Martin Lilleker, whose book *Beats Working for a Living* was responsible for the discovery of the first clue in the Ken Patten mystery. Thanks also go to James Leesley, Graham Wrench, Anaïs Roumens, Gabriel Edvy, Caroline Cooper Charles, Sean Bean, Enda Mullen and Ryan Howes for collaborating

Acknowledgements

on the documentary *A Film about Studio Electrophonique*, which became a lost classic before it was even a classic. I would also like to acknowledge the following people who were essential to this tale but are sadly no longer with us: Ken, Lorna and Michele Patten, Veronica and Chris Wilkinson, Stephen 'Judd' Turner, Mark Civico, Haydn Boyes-Weston, Richard H. Kirk, David Sydenham, Andy Gill, Martin Lilleker and Sarah Doole.

Thanks to Laura for tolerating years of unrewarded musing and to my parents and Greenhill Library for providing years of nourishment.

ILLUSTRATIONS

Illustrations

NOTES

Preface: young meteors

1 Steven Bach, *Dreams and Disaster in the Making of Heaven's Gate* (London: Jonathan Cape Ltd, 1985).

2 Tom Wolfe, *The Right Stuff* (New York: Farrar, Straus and Giroux, 1979).

1 Death of a futurist

1 Richard Hoggart, *The Uses of Literacy* (London: Chatto & Windus, 1957).

2 Louis-Ferdinand Céline, *Death on The Instalment Plan* (London: Chatto & Windus, 1938).

3 Søren Kierkegaard, *The Sickness unto Death* (Princeton: Princeton University Press, 1941).

4 James Strong, 'Heaven 17: The Story of Penthouse and Pavement', BBC Two, 17 May 2010, www.bbc.co.uk/programmes/b00shclx (accessed 18 July 2024).

2 Ballifield year zero

1 Paul Mather, 'Volume Interview with Jarvis Cocker', *Acrylic Afternoons Press*, November 1991, www.acrylicafternoons.com/volume02.html (accessed 18 July 2024).

Notes

2 Alexander Walker, *Stanley Kubrick Directs* (San Diego: Harcourt, Brace & Jovanovich, 1971).

3 Tedd George, 'Remembering the Last Night at Sheffield Playhouse – 50 Years after It Closed with Promise of City's First Full Nude Scene', *The Star*, 3 June 2021, www.thestar.co.uk/wh ats-on/arts-and-entertainment/remembering-the-last-night-at-shef field-playhouse-50-years-after-it-closed-with-promise-of-citys-firs t-full-nude-scene-3261016 (accessed 18 July 2024).

4 John Firminger, *Not Like a Proper Job: The Story of Popular Music in Sheffield 1955–1975 as Told by Those Who Made It* (Sheffield: Juma, 2001).

5 Simon Reynolds, *Rip It Up and Start Again: Postpunk 1978–1984* (London: Faber & Faber, 2005).

6 Rob Waugh, 'Sheffield's Rare and Racy: The Independent Music Store Jarvis Cocker Says It Would Be "a Crime to Destroy"', *The Guardian*, 31 March 2015, www.theguardian.com/cities/the-nor therner/2015/mar/31/rare-and-racys-closure-jarvis-cocker (acc-essed 18 July 2024).

3 The analogue trace

1 Jeffrey Pocock, 'Tape Recording', *BMG*, December 1960, https://classic-banjo.ning.com/page/bmg-magazines (accessed 18 July 2024).

2 Ibid.

3 Ian Helliwell, *Tape Leaders: A Compendium of Early British Electronic Music Composers* (Cambridge: Sound on Sound Ltd, 2016).

4 Ibid.

5 Ian Arnison and R. Brown, 'Sense of Proportion', *Tape Recording Monthly*, June 1957, www.worldradiohistory.com/Tape-Record ing-UK.htm (accessed 18 July 2024).

6 Ian Arnison and R. Brown, 'Poor Mike Can't Take Noisy Parties', *Tape Recording Monthly*, January 1958, www.worldradiohistory. com/Tape-Recording-UK.htm (accessed 18 July 2024).

7 Ibid.

8 Ben Whalley, 'Synth Britannia at the BBC', BBC Four, 9 July 2022, www.bbc.co.uk/programmes/b00n93c6 (accessed 18 July 2024).

9 Lynsey Hanley, *Estates: An Intimate History* (London: Granta Books, 2007).

10 James Strong, 'Heaven 17: The Story of Penthouse and Pavement', BBC Two, 17 May 2010, www.bbc.co.uk/programmes/b00shclx (accessed 18 July 2024).

4 Untrained/undaunted

1 Arthur Rimbaud, Letter to Paul Demeny, Charleville, 15 May 1871.

2 Andy Gill, 'This Week's Sheffield – Sheffield', *NME*, 8 September 1979.

3 Ibid.

4 William Blake, *Jerusalem: The Emanation of the Giant Albion* (London: Joseph Johnson, 1820)

5 The décor of tomorrow's hell

1 Robert Ardrey, *African Genesis: A Personal Investigation into the Animal Origins and Nature of Man* (Glasgow: Collins, 1961).

2 Robert Hughes, 'Cinema: The Décor of Tomorrow's Hell', *Time Magazine*, December 1971, https://time.com/archive/6839473/cinema-the-dcor-of-tomorrows-hell/ (accessed 18 July 2024).

3 Lynsey Hanley, *Estates: An Intimate History* (London: Granta Books, 2007).

4 Ibid.

5 Ibid.

6 Ibid.

7 Ibid.

8 George Orwell, *The Road to Wigan Pier* (London: Victor Gollancz, 1937).

9 Ben Whalley, 'Synth Britannia at the BBC', BBC Four, 9 July 2022, www.bbc.co.uk/programmes/b00n93c6 (accessed 18 July 2024).

6 War chants

1 Phillip Larkin, *Collected Poems 1988* (London: Faber, 1951). Reproduced by permission of Faber. All rights reserved.

Notes

2 In 1973, Ashleigh Technical School was renamed Atlee School for the duration of the filming of a Barry Hines TV play called 'Speech Day' which starred Brian Glover and Bill Dean.

7 This is tomorrow

1 Paul Mather, 'Volume Interview with Jarvis Cocker', *Acrylic Afternoons Press*, November 1991, www.acrylicafternoons.com/volume02.html (accessed 18 July 2024).
2 One of the many highlights of Pulp's 'Sheffield Sex City' is Jarvis yelping 'Peace Gardens!' in a moment of rhapsodic abandon.
3 Mark Civico and Ian Craig Marsh (Musical Vomit), 'Denim Mind' (unreleased).
4 Martin Lilleker, *Beats Working for a Living: Sheffield Popular Music 1973–1984* (Sheffield: Juma, 2005).
5 Ibid.
6 Ibid.
7 Brian Baker, 'The Blue Marble: Art and Pop in the Space Age', *Foundation* 142 (2022), 41–48.
8 Martin Lilleker, *Beats Working for a Living: Sheffield Popular Music 1973–1984* (Sheffield: Juma, 2005).
9 Ibid.

8 Knock three times and ask for Big Jake

1 Stanley Cook, *Wood beyond a Cornfield: Collected Poems* (Sheffield: Smith/Doorstop Books, 1995).
2 Martin Lilleker, *Beats Working for a Living: Sheffield Popular Music 1973–1984* (Sheffield: Juma, 2005).
3 Paul Boddy, 'VICE VERSA Interview', *Electricity Club*, November 2015, www.electricityclub.co.uk/vice-versa-interview/ (accessed 18 July 2024).
4 Martin Lilleker, *Beats Working for a Living: Sheffield Popular Music 1973–1984* (Sheffield: Juma, 2005).
5 Ibid.
6 Barry Hines, *The Artistic Life* (Claremont: Pomona Press, 2009).
7 Ibid.

9 Musical Vomit

1 *Sheffield Star* (28 May 1974).
2 Martin Lilleker, *Beats Working for a Living: Sheffield Popular Music 1973–1984* (Sheffield: Juma, 2005).
3 Charles Shaar Murray, 'A Big Hand for The Human League', *NME*, 12 July 1980.
4 Martin Lilleker, *Beats Working for a Living: Sheffield Popular Music 1973–1984* (Sheffield: Juma, 2005).
5 Ibid.
6 Michel Sanouillet and Elmer Peterson, *The Writings of Marcel Duchamp* (New York: Oxford University Press, 1973).
7 Hans Richter, *Dada (World of Art): Art and Anti-Art* (London: Thames and Hudson, 1965).
8 Ibid.
9 Ibid.
10 Francis Picabia, *Manifeste Cannibale Dada* (1920).
11 Ibid.

10 Adolphus rising

1 Hans Richter, *Dada (World of Art): Art and Anti-Art* (London: Thames and Hudson, 1965).
2 Martin Lilleker, *Beats Working for a Living: Sheffield Popular Music 1973–1984* (Sheffield: Juma, 2005).
3 Ibid.
4 Ibid.
5 Simon Reynolds, *Rip It Up and Start Again: Postpunk 1978–1984* (London: Faber & Faber, 2005).
6 Paul Morley, 'The Heart and Soul of Cabaret Voltaire', *NME*, 29 November 1980.
7 Ibid.
8 Ibid.

11 New ruins

1 Charles Shaar Murray, 'A Big Hand for The Human League', *NME*, 12 July 1980.

Notes

2 Martin Lilleker, *Beats Working for a Living: Sheffield Popular Music 1973–1984* (Sheffield: Juma, 2005).
3 Ibid.
4 Ibid.
5 Ibid.
6 Eve Wood, *Made in Sheffield*, documentary feature, 2001.

12 No illegal connections

1 Colleen 'Cosmo' Murphy, 'Sounds of a City: The Human League-Travelogue', BBC Radio 6, May 2015, www.bbc.co.uk/pro grammes/b05t2djc (accessed 18 July 2024).
2 Charles Shaar Murray, 'A Big Hand for The Human League', *NME*, 12 July 1980.
3 Ron would later reside in a underheated Victorian ruin in Upperthorpe called 'Hula Kula' with various young bohemians (including Stephen Mallinder). He named his band Hula after this haunted Sheffield commune.
4 Andy Gill, 'Gig Review', *NME*, 14 January 1978.

13 Fast products

1 W. H. Auden, *The Age of Anxiety* (New York: Random House, 1947). Reproduced by permission of Curtis Brown. All rights reserved.
2 Giovanni Dadomo, 'The Humour League Have Not Broken Up', *Sounds*, December 1979, http://w.the-black-hit-of-space.dk/arti cles_1979_sounds.htm (accessed 18 July 2024).
3 Michael Moorcock, *The Cornelius Chronicles* (New York: Avon, 1977).
4 Ben Whalley, 'Synth Britannia at the BBC', BBC Four, 9 July 2022, www.bbc.co.uk/programmes/b00n93c6 (accessed 18 July 2024).
5 Martin Lilleker, *Beats Working for a Living: Sheffield Popular Music 1973–1984* (Sheffield: Juma, 2005).
6 Ben Whalley, 'Synth Britannia at the BBC', BBC Four, 9 July 2022, www.bbc.co.uk/programmes/b00n93c6 (accessed 18 July 2024).

7 Charles Shaar Murray, 'A Big Hand for The Human League', *NME*, 12 July 1980.

8 Ibid.

9 Ibid.

10 Kate Meynall, 'Young Guns Go for It: The Human League', BBC Four, 8 January 1999, www.bbc.co.uk/programmes/b00shyg4 (accessed 18 July 2024).

11 *Sheffield Telegraph*, 29 January 1978.

12 Paul Bower, *Gun Rubber* fanzine, issue 7, Christmas 1977.

13 Simon Reynolds, *Rip It Up and Start Again: Postpunk 1978–1984* (London: Faber & Faber, 2005).

14 Ibid.

15 Martin Lilleker, *Beats Working for a Living: Sheffield Popular Music 1973–1984* (Sheffield: Juma, 2005).

16 Improbable fact – Howard Kendall played in the same school football team as Bryan Ferry. They both attended and turned out for Washington Grammar School in the late 1950s. Kendall remembered Ferry as a 'wimpy right winger'.

17 Jarvis Cocker, *Good Pop Bad Pop* (London: Jonathan Cape, 2022).

18 Martin Lilleker, *Beats Working for a Living: Sheffield Popular Music 1973–1984* (Sheffield: Juma, 2005).

19 Giovanni Dadomo, 'The Humour League Have Not Broken Up', *Sounds*, December 1979, http://w.the-black-hit-of-space.dk/arti cles_1979_sounds.htm (accessed 18 July 2024).

20 Martin Lilleker, *Beats Working for a Living: Sheffield Popular Music 1973–1984* (Sheffield: Juma, 2005).

21 Roger Quail, 'Gig 9. Cabaret Voltaire, Deaf Aids, Molodoy, The Push. The Limit club, Sheffield, 15th August 1978', *My Life in the Mosh of Ghosts*, 1 July 2019, https://podcasts.apple.com/ gb/podcast/my-life-in-the-mosh-of-ghosts-gig-9-cabaret/id146 4213757?i=1000443643796 (accessed 18 July 2024).

22 Only fourteen people turned up to see U2 at The Limit in 1980 and Bono split his leather trousers reaching up to touch the low ceiling.

23 Giovanni Dadomo, 'The Humour League Have Not Broken Up', *Sounds*, December 1979, http://w.the-black-hit-of-space.dk/arti cles_1979_sounds.htm (accessed 18 July 2024).

Notes

24 Charles Shaar Murray, 'A Big Hand for The Human League', *NME*, 12 July 1980.

14 Notes from a condemned terrace

1 In January 1977, *The Guardian* reported on the death of 'the best-known tramp in Sheffield', Cyril Griffin, who had been found lifeless in a shop doorway after a freezing night during the Christmas period. Cyril, who died at the age of fifty-two, had been living on the streets for ten years since the death of his parents and made his pitch in the 'hole in the road' at the end of Arundel Gate, existing on a diet of tea, fish and chips, and cheap cigarettes. He even carried his own set of cutlery attached to a silver chain inside his moth-eaten coat.

2 Andrew Harrison, 'ABC: Suave to the Rhythm – Martin Fry Interviewed', *Bigmouth Mag*, 18 May 2016, https://bigmouthmag. wordpress.com/2016/05/18/abc-martin-fry-suave-to-the-rhythm/ (accessed 18 July 2024).

3 Ibid.

4 Martin Lilleker, *Beats Working for a Living: Sheffield Popular Music 1973–1984* (Sheffield: Juma, 2005).

5 Paul Morley, 'A Career in Electronics Can Be Yours', *NME*, 31 March 1979.

6 Ibid.

7 Martin Lilleker, *Beats Working for a Living: Sheffield Popular Music 1973–1984* (Sheffield: Juma, 2005).

8 Ibid.

9 Ibid.

10 Andrew Harrison, 'ABC: Suave to the Rhythm – Martin Fry Interviewed', *Bigmouth Mag*, 18 May 2016, https://bigmouthmag. wordpress.com/2016/05/18/abc-martin-fry-suave-to-the-rhythm/ (accessed 18 July 2024).

11 Paul Morley, 'A Career in Electronics Can Be Yours', *NME*, 31 March 1979.

12 Single Reviews, *Sounds*, June 1979.

13 Roger Quail, 'Gig 24. Artery, Shy Tots, the Blitz Club, Sheffield, 18th December 1979', *My Life in the Mosh of Ghosts*, 28 December 2019, https://podcasts.apple.com/gb/podcast/my-life-in-the-mosh-of-ghosts-gig-24-artery-shy/id1464213757?i= 1000460985752 (accessed 18 July 2024).

15 Dreams of leaving

1 Thomas H. Green, 'Mutant Disco from Planet ZE', *The Telegraph*, 13 August 2009, www.telegraph.co.uk/culture/music/rockandp opfeatures/5978110/Mutant-disco-from-planet-ZE.html (accessed 18 July 2024).

2 Paul Boddy, 'VICE VERSA Interview', *Electricity Club*, November 2015, www.electricityclub.co.uk/vice-versa-interview/ (accessed 18 July 2024).

3 Andy Gill, 'Gig Review', *NME*, 14 January 1978.

4 Colleen 'Cosmo' Murphy, 'Sounds of a City: The Human League-Travelogue', BBC Radio 6, May 2015, www.bbc.co.uk/pro grammes/b05t2djc (accessed 18 July 2024).

5 Ibid.

6 Ibid.

7 David McCullough, 'Paradoxes in Industry Chic', *Sounds*, 24 May 1980, www.rocksbackpages.com/Library/Article/the-human-lea gue-itraveloguei-virgin-v2160- (accessed 18 July 2024).

8 Paul Morley, 'A Career in Electronics Can Be Yours', *NME*, 31 March 1979.

9 Roger Quail, 'Gig 33. Futurama 2 festival, Queens Hall, Leeds. 13th September 1980', *My Life in the Mosh of Ghosts*, 29 May 2020, https://podcasts.apple.com/gb/podcast/my-life-in-the-mosh-of-ghosts-gig-33-futurama-2/id1464213757?i=1000476268738 (accessed 18 July 2024).

10 Kate Meynall, 'Young Guns Go for It: The Human League', BBC Four, 8 January 1999, www.bbc.co.uk/programmes/b00shyg4 (accessed 18 July 2024).

11 James Strong, 'Heaven 17: The Story of Penthouse and Pavement', BBC Two, 17 May 2010, www.bbc.co.uk/programmes/b00shclx (accessed 18 July 2024).

12 Ibid.

13 Ibid.

14 Ibid.

15 John Shearlaw, 'More Cabs', *Record Mirror*, 26 April 1980.

16 Paul Morley, 'The Heart and Soul of Cabaret Voltaire', *NME*, 29 November 1980.

17 Roger Quail, 'Gig 52. Bow Wow Wow, The Lyceum Theatre, Sheffield, 29th October 1981', *My Life in the Mosh of Ghosts*,

7 October 2021, https://podcasts.apple.com/gb/podcast/my-li fe-in-the-mosh-of-ghosts-gig-52-bow-wow-wow/id146421375 7?i=1000537825025 (accessed 18 July 2024).

18 Sleeve notes for Cabaret Voltaire, *Methodology '74/'78. Attic Tapes* (Mute Records, 2015).

16 The wall in the head

1 Dave McCullogh, *Sounds*, 14 February 1981.

2 The Sony Walkman was originally launched in the UK as the Sony Stowaway.

3 Roger Quail, 'Gig 52. Bow Wow Wow, The Lyceum Theatre, Sheffield, 29th October 1981', *My Life in the Mosh of Ghosts*, 7 October 2021, https://podcasts.apple.com/gb/podcast/my-life-in-the-mosh-of-ghosts-gig-52-bow-wow-wow/id1464213757? i=1000537825025 (accessed 18 July 2024).

4 Martin Lilleker, *Beats Working for a Living: Sheffield Popular Music 1973–1984* (Sheffield: Juma, 2005).

5 Andy Gill, 'Gig Review', *NME*, 14 January 1978.

6 Ben Whalley, 'Synth Britannia at the BBC', BBC Four, 9 July 2022, www.bbc.co.uk/programmes/b00n93c6 (accessed 18 July 2024).

7 Simon Reynolds, *Rip It Up and Start Again: Postpunk 1978–1984* (London: Faber & Faber, 2005).

8 Roger Quail, 'Gig 52. Bow Wow Wow, The Lyceum Theatre, Sheffield, 29th October 1981', *My Life in the Mosh of Ghosts*, 7 October 2021, https://podcasts.apple.com/gb/podcast/my-life-in-the-mosh-of-ghosts-gig-52-bow-wow-wow/id1464213757? i=1000537825025 (accessed 18 July 2024).

9 Andrew Harrison, 'ABC: Suave to the Rhythm – Martin Fry Interviewed', *Bigmouth Mag*, 18 May 2016, https://bigmouthmag. wordpress.com/2016/05/18/abc-martin-fry-suave-to-the-rhythm/ (accessed 18 July 2024).

10 Ibid.

11 Ibid.

12 Lynsey Hanley, *Estates: An Intimate History* (London: Granta Books, 2007).

13 Richard Hoggart, *The Uses of Literacy* (London: Chatto & Windus, 1957).

14 Martin Dawes, *Sheffield Star*, 14–20 November 1981.

17 Buried dreams

1 Roger Quail, 'Gig 41. New Order, Atmosphere club night at Romeo's & Juliet's, Sheffield, 22nd April 1981', *My Life in the Mosh of Ghosts*, 25 November 2020, https://podcasts.apple.com/gb/podcast/my-life-in-the-mosh-of-ghosts-gig-41-new/id1464213757?i=1000500295198 (accessed 18 July 2024).
2 Pulp, *Last Day of the Miner's Strike* (London: Island Records, 2002).
3 Jarvis Cocker, *Good Pop Bad Pop* (London: Jonathan Cape, 2022).
4 Martin Lilleker, 'Patten's Platter', *Sheffield Telegraph*, 1984.
5 Ibid.
6 Paul Mather, 'Volume Interview with Jarvis Cocker', *Acrylic Afternoons Press*, November 1991, www.acrylicafternoons.com/volume02.html (accessed 18 July 2024).
7 Martin Lilleker, *Beats Working for a Living: Sheffield Popular Music 1973–1984* (Sheffield: Juma, 2005).
8 Kate Meynall, 'Young Guns Go for It: The Human League', BBC Four, 8 January 1999, www.bbc.co.uk/programmes/b00shyg4 (accessed 18 July 2024).

INDEX

Index

Index

Studio Electrophonique

Mackay, Andy 80, 137
MacNeice, Louis 35
McCloskey's Apocalypse 24,
  66
McCulloch, Ian 226
McCullough, Dave 223, 237
McDowell, Malcolm 53
Mainwaring, Richard 219
Magritte, René 156
Maile Hawaiians, The 61–4,
  68–9, 112
Mallinder, Stephen 46–9, 70–1,
  77–9, 117, 133, 136–8,
  143–6, 148, 163, 171–3,
  186–7, 194, 205, 209, 211,
  223–4, 242, 254, 264,
  266
Man Ray 118, 122
Man Who Fell To Earth, The
  142–3
Manzanera, Phil 82
Marsh, Ian Craig 8, 112–13,
  116–17, 134, 141, 146, 148,
  152–3, 155, 159–60, 164,
  167–8, 174, 181, 184, 188,
  220, 227–8, 238, 263
May, Violet 47, 149
Mayfield, John 92–3
Marsden, John 60–9, 200
Meatwhistle 21, 97–102,
  112–14, 117, 120, 122,
  127–8, 134, 139, 151–2,
  165, 167, 173, 228, 231, 266
Meek, Joe 47
Mekons, The 161
Men, The 220
Mitchell, Ed 73
Modern Drugs 192, 195, 201,
  216

Molodoy 54, 184–5
Moloko 54
Mondrian, Piet 49
Monkees, The 222
Monumental Studios 187–8,
  208, 219, 233
Moorcock, Michael 24, 50, 81,
  105, 133, 165–6
Morley, Paul 195–6, 224–5,
  229–30
Moroder, Giorgio 81, 205
Morrissey, Steven 150
Mother Teresa 121
Mr Kite's Wine Bar 204,
  244
Musical Vomit 75, 98, 112–15,
  127
Myers Grove School 112
My Pierrot Dolls 8, 30, 93,
  266–7, 248

Naughtiest Girl was a Monitor,
  The 8, 92, 233,
Neutron Records 214, 216
New Arts Lab 96
New Model Soldier 248
New Order 223–4
Newton, Adi 8, 18–20, 58,
  122–8, 134, 139–43,
  148–63, 185, 189–91,
  194–7, 206, 225–7, 231,
  238–41, 262, 264–6
New Worlds Group 50
New York Dolls 115, 133
Nice, The 50
Normal, The 179
Now Society, The 161, 184,
  190, 193
Numan, Gary 220, 226, 247

288

Index

Index

EU authorised representative for GPSR:

Easy Access System Europe, Mustamäe tee 50, 10621 Tallinn, Estonia gpsr.
requests@easproject.com